UNIX for Programmers
An Introduction

UNIX for Programmers

An Introduction

DANIEL FARKAS

Pace University

WILEY

JOHN WILEY & SONS

New York / Chichester / Brisbane / Toronto / Singapore

Library of Congress Cataloging in Publication Data:
Farkas, Daniel, 1947–
    UNIX for programmers.

    Bibliography: p.
    1. UNIX (Computer operating system) I. Title.
QA76.76.063F37 1988   005.4'3   87-29824
ISBN 0-471-83799-7
ISBN 0-471-83812-8 (pbk.)

Printed in the United States of America

10 9 8 7 6 5 4 3 2 1

Trademark and Product Acknowledgments
Amdahl Corporation: Amdahl, UTS
AT&T: UNIX, UNIX System V, Writer's Workbench, PC 6300, PC 6300 Plus, UNIX PC, 7300 PC.
The Board of Regents of the University of California at Berkeley: 4.2BSD
CompuServe Inc.: CompuServe
COSI, Inc.: Synchrony
Digital Equipment Corporation: DEC, Ultrix, VAX, PDP-11, VMS, MicroVAX
Dow Jones Company, Inc.: Dow Jones News/Retrieval
Hewlett-Packard Inc. HP, HP-UX
International Business Machines Corporation: AIX, CMS, MVS, IBM, IBM PC, IBM PC/AT, PC/IX,
    IBM PC/RT, IBM PC/XT
The Mark Williams Company: Cohonent
The Santa Cruz Operation, Inc.: SCO XENIX, SCO XENIX System V
Source Telecomputing Corporation: The Source
Sun Microsystems, Inc.: Network File System, NFS, Sun Microsystems, Sun Workstation
TouchStone Corporation: PCworks
VenturCom, Inc.: Prelude, VENIX
The Wollongong Group: WIN, WINS, WINPC

To my mother, Frieda, and in memory of my father, Emil

Preface

The motivation for this book originated during the two years I spent traveling around the country delivering UNIX seminars. Like a tent show traveling from city to city, I presented my vision of a new world for the computer industry, proselytizing the beauty of the UNIX operating system. I described how its richness goes beyond the commands and utilities, providing an environment for development that incorporates a methodology for constructing systems as well as the tools. UNIX is the system of choice for many developers today because of its tools approach, the elegant integration of input/output processing with the file system, and the powerful user interface, the shell. It was only natural that my enthusiasm coupled with UNIX's power and sophistication should spawn this book.

It became apparent speaking to seminar participants, some of whom were very experienced, that learning UNIX required a special type of commitment. It wasn't as easy to learn as they had originally expected. Not only was there a wide variety of functions, but the documentation was impossible to understand, even when one understood the concepts being explained. It's almost as if reading the documentation was a test in which passing gave one entrance to the world of UNIX insiders. The books that were available were mostly for beginners, briefly mentioning or leaving out the material a programmer or system developer would be interested in.

As I traveled around the country, more and more of the seminar attendees were in workstation environments, and it became clear that UNIX was going to become the operating system of choice for the many personal computer-based workstations that had been coming on the market.

The result of all of these discoveries is this book. It is an attempt to provide an introduction to UNIX for the intelligent computer user (Part I), an exploration of some of the system development tools and techniques for the programmer (Part II), and finally, a guide to the workstation user who must manage his own environment from installation to system administration (Part III). While not a replacement for your system documentation, I hope to make it more usable and easier for you, the reader, to also become an insider—to appreciate and exploit the power and elegance of the UNIX Operating System.

In writing this book, it was both necessary and desirable to depend on a number of people and organizations for advice and support. In most cases I took the advice, and always more than welcomed the support. However, very few of the people who helped me actually read the entire manuscript, but rather they gave organizational suggestions, access to machines, and demo software. In short, these acknowledgments do not represent their endorsements, but rather my appreciation of the enthusiastic sharing of ideas and resources within the UNIX community.

First, I am grateful to the help of a number of organizations who always seemed to come up with the right person or software package just when I needed it. These include AT&T Information Systems, The IBM Corporation, The Santa Cruz Operation, Inc., The Mark Williams Company, Inc., Catalytix, Inc., CSRI, Inc., /usr/group, VenturCom, Inc., and The Wollongong Group, Inc.

There have been a number of individuals within the UNIX community without whose support the book would not have been possible. These are professionals who have been involved with UNIX for many years and were gracious enough to accept me into the fold: Don French, Gig Graham, Dave Langlais, Lizabeth Reilly, Bill Rieken and BillieAnn Rice.

Last, I also want to thank, for continued support over several years and changes, my editors, Paul Farrell, Maria Taylor, and Diane Cerra. Most importantly, Felicia Eth, formerly of Writer's House, was an author's dream literary agent.

DANIEL FARKAS

November 1987
Katonah, New York

Contents

UNIX *for Programmers*
An Introduction

PART *I*

UNIX Basics

*The chapters in this part of the book present what you will need to know
as a beginning user of UNIX. If you have had some experience with UNIX,
or prefer to get into the advanced material right away, you should skim
these chapters and come back for reference when necessary.*

*The chapters cover the basics of the shell, editing, the file system, and
file manipulation tools.*

1

The UNIX System

In this chapter we introduce the UNIX operating system. Whether you are an experienced computer user or not, UNIX will provide a powerful computing environment not matched elsewhere in the computer world. In order to fully exploit its capabilities, you must understand how it works and what it does and does not do. That is the purpose of this book.

If you have been programming for a while, you will have a basic understanding of computer systems, specifically computer operating systems. Users in workstation environments may be responsible for installing and maintaining their own installation. Our objective, then, is to present an introduction to UNIX to experienced programmers and system developers.

This chapter discusses what UNIX is in the context of the general computing environments, covering concepts such as:

UNIX Background and History
UNIX Versions
The UNIX Kernel and the Shell
UNIX Documentation

1.1 Why UNIX?

UNIX has been hailed as the operating system standard of the 1980s. Every day, more manufacturers come out with new versions of UNIX for their hardware, and the trade papers and magazines are filled with articles on its emerging importance. There are many reasons for this interest and enthusiasm. First, since UNIX runs on a variety of hardware, designers can create systems on one machine to run on another. Installations with multiple hardware configurations can design or purchase software which runs on all their systems.

A second, and related reason is that UNIX is written primarily in the C language. This makes modification and maintenance easier. Furthermore, systems written in C will migrate without difficulty to other new UNIX (and non-UNIX) environments.

Another aspect of UNIX is the wealth of development tools which come as part of the distribution package. In addition to the traditional editors, compilers, and debuggers, there are advanced development tools and a command system and structure which provides a powerful environment for creating and tailoring software. The designers of UNIX have incorporated many modern techniques and concepts formerly limited to experimental operating systems, which have made UNIX manageable and understandable, unlike many of the mainframe operating systems in the marketplace today.

Lastly, UNIX is now available on a variety of microcomputer systems, which makes it the ideal system to host a personal workstation environment. This is opening up a new range of users, applications, and markets. This is discussed in Part III, ''Workstation Issues.''

1.2 Why an Introduction for Programmers?

As UNIX becomes more widely known and used, more and more books are published to provide ''how to's'' which are sorely needed guides to the traditional multivolumed cryptic documentation. In this context, the present volume is *yaub*, ''yet another UNIX book'' (look up **yacc** in the command section of your UNIX system documentation).

If you are a beginning user of UNIX, you will be able to benefit from this presentation which describes basic system usage. However, the book is aimed at experienced programmers who need and desire less handholding. Users who rely on documentation for details, not concepts. In short, professionals who:

- Have some experience with computers, programming, and operating systems.
- Want to learn the basics of the UNIX operating system and how it compares and contrasts with the systems they are familiar with, including mainframe systems and personal computers (e.g., MS-DOS).
- Have acquired a UNIX-based personal computer and must develop applications in a workstation environment.
- Want to network or establish a networked environment including mainframes and personal computer workstations.
- Have had experience with one or more operating systems and so do not need a beginner's introduction but, rather, a presentation which assumes a certain degree of sophistication.
- Are using UNIX in an environment which does not provide documentation to each user and they require a book which goes beyond most introductory texts.
- Are responsible for maintaining their own systems and require a basic understanding of system administration.
- Need a basic understanding of UNIX communications facilities.

In addition to providing a clear and concise description of the basic UNIX system, the text goes beyond basic introductory manuals by including:

1. A tutorial introduction to basic UNIX concepts and features (shell, editing, file system).
2. A detailed description of the utilities (regardless of UNIX version).
3. An in-depth presentation of program development and systems programming, including **adb, make,** SCCS.
4. An introduction to communications and access to UNIX and non-UNIX systems.
5. A description of the important system administration activities which personal computer workstation users must recognize (diskette handling, backups, setting up users, etc.).
6. A comparison of UNIX to MS-DOS.
7. A comprehensive reference to UNIX commands.

1.3 Organization of this Book

The book is divided into three parts. Part I is tutorial and covers all the major aspects of UNIX in a functional and conceptual way. By reading the chapters in Part I, you can become fully acquainted with the UNIX operating environment. If you have been exploring UNIX on your own for a while, you may want to skim these chapters and go directly to Part II. Chapter 2 describes the basic UNIX shell. Chapter 3 contains a complete description of the UNIX editors (ed, ex, and vi) as well as a discussion of regular expressions which become more important later on in other UNIX utilities. Chapter 4 covers the UNIX file system and the associated file manipulation commands. With these chapters to reference, experienced users can begin to effectively use the system. Chapter 5 is an alphabetically organized tutorial to the UNIX file utilities.

Part II covers the more advanced aspects of UNIX, features which most readers will recognize in other operating systems. Chapter 6 covers the basics of UNIX document processing, presenting the elements of **nroff/troff** and the basic macro packages. Chapters 7 and 8 cover advanced shell topics and shell programming. The Bourne shell, standard with System V, is discussed in Chapter 7, and the C-shell, which is part of XENIX and the Berkeley systems, is described in Chapter 8. Chapters 9 and 10 get down to programming issues. C language programming tools are discussed in Chapter 9 and programming techniques in Chapter 10.

Because of the proliferation of inexpensive desktop personal computers and workstations which run UNIX, Part III of the book is devoted to workstation issues. Chapter 11 discusses basic system administration for users who will have to maintain their own systems. Chapter 12 addresses communications issues, including UNIX-based communications, networking, and connecting to mainframes. A final chapter discusses some of the different types of UNIX workstations on the market, as well as a comparison of UNIX to MS-DOS.

1.4 A Special Section on Workstations

The most important development in the computer industry as well as the UNIX marketplace has been the introduction of low-cost, single (or few) user desktop workstations. The term workstation has different connotations for different people, and lately has become a buzzword. For the most part, a personal workstation is a computer used and administered by a single user. The workstation may be in an office, used for standard office automation applications, or it may be in a development environment, used by programmers and application designers.

An interesting recent development has been the introduction of low-cost, high-performance engineering and scientific workstations. While the focus of this section is on personal computer-based workstations, IBM's entry into this marketplace (IBM PC/RT)—along with Sun Microsystems,

DEC, and Apollo—has made these machines quite important. Chapter 13 addresses these machines.

The microcomputer-based workstations that we are considering have enough disk storage to hold the UNIX system (minimum 10M), and enough main storage for efficient multiprogramming (minimum 256k). They will support a variety of peripheral devices and forms of communications. Typical entries in this product area include the IBM PC/XT, IBM PC/AT, AT&T 6300 Plus, AT&T 7300, TANDY 3000, and others.

1.5 UNIX Background and History

The development of UNIX began in the research environment of Bell Labs in the late 1960s. Ken Thompson developed an operating system for his own use, written in assembly language, for the DEC PDP-7. The advent of the PDP-11 in 1970, combined with the development of the C language by Dennis Ritchie, also a member of the original Bell Labs group, added impetus to the development of UNIX. In 1973, UNIX kernel was written in C and UNIX as we know it was born.

As UNIX systems appeared throughout Bell Labs and in universities, its popularity and user community grew. Initially, UNIX was distributed by Bell Labs on an as-is basis with no support. These releases had version numbers, the last of which was UNIX Version 7. Shortly thereafter, a similar version emerged called the Programmers Workbench (PWB), which had additional program development tools. These folded into a single system, UNIX System III, but it was still distributed unsupported. Then, in January 1983, Bell Labs announced a fully supported UNIX System V.

During the 1970s and early 1980s, the University of California at Berkeley was creating and distributing enhancements to licensed UNIX holders. The enhancements (current as of this writing) became known as Berkeley 4.2bsd and added to UNIX a more powerful interface (the C-shell) and an expanded context and full-screen editor (ex and vi), among other features.

On another track, independent hardware and software companies were either licensing UNIX from AT&T and developing their own versions, or they were designing lookalikes (e.g., Coherent from the Mark Williams Company). As the number of machines running UNIX expanded, so did its popularity and variations. Today, almost every major computer manufacturer has product lines which incorporate UNIX in one form or another. AT&T System V seems to have emerged as the measure of standardization. While the notion of different UNIX versions is still important, it has become less so as manufacturers try to embrace the AT&T standard. Table 1.1 lists some current versions.

TABLE 1.1
Some UNIX Versions

UNIX Version	Vendor/Manufacturer
System V	AT&T
Berkeley 4.2	UC Berkeley
PC/IX	IBM
AIX	IBM
Ultrix	DEC
HP-UX	Hewlet Packard
XENIX	Microsoft
VENIX	VentureCom
UTX	Amdahl

1.6 UNIX Versions

While reading all the different names, numbers, and manufacturers, UNIX systems may be confusing to the UNIX user. AT&T has established its version, System V, as the standard UNIX. Most vendors and hardware manufacturers are beginning to release their own versions with the distinguishing "System V" appellation, which should reduce most of the confusion in the years to come (e.g. XENIX System V).

The standardization applies to the way in which the kernel manages its resources and application and system programs communicate with UNIX. It does not mean that every version of System V UNIX will contain the same commands; instead, functions such as input/output or resource sharing at the programming level will be compatible across System V versions.

In this book, we take the view that to the beginning user, even the computer literate one, it is not necessary to become so system specific as to describe functions particular to each version, but rather to approach UNIX as a generic system under the assumption that the trend by proprietary vendors is to incorporate the best from all the available systems.

It is still not unreasonable to be aware of where a version of UNIX has been developed since you may still find vendors, documentation, articles, and books which promote one UNIX system over another. Keep in mind that AT&T UNIX System V seems to be the major force to which other vendors look for standardization.

1.7 The UNIX Kernel and the Shell

All computer systems provide a *user interface,* to permit the user to specify the functions to be performed by the operating system. This usually involves executing programs and managing files, but it also includes communications and system administration functions. In the UNIX operating system, the user interface is a program called the *shell*, and it comes in several different forms depending on the version of UNIX you are using. Most UNIX versions come with multiple shell versions.

The *shell* is a sophisticated interpreter, separate from the operating system, which allows the UNIX user to interact with the computing system. This concept, which may be familiar to users of MS-DOS, provides for a significant degree of flexibility. The shell is a program running as an operating system process. Therefore, any program can be used as a shell, and in multiprogramming environments (such as UNIX), it is possible for a single user to be running several shells superimposed upon each other. For example, by running the shell from the editor, it is possible to temporarily exit the utility and perform operating system commands, then re-enter the shell. Your system will have the standard *Bourne* shell and possibly the enhanced *C-shell*. Chapter 2 discusses concepts common to both, while advanced shell topics are described fully in Chapters 7 and 8.

All the resource management programs are combined into a collection of programs called the *kernel*. The kernel is small since it does not include all the programs which come with a UNIX system, but only those which manage the computer system's resources. You communicate with UNIX by using the shell, which basically sets up other programs to run, including all the commands and any other application you may write.

Chapter 2 introduces the shell and how it is used to execute commands and programs.

1.8 Your Documentation

A UNIX system is distributed with more than 200 commands and utilities. Utilities may have many subcommands, or they may be a type of programming language. The documentation which comes with your system is likely to be large and comprehensive but, like most documentation in the computer field, offers poor user instructions. It is not our goal to replace your system documentation but rather supplement it.

The original UNIX Command Reference Manual was organized into eight sections (see Table 1.2a). Many of the new workstation systems (e.g., XENIX, VENIX) have given functional organization to the manual as illustrated in Table 1.2b. Topics or commands are organized alphabetically within a section. Each entry consists of the topic or command, its syntax, a description of what the command does, its options, and examples of usage. If there are any known bugs, they may also be indicated in the manual entry. Since some of the entries come from the original development days of UNIX, you may find some interesting passages!

TABLE 1.2a
Manual Sections

Section	Description
1	Commands
2	System calls
3	Subroutines
4	Special files
5	File formats
6	Games
7	Miscellaneous facilities
8	System maintenance

At the end of each chapter in this book there is a list of terms and commands which are references to your system documentation.

1.9 Further Exploration

Many of the utilities which come with your UNIX system are sophisticated systems in themselves. Your manuals will explain how to invoke the subsystem, but they will not give much information on how it is used. Your system documentation may contain reprints of articles which describe the utilities, but these sometimes require more experience than the beginner or novice possesses. You may find some of the references listed in the index to be helpful. Table 1.3 lists some of these subsystems. The entries preceded by an asterisk are covered in this book.

TABLE 1.2b
XENIX Subdivisions

Section	Description
C	Commands
M	Miscellaneous
F	Formats
CP	Program development
S	System/subroutines
CT	Text processing

TABLE 1.3
Utilities and Subsystems

Command	Subsystem or Utility
*adb	Absolute debugger
*awk	Pattern processing
bc	Arithmetic language
*cc	C compiler
dc	Desk calculator
*ed	Line editor
*eqn	Text equation processor
*ex	Berkeley line editor
lex	Lexical analyzer language
*lint	C program checker
m4	General macro language
*make	Large program manager
*mm	Macro processor (nroff)
mmt	Macro processor (troff)
*nroff	Line printer text processor
sdb	Symbolic debugger
*tbl	Text table processor
troff	Typesetter text processor
*sccs	Source code control sys
yacc	Compiler compiler

2

The UNIX Shell

In this chapter the user environment and the basic functions of the UNIX command language are described. This will enable you to begin using the system effectively while laying the foundation for more advanced topics.

This chapter is for beginners. While we assume that you have an understanding of computer systems, we expect that you have little exposure to UNIX. Very sophisticated readers may want to skim this chapter before going to Chapters 7 and 8, which provide an advanced presentation of UNIX shell concepts and programming.

Throughout this chapter it is assumed that your UNIX system is installed and operational. If it is not, see Chapter 11 for instructions for setting up the system. You should be comfortable with the basics of logging on and using the keyboard to enter and execute commands.

This chapter introduces several important concepts—some peculiar to UNIX, others not. You should pay particular attention to the following key concepts:

Command Line Editing
Terminal Control
Command Line Format
UNIX Help Facilities
Filename Generation

Quoting Special Characters
Standard Input and Output
Redirection of I/O
Command Substitution
Pipes and Filters

2.1 *Command Syntax Philosophy*

The UNIX command interface (shell) is designed to be terse with commands, typically no more than two or three characters in length. Furthermore, responses from the system are kept to a minimum. This is intentional. In a development environment, users are interested neither in long mnemonic commands nor in multiline error messages. A ''?'' is usually sufficient for the experienced user to know a parameter is incorrect. More often than not, when a command operates correctly, no message will be displayed. For example, if there are no syntax errors in a C language compilation, there is no system message to acknowledge it except the shell prompt for the next command.

UNIX uses brief responses—or no response at all—for a second reason. Later in this chapter you will learn how a pipe enables you to use the output of one command as direct input to another command. If the output has extraneous information such as page numbers, dates, headings, and so forth, it will have to be ignored by programs using the data. Therefore, as a general rule, output contains only the specific information requested. For example, the **who** command lists users on the system with one line of output for each user. On single user systems, only your user-id information will print.

```
$ who
farkas      tty02      Mar 10 09:35
smith       tty03      Mar 10 09:45
jones       tty04      Mar 10 10:35
root        console    Mar 10 09:12
$
```

First notice the dollar sign prompt symbol, $. This is the default prompt for the Bourne shell. If you are using the C-shell (e.g. XENIX or Berkeley 4.2bsd), the default is the percent sign, %. There are no column headings to help you understand the meaning of the output. You will have to consult the manual. In this case, **who** with no options displays the user-id, the terminal, and the date and time of login for each active user. If you're sitting at a workstation which is not attached to a larger UNIX system, you're the only user and only one line will be displayed.

While the terse quality of the shell's responses may be initially disconcerting to some users, most become familiar and comfortable with the system's lack of "friendliness" and, in fact, become impatient with wordier systems. Some versions of UNIX have alternative interfaces (e.g., menu driven), and since the shell is programmable, tailoring a specific user view is not difficult. This important aspect of the UNIX shell will be covered in depth in Chapters 7 and 8.

2.2 Command Syntax

UNIX command syntax is similar to many other systems. A command name consists of any combination of up to 14 ASCII characters. By convention, most UNIX commands are alphabetic lower case and two or three characters long.

A command may be entered with no arguments, as we've seen with **who,** or several arguments which are entered on the command line separated by blanks. While arguments may have many forms, they are usually filenames or options which determine the action of the command. Options also have different forms, but most commands accept them as single or multiple letters with no intervening blanks, preceded by a dash (-). Sometimes a single letter preceded by a dash can be followed by an option value which is supplied as a parameter to the command.

The lack of standardization is due to the nature of most of the commands. They are not, as in most systems, integrated parts of the operating system but rather programs which define and handle their own arguments. This is actually one of the UNIX system's advantages. It provides for expansion, modification, and straightforward tailoring of individual user environments by adding or changing command programs.

To illustrate command line syntax, we will use the **ls** command, which lists the contents of your *home directory.* The home directory is the collection of files accessible after you log in. It is similar to a user library in a time-sharing system or diskette directory in a microcomputer system. The broader aspects of the UNIX file system and the **ls** command will be explored in Chapter 4. Commands can be entered in a variety of ways as the following uses of **ls** demonstrate.

2.2.1 Simple Command with No Arguments

We have seen this already with **who.** The **ls** command with no arguments lists the contents of your directory displaying the filenames without any attributes.

```
$ ls
dfla.c
dfla.o
dfny.c
dfny.o
dfhsort.f
dfqsort.f
$
```

This output indicates that there are six files in the home directory. The letter following the period (.) is called an extension and, while optional from the UNIX file system perspective, some system programs require the extension to recognize the type of a file. For example, the extension *.c* indicates a C program, *.o* an object file, and *.f* a Fortran program.

Experienced users and many development environments use naming conventions to help identify files. In our examples, the first two characters of a filename are the creator's initials followed by a string which further identifies the file. As you gain experience with the system, you'll most likely work out a filenaming scheme of your own.

2.2.2 *Commands with File Arguments*

Most commands operate on files and can take one or more filenames as arguments. When the **ls** command has file arguments, it displays only the filenames in the directory which match the filenames specified on the command line. For the **ls** command, it is not an error if specified files are not found; they just aren't displayed.

```
$ ls dfqsort.f dfhsort.f dfssort.f
dfhsort.f
dfqsort.f
$
```

The command line in this example is checking whether three Fortran sort programs are in the directory. Note that the two actually present are listed.

2.3 *Commands with Options*

Options to UNIX commands are placed immediately after the command name and are specified in several different ways. The most common syntax for options is a dash (-) followed by a single letter which determines the type of action the command is to take. If there are multiple options, the option letters are placed together following the dash with no intervening blanks. Another notation is to specify the option letters without the preceding dash. In this case, the option letters are called *keys*. In either case, they function in the same way. The commands introduced in this chapter use the dash, but we will see in later chapters that some commands use the *key* notation.

The **ls** command **-r** option inverts the order of the listing. The output below illustrates a simple **ls** command with the default order (ascending by filename), and then reversed:

```
$ ls            $ ls -r
dfhsort.f       dfqsort.f
dfla.c          dfny.o
dfla.o          dfny.c
dfny.c          dfla.o
dfny.o          dfla.c
dfqsort.f       dfhsort.f
$               $
```

The **-s** option gives the size of each file. When multiple options are specified, the option letters can be in any order, so the commands **ls -sr** and **ls -rs** will display identical output:

```
$ ls -sr
10      dfqsort.f
12      dfny.o
15      dfny.c
17      dfla.o
16      dfla.c
20      dfhsort.f
$
```

A third type of specification includes options which take values. In this situation the option is followed by its value, with or without spaces depending on the individual command syntax. We will see examples of this type of option specification in later chapters.

2.3.1 Commands with File and Option Arguments

It is always possible to combine file and option arguments to select specific files and options. The filenames follow the options list.

```
$ ls -rs dfqsort.f dfhsort.f
10      dfqsort.f
20      dfhsort.f
$
```

2.3.2 *Multiple Commands on a Line*

Finally, it is possible to have more than one command on a command line. By using the semicolon as a separator, several operations may be entered as a single command. For example, to print the date and contents of the directory as one command, you can enter:

```
$ date; ls
Mon Mar 10 21:49:56 EST 1986
dfhsort.f
dfla.c
dfla.o
dfny.c
dfny.o
dfqsort.f
$
```

2.4 *Error Handling*

Occasionally, you will make an error entering a command. This may be the result of a typing error or incorrect usage. There are three different ways in which UNIX may respond to the error.

First, UNIX may display the command usage. Some commands do not trap every individual error, and they only give the general usage of the command to indicate that something is incorrect. For example, the **wc** command counts and displays the characters, words, and lines of a file. If you enter the command with an incorrect option, the proper form of the command is displayed.

```
$ wc -x dfqsort.f
usage: wc [ -clw ] [ file . . . ]
$
```

In this context, the square bracket indicates that supplying the parameter is optional. The usage message also indicates that the command **wc** has three possible options—**c** (number of characters), **l** (number of lines), **w** (number of words)—and may take one or more files. If the file *dfqsort.f* had 50 lines, the **wc** command with the -l option would return the following:

```
$ wc -l dfqsort.f
50
$
```

UNIX has a second way of dealing with errors: in some cases, it will display an error message. In this case the command name is given and followed by a message. If the file presented to **wc** doesn't exist, an error message is printed.

```
$ wc -x dfqsort
wc: file cannot open
$ wc -l dfqsort.f
50
$
```

In this example, the file was spelled wrong. The logically invalid arguments are syntactically correct, but at least an error message is displayed.

In some responses, UNIX may respond to an error by processing the command line as if there were no error at all. Needless to say, these are the hardest types of errors to discover. For example, if you reverse the options and filenames on the **ls** command, the options list will be interpreted as a filename beginning with dash.

```
$ ls dfqsort.f -l
dfqsort.f
$
```

Note that the misplaced **-l** option is taken as a filename, and since no such file is in the directory, it is not displayed. This further illustrates that UNIX filenames can be made up of any ASCII (even unprintable!) characters.

2.5 Help Facilities

There are two facilities to provide additional information about command usage and syntax. The **help** command gives information about some commands and, in some cases, further information about error message numbers coming from certain commands (e.g., SCCS, see Chapter 9).

The **help** command, however, is not the utility which describes command operation. This is done by the manual command, **man,** which displays user manual entries. Unfortunately, many workstation UNIX systems will not distribute the on-line manual due to disk space constraints; however, when available, this facility provides on-line access to the user manual. Typically, the **man** command is available and it is up to each installation to set up their own manual entries.

If you check your user documentation, you will notice that it is divided up into different sections which contain, in alphabetical order, information about different aspects of the UNIX system. AT&T UNIX divides the manual into the eight sections listed in Table 2.1.

The section number is an optional argument to **man**. If you do not specify a section number, the first section which contains an entry with a matching document name will be selected and displayed. If there are multiple documents in different sections with the same name, you may have to specify the section name. For example, if you want to learn how to use the **man** command, enter:

```
$  man man
```

or

```
$  man 1 man
```

In the above example, the 1 indicates section 1. Manual entries for items which may appear in one or more sections must contain the section number. For most commands, it is not necessary. If the **man** is available, the pages from the manual describing how to use the command will print on your screen. Try it.

2.6 Filename Generation

All text editors have the ability to search for character strings in a file. The string to be sought is always expressed as a sequence of alphanumeric characters. In most editing systems, the search is limited to a single string.

TABLE 2.1
Manual Sections

Section	Description
1	Commands
2	System calls
3	Subroutines
4	Special files
5	File formats
6	Games
7	Miscellaneous facilities
8	Maintenance programs and Procedures

The editor will search for lines which contain occurrences of the string and then perform some operation on the string or the line containing it. For example, the programmer may say "search for abc and change it to xyz."

UNIX's ability to match strings in general ways is one of its most useful features. In this section we will apply pattern matching to filenames, but later we shall see how UNIX incorporates this feature in many of its commands, editors, utilities, and subsystems.

2.6.1 Pattern Matching

Given the proper instructions, UNIX can search for strings according to a pattern specified by the user. In its most general format, these patterns are called *regular expressions*. In this chapter we discuss a restricted type of pattern matching which selects those filenames from the directory which matches the pattern specified by the user.

A pattern is simply a formal way of expressing a description of a file name. For example, if we take the filenames in our sample directory, we can describe collections of files as illustrated in Figure 2.1.

2.6.2 Wildcard Characters

There is a formal system for representing patterns in UNIX by special symbols of matching single characters, groups of characters, alternate characters, and so forth. Our first encounter with regular expressions is in the

Description	Filename Matches
All filenames	dfla.c
	dfla.o
	dfny.c
	dfny.o
	dfhsort.f
	dfqsort.f
Files ending in **.c**	dfla.c
	dfny.c
Files which have **sort** in them	dfhsort.f
	dfqsort.f
Files which have an **n** followed by any character followed by a period (.)	dfny.c
	dfny.o
Files which begin with **dfh**	dfhsort.f
Files ending in **.o** or **.c**	dfla.c
	dfla.o
	dfny.c
	dfny.o

Figure 2.1. File Search Descriptions

UNIX shell, which uses a variation of a formal regular expression language for matching filenames in a directory.

In the shell, special characters called *wildcard characters* are used to construct regular expressions for the search patterns. The characters are used in the following manner:

* * matches 0 or more of characters
* ? matches any single character
* [] matches any single character listed between the square brackets.

Readers familiar with MS-DOS will recognize similar usage for the asterisk and question mark. Figure 2.2 shows how we can rewrite the examples of Figure 2.1 using wildcard characters.

When the wildcard characters are used in arguments on a command line, the argument is expanded into all the filenames which can be derived from the string, and these are matched by filenames in the user directory. The filenames are substituted on the command line taking the place of the original argument.

Assume your directory contains the following files:

```
dfla.c
dfla.o
dfny.c
dfny.o
dfhsort.f
dfqsort.f
```

Description	Pattern	Filename Matches
All filenames	*	dfla.c
		dfla.o
		dfny.c
		dfny.o
		dfhsort.f
		dfqsort.f
Files ending in .c	*.c	dfla.c
		dfny.c
Files which have sort in them	*sort*	dfhsort.f
		dfqsort.f
Files which have a **y** followed by any character followed by a period (.)	*n?.*	dfny.c
		dfny.o
Files which begin with **dfh**	dfh*	dfhsort.f
Files ending in .o or .c	*.[oc]	dfla.c
		dfla.o
		dfny.c
		dfny.o

Figure 2.2. File Description Patterns

The **echo** command can be used to demonstrate how filename generation and argument substitution work. Echo displays its expanded arguments on the terminal. For example, **echo** with simple string arguments
will display them:

```
$ echo abc xyz
abc xyz
$
```

If an argument contains wildcard characters, the expanded, substituted
filenames are printed. If no files are selected, the wildcard character expression is echoed.

If you wanted to see all the files in the directory, you could type:

```
$ echo *
dfla.c dfny.c dfla.o dfny.o dfqsort.f dfhsort.f
$
```

If you wanted only sort programs, type:

```
$ echo *sort*
dfhsort.c dfqsort.c
$
```

For Fortran or C programs:

```
$ echo *.[cp]
dfla.c dfny.c dfqsort.f dfhsort.f
$
```

C language source and object programs:

```
$ echo *.[co]
dfla.c dfny.c dfla.o dfny.o
$
```

The advantage of using wildcard characters is that they can be used on any
command to specify a collection of files to be processed. For example, the
cc command invokes the C compiler. To compile all the C programs in the
directory (perhaps all the source programs for a particular application):

```
$ cc *.c
```

To look for all sort programs:

```
$ ls *sort*
```

In the last example, we knew that the string, sort, was imbedded in all sort program files.

2.7 Standard Input and Output

The UNIX shell is an interactive program, communicating with you through your terminal. Inside the shell program are three files that control the interaction between the commands you execute and the shell itself:

1. *Standard Input.* When this file is read, your keyboard is being accessed.
2. *Standard Output.* When this file is written, output is displayed on your screen.
3. *Standard Error.* When this file is written, output is displayed on your screen. The shell, commands, and programs use this file for error messages.

When you log in, these three files are set up to communicate with the terminal. The shell also makes them available to any command or program you execute.

2.8 Redirection of Standard Input and Output

UNIX provides, through the shell, a mechanism for changing the standard input, output, and error files. This feature should be familiar to MS-DOS users. The special characters < and > are used on the command line to specify how output or input are to be redirected. Files can be copied (with > or <) or appended to (with > >) other files, as in these examples:

>	*newout*	redirect standard output to the file newout
> >	*newout*	append standard output to the file newout
<	*newin*	redirect standard input from the file newin

Try some of the following examples on your system. Print the directory contents on standard output, the terminal screen (this is the default):

```
$ ls
dfla.c
dfla.o
dfny.c
dfny.o
dfhsort.f
dfqsort.f
$
```

The following example writes the directory contents to the file *dfdir*. The original contents of *dfdir*, if any, are destroyed. If you are using the C-shell, a system variable may prevent wiping out existing files. For now just use different filenames (e.g., *dfdir1*, *dfdir2*, etc.). The C-shell is discussed in Chapter 8.

```
$ ls > dfdir
```

Write both the date and the directory contents (in that order) to the file *dfdir*:

```
$ date > dfdir
$ ls >> dfdir
```

To see the results and the flexibility with which UNIX redirects input and output, we will use the **cat** (concatenate) command, which in its simplest form is used to display the contents of a file. In the following example, **ls** lists the C programs on the file *dfdir* (redirected output) followed by **cat** which lists the contents of *dfdir* on standard output, the terminal.

```
$ ls *.c > dfdir
$ cat dfdir
dfla.c
dfla.o
dfny.c
dfny.o
dfhsort.f
dfqsort.f
$
```

If the **cat** command has no file arguments, it reads standard input as its input file:

```
$ cat
_
```

Since standard input is from the terminal keyboard, any lines typed will represent the file to list. Similarly, standard output is also the terminal. Therefore, after all the lines have been read in and terminated by the end-of-file character, *ctrl-D* (hold down the control key and type D), the same lines will be displayed on the screen. For example,

```
$ cat
now is
the
time
ctrl-D

now is
the
time
$
```

2.9 Creating a Personal Telephone Index

These concepts can be incorporated into the following useful example, the creation of a personal telephone index. To create the index, we will use the terminal as standard input, and redirect output to a file called *tel*.

```
$ cat > tel
Smith      Robert    212 555-1234
Jones      William   914 555-1234
Blake      Michael   212 555-4321
ctrl-D
$
```

To see the contents we enter the **cat** command. If **cat** has any arguments, they are assumed to be files. An alternative specification could use input redirection, but it is a convention (not a rule) for a command to take its file arguments for input. When there are no arguments, then the command looks to standard input.

```
$ cat tel
Smith      Robert    212 555-1234
Jones      William   914 555-1234
Blake      Michael   212 555-4321
$
```

To add names to the index, we want to redirect standard output, but in this case the data is appended (> >) to the existing file (using > would overwrite the original file and destroy its contents):

```
$ cat >>tel
Sugarman   David     212 555-2394
Loxley     Robert    212 555-1921
Abramov    Roz       212 555-1365
ctrl-D
$
```

Now listing the file displays the entire telephone index:

```
$ cat tel
Smith      Robert    212 555-1234
Jones      William   914 555-1234
Blake      Michael   212 555-4321
Browne     Peter     203 555-1234
Sugarman   David     212 555-2394
Loxley     Robert    212 555-1921
Abramov    Roz       212 555-1365
$
```

While all we can do now is create an index, add names, and list the entire contents, we'll soon be able to use shell facilities and standard UNIX commands to search and delete entries as well as perform other operations.

2.10 Pipes

So far we've seen how UNIX can be used to redirect entire files. It can also be used, however, to redirect the standard output of one command directly as standard input to another command. The facility that makes this redirection is called a *pipe,* since it is a connection between the two commands, as shown in Figure 2.3.

A pipe is represented by the symbol | between the two commands being connected. Using the **ls** command and the **wc** (word count) command, we can create a new function which displays the number of files in a directory. Before we create this new function, however, let's first see how this is done without using a pipe. First, a file called *temp* is created, then **wc** is used

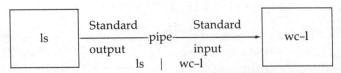

Figure 2.3. A Simple Pipe from **ls** to **wc**

with the lines option, **-l**. This creates a temporary file which contains all the directory filenames, and **wc** counts and displays the number of lines in the file:

```
$ ls > temp
$ wc -l temp
6
$
```

Using a pipe, the same result is achieved in a simpler manner, and no extra files are needed.

```
$ ls | wc -l
6
$
```

2.11 Quoting

As we will see in the next section and throughout the book, arguments to commands may contain wildcard characters which will cause the shell to try to expand them into filenames. In order to inhibit this expansion, it is necessary to quote the character or string containing the special characters. This is done in one of three ways, each having a slightly different meaning to the shell.

The simplest form of quoting uses the backslash, \, which tells the shell to treat the following character as just that character and not some special symbol. The quoting symbol cancels any special action the special character may have caused and is used throughout the UNIX system. It is a UNIX convention used in the shell, the standard editors, and many utilities.

For example, suppose we wanted to display a message on the screen with the **echo** command (this is usually done from shell scripts described in Chapters 7 and 8):

```
echo ***Error, re-enter***.
```

This message would cause each occurrence of an asterisk to be replaced by all the filenames in the directory. To rewrite the message and have it display properly, each asterisk must be quoted:

```
echo \*\*\* Error, re-enter \*\*\*
```

Since this can be rather cumbersome, an alternative is to quote the entire string. Single quotes, ' are used to quote entire strings:

```
echo '*** Error, re-enter***'
```

As we will see in later chapters on advanced shell usage, there are some special characters we will want interpreted (e.g., $ for parameter substitution). The use of double quotes, ", causes the shell to continue to interpret these special characters but to inhibit the wildcard characters. In our example above, we only have the single wildcard character, asterisk, so the use of double or single quotes could be used interchangeably.

2.12 Command Substitution

This refers to substituting the output of a command as an argument on the command line. The accent grave, `, indicates command substitution. For example, to echo a message on the number of users logged in, we want the output of **who** piped into **wc**:

```
$ echo ''The number of users is: '' ' who / wc -1 '
The number of users is: 5
$
```

This will become useful when we do shell programming in later chapters.

2.13 Background Execution

UNIX supports a type of background execution which exploits its multiprogramming capability to the fullest. The mechanism of how this works is discussed in Chapter 10. Very simply, if you append a command line with an ampersand, &, the command will be run in the background and you can continue to work at the terminal.

Since all you have done with the ampersand is direct the shell to continue processing while the command is processing, unpredictable results will occur if the background process is writing to standard output (or reading from standard input). The output of many commands can be erroneously interleaved. When used properly, this is a powerful feature:

```
$ cc *.c &
$ nroff *.doc > textbook &
$ vi newtext.doc
```

In the above example, we are compiling a C language system and creating a document in the background while doing some editing in the foreground. The limits on the number of background processes are established by the system administrator and the capacity of your machine.

2.14 Filters

In UNIX, a *filter* is a command which transforms a file in some way. We will see many examples of filters in Chapter 5. Complex functions can be created by connecting several filters and commands with pipes.

To illustrate this we will introduce **grep,** a filter which performs a pattern match similar to the pattern match performed by the shell when it checks the filenames in the user directory. However, **grep** compares each line of a file (not the file name) to the pattern. If there is a match, the entire line is printed on standard output.

The format for **grep** is:

```
grep pattern filename(s)
```

While **grep** can handle patterns with a more general, regular expression notation than the shell, we will use patterns which are absolute strings (no special characters) and leave our more complete discussion for Chapter 5. For example, suppose we created a file of filenames using I/O redirection and the **ls** command:

```
$ ls > dfdir
```

Utilizing the directory in previous examples, we could use **grep** to print the sort programs on standard output:

```
$ grep sort dfdir
dfhsort.f
dfqsort.f
$
```

Note that this would usually be done directly: **ls *.c.**

In general, commands or programs which change the input by rearranging it, modifying it, or selecting certain lines are called filters. The command **grep** is a filter because it transforms its standard input by selecting matched lines before sending it to standard output. The analogy comes from chemistry where a filter is used to change a chemical from one compound into another. This is illustrated in Figure 2.4.

```
$ ls | grep sort | wc -l
2
$
```

The above command line uses **grep** as a filter to extract sort programs and the filtered result is sent to **wc** which prints how many there are.

It is useful at this point to recall the telephone index example. At first we were only able to create the index, add names, and list the entire contents. Now, with **grep,** we can search for numbers based on any single attribute (first name, last name, area code, etc.):

```
$ grep Roz tel
Abramov    Roz    212 555-1365
$
```

2.15 Tee Pipes

Since a pipe may have several connections, and all standard output is being directed into the standard input of the next command, we may want to extract information during its execution. The **tee** command redirects a copy of standard output of the last command executed into a file for later inspection. As illustrated in Figure 2.5, the tee command sends a copy of the standard output of **ls,** to dfdir and displays the number of files in the directory on the terminal.

```
$ ls | tee dfdir | wc -l
6
$ cat dfdir
dfla.c
dfla.o
dfny.c
dfny.o
dfhsort.f
dfqsort.f
$
```

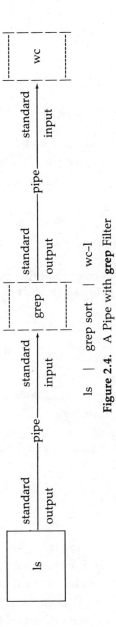

ls | grep sort | wc-l

Figure 2.4. A Pipe with **grep** Filter

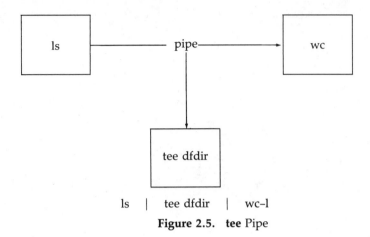

ls | tee dfdir | wc–l

Figure 2.5. **tee** Pipe

2.16 Further Exploration

This chapter has covered the basic concepts you will need to begin using your UNIX system. After logging in, practice using the shell. Perform some of the following exercises.

1. Check the time and date
2. List the contents of your directory
3. Create your own telephone index
4. Create your own appointment calendar
5. Explore the UNIX appointment calendar, **calendar**
6. Explore the UNIX calendar display command, **cal**
7. Check whether there is a **help** or **man** command

2.17 Manual References

cal	display calendar
calendar	appointments calendar
cc	invoke a C compiler
date	displays and sets the date and time
echo	repeat command line arguments
grep	line by line pattern search
help	provide additional online help
ls	list directory contents

login	invoke the login program
man	retrieve online manual
tee	redirect to a file in a pipe
wc	character, line, and word count
who	display users

3

UNIX Editors

Editing is the primary process by which you create files for programs, data, and documents. UNIX provides several powerful editors to support this process. Today, most UNIX systems come with some type of full screen editor, and basic editing can be accomplished without too much difficulty. However, even the advanced editors have their roots in the original UNIX line editors (**ed** and **ex**) and I feel that to be a real UNIX programmer, you should learn editing from the ground up. I still use the primitive **ed** (only compared to some UNIX other editors) for some simple tasks and feel that a solid understanding of the UNIX editors will give you a foundation for things to come. If there is a topic to cut one's teeth by, UNIX editing is it.

Line Editing
Full Screen Editing
Creating a File
The Current Line
Listing Lines
Deleting Lines
Context searching
Changing Lines
Cut and Paste
Saving Changes

There are three types of editors which come with your UNIX system. The first type is the *line editor*, which addresses the file one line at a time. A second type is called a *full screen editor*, in which you may position the cursor anywhere on the screen and enter commands or change text. The third type of editor is a *stream editor* operating like a command or filter, performing editing functions to selected lines in the specified files. We leave our discussion of this editor, **sed**, to Chapter 5, which covers a variety of file manipulation utilities.

Since the original UNIX editor, **ed,** is the basis for other UNIX editing systems and utilities, we begin our discussion with it. While there are a number of full screen editors available for UNIX-based systems, we will describe the most common, the Berkeley editor, **vi,** and its associated line oriented editor, **ex,** both of which are integral parts of System V, Berkeley 4.2, XENIX, VENIX, and other PC-based UNIX systems.

3.1 The *ed* Editor

The standard UNIX editor, present on all UNIX systems is called **ed.** It is a line-oriented context editor which is fast, comprehensive and has powerful features for pattern recognition, but is also quite terse and, therefore, for many beginners, awkward to use. Becoming familiar with **ed** will help you pick up other editors more quickly, since in one form or another, it is a subset of most editing systems you will find. Also, **ed** is an entry point into the mindset of the UNIX programmer.

3.1.1 Creating a File and Entering Data

One enters the editor by using the **ed** command with the name of a file to edit. If the file does not exist, **ed** will create it. **ed** uses the asterisk as a prompt, if it has been toggled on. The prompt command, **P,** acts as the toggle switch which turns the prompt on and off. There are versions of **ed** for which **P** is a synonym for **p** and no prompt is available. Most of our later examples will not show the prompt.

```
$ ed myfile
1230
*
```

In the above example, the editor is entered with the file, *myfile*. The number of characters in the file is displayed. Files, as we will explore in the next chapter, consist of a sequence of unformatted bytes whose sizes are measured in bytes or characters. If *myfile* was a new file, the size would be zero. On some systems an error message appears indicating that the file did not originally exist:

```
$ ed myfile
?myfile
*
```

In the above example, *myfile* didn't exist. While **ed** treats this as an error, it is really just a message that a new file is being edited.

The default mode of **ed** is usually set to display only a question mark when there is an error. This can be toggled and individual messages can be displayed with the **ed** help, **H**, command. Most users, once they have been using ed awhile, prefer to not have the extra lines of output print on the screen.

3.1.2 Entering Data

The editor has two modes of operation: insert mode, in which lines entered at the keyboard are placed in the file, and command mode. To initiate the insert mode, there are two commands you can use. If the file is empty, you enter the **a** command which will append the lines entered to the current position in the file, the beginning:

```
* a
Smith Robert 212 555-1234
Jones William 914 555-2345
Blake Michael 312 555-3456
Browne Peter 203 555-4567
.
*
```

To change back to the command mode the dot is used on a line by itself. *ctrl-D* will also change you back to command mode.

3.1.3 Basic Command Format

The basic command format for the UNIX line editors is:

```
address command arguments
```

The *address* is a specification of absolute line numbers, or context patterns, which delimit the range of an editor command. The *command* is a single letter representing an **ed** function to perform, and the arguments denote the manner in which the operation takes place. In the sections that follow, we explain how to specify line references and most of the important **ed** commands.

3.1.4 Referencing Lines

To reference lines in a line-oriented editor, it is necessary to give the address of the line or line range desired. If omitted, the current line is addressed by default. In **ed**, line addresses begin a command line and consist of the start of the range, separated by a comma from the end of the range. Figures 3.1a-b show the different ways in which lines can be referenced. In the examples, the **n** command is used, which prints the lines with line numbers. If we used the **p** command, the relative line number would not print. A third command, **l**, would list the line showing the ASCII equivalent of special control sequences (e.g., line feed). The line numbers in Figure 3.1a are not part of the actual file, but are used for identification in the rest of the examples.

Figure 3.1b shows examples of absolute line range specifications. The end of the range must exist; otherwise, the editor will issue an error message. As shown in Example 2, if the second part of the range is not present, a single line defaults.

3.1.5 The Current Line

Since **ed** is a line-oriented context editor rather than a full-screen editor, it keeps one line as a reference point. Many ed commands use that line as a

```
 1 Smith Robert 212 555-1234
 2 Jones William 914 555-2345
 3 Blake Michael 312 555-3456
 4 Browne Peter 203 555-4567
 5 vanWormer Judy 914 555-9876
 6 Condliffe Jane 212 555-8901
 7 Sugarman David 212 555-5678
 8 Loxley Robert 212 555-1365
 9 Driver Martha 212 555-7890
10 Condliffe Jane 212 555-8901
11 Steffens Pieta 212 555-9012
12 Jones William 914 555-2345
13 Weber Vanessa 312 555-0123
14 Roberts Judy 213 555-0987
15 Blake Michael 201 555-3456
```

Figure 3.1a. Sample Edit File

1. Display lines 5 through 10:

```
5,10n
 5   vanWormer Judy 914 555-9876
 6   Condliffe Jane 212 555-8901
 7   Sugarman David 212 555-5678
 8   Loxley Robert 212 555-1365
 9   Driver Martha 212 555-7890
10   Condliffe Jane 212 555-8901
```

2. Display only line 5:

```
5n
5 VanWormer Judy 914 555-9876
```

Figure 3.1b. Absolute Line References

base to perform their operations. Referring to Figure 3.1c, the dot is used in context to represent the current line. The first example shows a simple reference to the current line. The second example shows how to reference a line range relative to the current line—in this case, from line 1. The second example also shows a relative reference to a forward line number.

3.1.6 *Your Position in the File*

In general, the position of the current line is placed at the last line referenced by a command. The value of the current line can be printed by using the = command, which prints the value of the address entered. The = is used with the current line symbol, the dot, to show its value after each of the examples.

   To change the current position directly, you can enter either an absolute line number or a relative line number. A carriage return advances the current position 1 line and displays it. Minus ($-$) and plus ($+$) move the current position back and forward, respectively. Without any values, the relative movement is one line at a time. Followed by a number, the current line is changed by the specified number of lines:

$$+10 \quad \text{forward ten lines}$$
$$-5 \quad \text{back five lines}$$

3.1.7 *The Last Line Reference: $*

Another shorthand notation is the $ for the last line of the file. This symbol can be used anywhere that an absolute line reference can be made. In Figure 3.1d, the first example shows how to list the entire contents of the file

1. Display the current line:

```
.n
5 vanWormer Judy 914 555-9876
```

2. Line ranges around the current line (5):

```
1,.n
1   Smith Robert 212 555-1234
2   Jones William 914 555-2345
3   Blake Michael 312 555-3456
4   Browne Peter 203 555-4567
5   vanWormer Judy 914 555-9876
.=
5
```

```
.,10n
 5  vanWormer Judy 914 555-9876
 6  Condliffe Jane 212 555-8901
 7  Sugarman David 212 555-5678
 8  Loxley Robert 212 555-1365
 9  Driver Martha 212 555-7890
10  Condliffe Jane 212 555-8901
.=
10
```

3. Relative references around the current line (5):

```
-5,.n
 5  vanWormer Judy 914 555-9876
 6  Condliffe Jane 212 555-8901
 7  Sugarman David 212 555-5678
 8  Loxley Robert 212 555-1365
 9  Driver Martha 212 555-7890
10  Condliffe Jane 212 555-8901
.=
10
```

```
.,+5n
10  Condliffe Jane 212 555-8901
11  Steffens Pieta 212 555-9012
12  Jones William 914 555-2345
13  Weber Vanessa 312 555-0123
14  Roberts Judy 213 555-0987
15  Blake Michael 201 555-3456
.=
15
```

Figure 3.1c. Current Line References

1. List the entire file:

```
1,$n
1   Smith Robert 212 555-1234
2   Jones William 914 555-2345
3   Blake Michael 312 555-3456
        .
        .
        .
13  Weber Vanessa 312 555-0123
14  Roberts Judy 213 555-0987
15  Blake Michael 201 555-3456
. =
15
```

2. List from the current line to the end:

```
.,$n
10  Condliffe Jane 212 555-8901
11  Steffens Pieta 212 555-9012
12  Jones William 914 555-2345
13  Weber Vanessa 312 555-0123
14  Roberts Judy 213 555-0987
15  Blake Michael 201 555-3456
. =
15
```

Figure 3.1d. End of File Reference

from the first line to the last. The second example displays a line range relative to the current line.

3.1.8 Inserting and Deleting Text

When creating a file, it is necessary to enter the append mode of **ed** to enter text. There are three commands for entering data: **a**, which appends, or inserts, text following the current line, **i**, which inserts lines before the current line, and **c**, which replaces the addressed lines. **c** is the equivalent of a delete followed by an append. Figure 3.2 illustrates each type of insert. Remember: you must enter a dot to tell the editor to return to command mode.

To delete lines you use the **d** command. The command syntax is similar to the print command. A single line or line range followed by the command is specified and all the lines in the range are deleted, as illustrated in Figure 3.3:

5d	deletes line 5
5,10d	deletes lines 5–10
1,$d	deletes all the lines

```
5n
5   VanWormer Judy 914 555-9876
i
Russell Judith 212 555-2424
Klain Stephen 232 555-4353
.
3,8n
3   Blake Michael 312 555-3456
4   Browne Peter 203 555-4567
5   Russell Judith 212 555-2424
6   Klain Stephen 232 555-4353
7   vanWormer Judy 914 555-9876
8   Condliffe Jane 212 555-8901
```

Figure 3.2a. Insert Two Lines

```
5n
5   vanWormer Judy 914 555-9876
a
Russell Judith 212 555-2424
Klain Stephen 232 555-4353
.
3,8n
3   Blake Michael 312 555-3456
4   Browne Peter 203 555-4567
5   vanWormer Judy 914 555-9876
6   Russell Judith 212 555-2424
7   Klain Stephen 232 555-4353
8   Condliffe Jane 212 555-8901
```

Figure 3.2b. Append Two Lines

```
5n
5   vanWormer Judy 914 555-9876
5,6c
Russell Judith 212 555-2424
Klain Stephen 232 555-4353
.
3,8n
3   Blake Michael 312 555-3456
4   Browne Peter 203 555-4567
5   Russell Judith 212 555-2424
6   Klain Stephen 232 555-4353
7   Sugarman David 212 555-5678
8   Loxley Robert 212 555-1365
```

Figure 3.2c. Change Lines 5 and 6

1. Delete line 5:

```
5d
3,7n
3   Blake Michael 312 555-3456
4   Browne Peter 203 555-4567
5   Condliffe Jane 212 555-8901
6   Sugarman David 212 555-5678
7   Loxley Robert 212 555-1365
```

2. Delete lines 5 throught 10:

```
5,10d
3,8n
3   Blake Michael 312 555-3456
4   Browne Peter 203 555-4567
5   Steffens Pieta 212 555-9012
6   Jones William 914 555-2345
7   Weber Vanessa 312 555-0123
8   Roberts Judy 213 555-0987
```

3. Delete all lines in the file:

```
1,$d
1,$n
?
```

Figure 3.3.   Delete Lines

These commands automatically renumber the file, since line numbers are relative to the beginning of the file and not part of the text itself.

3.1.9 Context Searching and Pattern Matching

Sometimes you may want to address lines by their context, rather than by their line numbers. The substitute command, **s,** and the context search specification incorporate patterns similar to the regular expressions we used in Chapter 2. The UNIX editor takes advantage of full regular expression notation to establish patterns for context searching. In fact, the special symbols used are a little different from the wildcard characters of the shell, but they are more general and, as we shall see, they are used in other pattern-matching utilities.

.	match a single character
*	repetition of the previous character
[ ]	match any single character in the set listed between brackets.

In addition to the above, the regular expression may contain symbols which represent the beginning and end of a line:

∧	match beginning of a line
$	match end of a line

Patterns to be matched are created by using combinations of normal and special characters. These patterns are then used in context-search and string-substitution commands. Figure 3.4 shows how these special characters are used to create patterns for searching.

3.1.10 Searching for a String

A string between slashes, /, is a type of line reference which indicates lines with a specific pattern to be matched. For example, if we want to search our telephone directory for the first occurrence of the area code 201, we would enter the following command:

/201/

The search begins at the line following the current line and continues until the first occurrence of the string, wrapping around to the beginning, if necessary. If the string isn't found, **ed** prints an error message. If **ed** does find it, the line containing it is displayed and changed to the current line.

Figure 3.5 shows how the context search can be used on our telephone directory in a variety of interesting ways using the regular expression characters. If the delimiter is **?** instead of /, the search starts back through the file towards the beginning.

When a regular expression symbol is part of the search string, the backslash, \, is used to quote it. This is very inconvenient and care should be taken, especially when editing text such as C programs which use many of the special characters.

Pattern	Description
914	914
f*	multiple f's
[23]12	212 or 312
2.3	2 followed by any character, followed by 3: 203, 213, . . . also 2a3, 2b3, etc.
∧D	D at the start of a line
5$	5 at the end of a line

Figure 3.4. Sample Patterns

If the search string is preceded by a **g,** then every line containing the search string is printed. The **grep** program we introduced in the last chapter uses this function of the editor. It gets its name from the editor command which performs the same function, **g/re/p.** This says to search the file for the regular expression between the slashes and print each line encountered. If the **p** command is not present, it defaults. In our examples, the **n** command is used which also prints the identifying relative line number.

3.1.11 Pattern Ranges

A pattern range can be specified in the same way as a line range. In fact, this is the generalization on the use of search strings. If two patterns are used in an address range, separated by commas, the lines selected include the line matched by the first pattern through the line which matches the second pattern. Once the first range has been selected, the editor will begin the search for a second start/stop pair of pattern matches.

1. Search on a fixed string:

   ```
   /914/n
   2   Jones William 914 555-2345
   ```

2. Search using * notation:

   ```
   /f*/n
   10   Condliffe Jane 212 555-8901
   ```

3. Search using [ ] notation:

   ```
   /[23]12/n
   1   Smith Robert 212 555-1234
   ```

4. Search using . notation:

   ```
   /2.3/n
   4   Browne Peter 203 555-4567
   ```

5. Search using start of line notation:

   ```
   /^D/n
   9   Driver Martha 212 555-7890
   ```

6. Search using end of line notation:

   ```
   /5$/n
   8   Loxley Robert 212 555-1365
   ```

   Figure 3.5a. Context Searching

1. Global absolute string:

```
g/914/p
  Jones William 914 555-2345
  vanWormer Judy 914 555-9876
  Jones William 914 555-2345
```

2. Global multiple character:

```
g/f*/n
 6   Condliffe Jane 212 555-8901
10   Condliffe Jane 212 555-8901
```

3. Global character class:

```
g/[23]12/n
 1   Smith Robert 212 555-1234
 3   Blake Michael 312 555-3456
 6   Condliffe Jane 212 555-8901
 7   Sugarman David 212 555-5678
 8   Loxley Robert 212 555-1365
 9   Driver Martha 212 555-7890
10   Condliffe Jane 212 555-8901
11   Steffens Pieta 212 555-9012
13   Weber Vanessa 312 555-0123
```

4. Global any character:

```
g/2.3/n
 4   Browne Peter 203 555-4567
14   Roberts Judy 213 555-0987
```

5. Global start of line:

```
g/^S/n
 1   Smith Robert 212 555-1234
 7   Sugarman David 212 555-5678
11   Steffens Pieta 212 555-9012
```

6. Global end of line:

```
g/5$/n
 2   Jones William 914 555-2345
 8   Loxley Robert 212 555-1365
12   Jones William 914 555-2345
```

Figure 3.5b. Global Context Searching

3.1.12 Changing Lines

Making changes to lines involves specifying the portion of the line to modify and the text to substitute. The general format for changing the current line uses **s,** the substitute command:

s/regular expression/new string/

The command uses the regular expression as a search string, and if a pattern is matched in the current line, it replaces the regular expression with the new string. To see the result of the substitution, you have to append a print, **p**, or number, **n**, to indicate a display of the change after the substitution. The examples in Figures 3.6a-b use the number command, **n**, and show how the substitute command can be used on our telephone index. In all of the examples, line 5 is assumed to be the current line unless otherwise indicated.

The examples in Figure 3.6a make substitutions to the current line. Example 1 changes lower case ''v'' to upper case while Example 2 uses the repetition symbol, *****, to change 555- to 333-. The last example shows an error displayed when the pattern is not found. In this case, the search included the lower case ''j'' rather than the upper case. Note that throughout the UNIX system, the distinction is made between upper and lower case characters.

It is possible to have the range of the substitutions go beyond the current line and beyond the first occurrence of the pattern on the line. There are several different ways to accomplish this, each with a slight variation. Figure 3.6b shows global changes both on the line and over a range of lines. Note the global command, **g,** append to the substitution indicates the operation should effect multiple occurrences on the same line. This is illustrated in Example 4. the **g** preceding a context address, illustrated in Example 5, indicates that the search should include all lines.

1. Simple substitute, change v to V in current line:

```
5n
5   vanWormer  Judy  914  555-9876
s/v/V/n
5   VanWormer  Judy  914  555-9876
```

2. Substitute with regular expression, change 555 to 333:

```
5n
5   vanWormer  Judy  914  555-9876
s/5*-/333-/n
5   VanWormer  Judy  914  333-9876
```

3. Substitute with regular expression not found:

```
5n
5   vanWormer  Judy  914  555-9876
s/judy/Judith/n
?
```

Figure 3.6a. Single Line Substitutions

1. Single change on a line:

```
5n
5   vanWormer Judy 914 555-9876
s/5/4/n
5   vanWormer Judy 914 455-9876
```

2. Multiple change on a line:

```
5n
5   vanWormer Judy 914 555-9876
s/5/4/ng
5   vanWormer Judy 914 444-9876
```

3. Global change using range, first occurrence per line:

```
1,$s/4/5/n
 1   Smith Robert 212 455-1234
 2   Jones William 914 455-2345
 .
 .
 .
14   Roberts Judy 213 455-0987
15   Blake Michael 201 455-3456
```

4. Global change using range, all occurrences per line:

```
1,$s/4/5/ng
 1   Smith Robert 212 444-1234
 2   Jones William 914 444-2345
 .
 .
 .
14   Roberts Judy 213 444-0987
15   Blake Michael 201 444-3456
```

5. Global change using search string:

```
g/555/s//888/n
 1   Smith Robert 212 888-1234
 2   Jones William 914 888-2345
 .
 .
 .
14   Roberts Judy 213 888-0987
15   Blake Michael 201 888-3456
```

Figure 3.6b. Global Changes

In the last example, the search argument of the **s** command is null. By default, **s** uses the "555" of the context search as the source string. The same command could be expressed:

```
g/555/s/555/888/n
```

3.1.13 *Moving Blocks of Text: Cut and Paste*

Two **ed** commands are used for moving blocks of text. In each case, the lines referenced by the line address part of the command are placed after the target line specified. The move command, **m,** removes the original addressed lines, and the copy command, **t,** takes a copy of them. Figure 3.7 illustrates both move and copy. In each of the examples, the asterisk preceding some of the lines flag the lines affected by the move or copy and are not actually a part of the line or **ed.**

The general form of a move or copy is:

start-line, end-line action target-line

The line range can be specified in one of three ways. You can use a line or context address similar to the technique described above. Figures 3.7a and 3.7b illustrate the move and copy with absolute line references. A second way to specify the line range is to use symbolic names for the lines. This is done using the mark command, **k,** to name lines. Thus, if the following sequence has been entered:

10ka	give line 10 the name a
15kb	give line 15 the name b
5kc	give line 5 the name c

You can do a move by using the line name rather than the line number:

'a,'bm'c   move a through b to c

Before Move		After Move	
		10,15m5	
1,$n		1,$n	
1	Smith Robert 212 555-1234	1	Smith Robert 212 555-1234
2	Jones William 914 555-2345	2	Jones William 914 555-2345
3	Blake Michael 312 555-3456	3	Blake Michael 312 555-3456
4	Browne Peter 203 555-4567	4	Browne Peter 203 555-4567
5	vanWormer Judy 914 555-9876	5	vanWormer Judy 914 555-9876
6	Condliffe Jane 212 555-8901	* 6	Condliffe Jane 212 555-8901
7	Sugarman David 212 555-5678	* 7	Steffens Pieta 212 555-9012
8	Loxley Robert 212 555-1365	* 8	Jones William 914 555-2345
9	Driver Martha 212 555-7890	* 9	Weber Vanessa 312 555-0123
*10	Condliffe Jane 212 555-8901	*10	Roberts Judy 213 555-0987
*11	Steffens Pieta 212 555-9012	*11	Blake Michael 201 555-3456
*12	Jones William 914 555-2345	12	Condliffe Jane 212 555-8901
*13	Weber Vanessa 312 555-0123	13	Sugarman David 212 555-5678
*14	Roberts Judy 213 555-0987	14	Loxley Robert 212 555-1365
*15	Blake Michael 201 555-3456	15	Driver Martha 212 555-7890

Figure 3.7a. Absolute Line Specification Move

Before Copy	After Copy
	`10,15t5`
`1,$n`	`1,$n`
`1   Smith Robert 212 555-1234`	`.1   Smith Robert 212 555-1234`
`2   Jones William 914 555-2345`	`2   Jones William 914 555-2345`
`3   Blake Michael 312 555-3456`	`3   Blake Michael 312 555-3456`
`4   Browne Peter 203 555-4567`	`4   Browne Peter 203 555-4567`
`5   vanWormer Judy 914 555-9876`	`5   vanWormer Judy 914 555-9876`
`6   Condliffe Jane 212 555-8901`	`* 6   Condliffe Jane 212 555-8901`
`7   Sugarman David 212 555-5678`	`* 7   Steffens Pieta 212 555-9012`
`8   Loxley Robert 212 555-1365`	`* 8   Jones William 914 555-2345`
`9   Driver Martha 212 555-7890`	`* 9   Weber Vanessa 312 555-0123`
`*10   Condliffe Jane 212 555-8901`	`*10   Roberts Judy 213 555-0987`
`*11   Steffens Pieta 212 555-9012`	`*11   Blake Michael 201 555-3456`
`*12   Jones William 914 555-2345`	`12   Condliffe Jane 212 555-8901`
`*13   Weber Vanessa 312 555-0123`	`13   Sugarman David 212 555-5678`
`*14   Roberts Judy 213 555-0987`	`14   Loxley Robert 212 555-1365`
`*15   Blake Michael 201 555-3456`	`15   Driver Martha 212 555-7890`
	`*16   Condliffe Jane 212 555-8901`
	`*17   Steffens Pieta 212 555-9012`
	`*18   Jones William 914 555-2345`
	`*19   Weber Vanessa 312 555-0123`
	`*20   Roberts Judy 213 555-0987`
	`*21   Blake Michael 201 555-3456`

Figure 3.7b. Absolute Line Specification Copy

Before Move	After Move
	`10ka`
	`15kb`
	`5kc`
	`'a,'bm'c`
`1,$n`	`1,$n`
`1   Smith Robert 212 555-1234`	`1   Smith Robert 212 555-1234`
`2   Jones William 914 555-2345`	`2   Jones William 914 555-2345`
`3   Blake Michael 312 555-3456`	`3   Blake Michael 312 555-3456`
`4   Browne Peter 203 555-4567`	`4   Browne Peter 203 555-4567`
`5   vanWormer Judy 914 555-9876`	`5   vanWormer Judy 914 555-9876`
`6   Condliffe Jane 212 555-8901`	`* 6   Condliffe Jane 212 555-8901`
`7   Sugarman David 212 555-5678`	`* 7   Steffens Pieta 212 555-9012`
`8   Loxley Robert 212 555-1365`	`* 8   Jones William 914 555-2345`
`9   Driver Martha 212 555-7890`	`* 9   Weber Vanessa 312 555-0123`
`*10   Condliffe Jane 212 555-8901`	`*10   Roberts Judy 213 555-0987`
`*11   Steffens Pieta 212 555-9012`	`*11   Blake Michael 201 555-3456`
`*12   Jones William 914 555-2345`	`12   Condliffe Jane 212 555-8901`
`*13   Weber Vanessa 312 555-0123`	`13   Sugarman David 212 555-5678`
`*14   Roberts Judy 213 555-0987`	`14   Loxley Robert 212 555-1365`
`*15   Blake Michael 201 555-3456`	`15   Driver Martha 212 555-7890`

Figure 3.7c. Marked Line Specification Move

Syntactically, you precede the line name with an apostrophe. Figure 3.7c shows how to name and reference marked lines with the **k** command. In any other command, wherever a line number can appear, the named or marked line can also appear. Thus, you can use this technique for deleting a block, displaying a block, and so forth.

3.1.14 Saving, Quitting, and File Manipulation

Perhaps the most important commands to learn save the file you are editing. It is a good idea when learning a new editor to save your file every few lines until you gain confidence that you won't lose several hours of work. The write command, **w,** is used by ed to save the file being edited. This command can be used with line addresses to save a line range or with a filename option to save the file or line range in another file.

Figure 3.8 shows the different uses of the write command. In the first example, we save the current file, *tel.* In the second example, a backup file, *newtel,* is saved, and in the third example, lines 5 through 10 of the file *parttel* are saved. You must be careful when using **w** without the file option. If you omit a filename, the file you are editing will be changed.

The opposite of writing out lines to a new file is merging text from an existing file into the file being edited. The read command, **r,** is used for

1. Saving the current file:

   ```
   w
   ```

2. Saving the file under a different name:

   ```
   w newtel
   ```

3. Saving part of the current file:

   ```
   10,15w parttel
   ```

4. Saving the current file and leaving ed:

   ```
   w
   q
   ```

5. Leaving the editor without saving:

   ```
   q
   ?
   q
   $
   ```

   or

   ```
   Q
   $
   ```

Figure 3.8. Leaving **ed**

this. Suppose we wanted to incorporate the file *tel2* after line 5 of *tel1*. The following command does this:

```
5rtel2
```

If no line address is given, the file is appended to the current file.

Leaving the editor, one uses the quit command, **q.** If you have not first saved the file with **w,** the ed will display a ?, but after the second **q,** the editor will exit. An upper case **Q** will exit the editor without the warning. In both cases, all changes since the last write will be lost. Be careful!

3.1.15 *Interfacing with the Shell from* ed

Sometimes it is desirable to execute a UNIX command without leaving the editor. For example, suppose you wanted to merge a file with the one being edited, but you forgot its name. You would have to leave the editor, do an **ls** command to check filenames, and re-enter the editor. This can be accomplished by using the editor escape command, **!,** which causes the UNIX command specified to be executed and the result to be displayed (on standard output) delimited by the exclamation point. (Note the prompt, ***,** has been turned on to distinguish between shell and **ed** modes.)

```
*  !ls
f1
f2
!
*  r  fl
```

Any UNIX command can be executed from ed in this way. In Chapter 6, we will view the shell as simply one of UNIX's commands. Because of this, it is possible to "escape" to the shell by entering the **sh** command.

```
*  !sh
$
```

Any and all UNIX functions and facilities can be invoked—even **ed.** When you are ready to return to the current edit session, simply terminate the shell by entering a *ctrl-D.*

```
$  ctrl-D
*
```

The **!** modifier on read and write subcommands also provides a powerful interface to the shell. With **w,** it writes the specified lines as standard input to the command:

```
*  1,10w  !pr
```

The **pr** command formats and prints on standard output the first 10 lines of the file being edited. To incorporate the output of a command in the current file, you enter **r !command**. For example, to include the date in the current file at the current location:

```
*  r  !date
```

Different UNIX versions respond by displaying the number of characters added to the file, the number of new lines, or the new text itself. This is illustrated in Figure 3.9.

3.1.16 Conclusion

These are not all of **ed**'s features. However, they will enable you to do more than many of the editors you may be familiar with. More importantly, many UNIX systems come with enhanced editors based on **ed** which provide greater ease of use. In the next sections, we look at the Berkeley editors, **ex** and **vi,** which add new features and a full screen capability to UNIX editing.

3.2 Full Screen Editing: vi and ex

While we have not covered all of the features of **ed,** you will be able to do more than many other text editors. Most likely, however, your system will come with a full-screen editor, and most of your editing will not be with

```
Set  number:
 1,4p
 1       Smith Robert 212 555-1234
 2       Jones William 914 555-2345
 3       Blake Michael 312 555-3456
 4       Browne Peter 203 555-4567
 r  !date
29
 1,5p
 1       Smith Robert 212 555-1234
 2       Jones William 914 555-2345
 3       Blake Michael 312 555-3456
 4       Browne Peter 203 555-4567
 5       Sun Sep 30 12:22:50 EDT 1984
```

Figure 3.9. Incorporating Filter Output

ed. The majority of UNIX versions will supply the Berkeley **vi** editor and its associated line-oriented editor, **ex.** Full-screen editing is philosophically different from line editing, and as you begin to understand how it works, it will be very difficult to go back to a line editor except for special situations.

3.2.1 Invoking vi

usage: **vi** [options] files . . .

This editor is invoked with the **vi** command and the file to be edited:

```
vi tellist
```

The screen on your terminal is cleared, and the top lines of the file are placed on the screen. This represents a window through which you can inspect and modify the file. If the file is empty, the screen will be blank. In **vi**, the tilde (~) is displayed at the beginning of each empty line at the end of the file. As illustrated in Figure 3.10, this notation is used to fill the last screen when displaying the file.

3.2.2 Full Screen Editing under vi

If you have always edited with a full-screen editor, then using **vi** may seem confusing at first. There are a few important differences between **vi** and

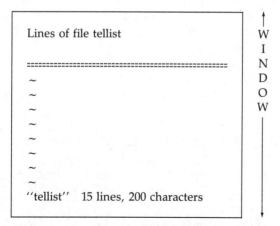

Figure 3.10.   Terminal Screen at the End of a File

most full-screen editors or word processors which you should keep in mind.

3.2.2.1 *Cursor and Screen Control.*

Word processing programs present one window of the document and provide for screen and cursor control commands which enable you to position yourself at any point in the document. Since many of the packages are written for specific computers (e.g., IBM-PC), they take advantage of that personal computer's special keyboard. Thus, *pgup, pgdn, home, end,* cursor arrows, and other keys will perform actions which are appropriate both to the package and the key.

On the other hand, **vi** has been written for a variety of terminals; therefore, its commands are designed to be keyboard independent. For the experienced word processor user, this is very inconvenient, especially compared to one of the better text or word processing packages. After a while, however, most users become as familiar with **vi**'s generic key sequences for control of the cursor and screen as they had been with special keys used by other packages. Furthermore, your version of **vi** may be tailored to utilize some of your terminal keyboard's special keys.

3.2.2.2 *Data Entry and Replacement.*

The second and perhaps most confusing difference between full-screen editing with **vi** and other full-screen editors is the way **vi** operates on a window of text. In reality, **vi** is an extension of a line editor. While it displays a window of text, it operates on one line at a time. The first disconcerting aspect of **vi** which new users observe is that the window is not "open" in the sense that you can enter text where the cursor is positioned. You enter commands which open the window at the current cursor position (in the current line), then add or replace text. The important point here is that you must indicate which operation you are performing before you enter text. You operate as if you were in a line editor and enter commands such as append at the current line, replace the next few lines, and so forth.

For example, suppose you want to replace three words in the middle of a line. The following actions must be performed:

- Position the cursor at the beginning of the words to be replaced. This is done with the **vi**'s generic key sequences rather than with the standard cursor control on your terminal.
- Enter a command to replace the next three words. The command is not displayed, but an indication of the scope of the replacement appears on the screen.
- Enter the text to replace the three words.
- Terminate the command and exit the insert mode.

3.2.2.3 Line Orientation. While most editors have some type of wrap-around facility, it is necessary in **vi** to enter a carriage return at the end of each line of text. While this will not cause any confusion when entering programs, it is cumbersome, especially when compared to the better word processors on the market for personal computers. Text is formatted with the text-formatting utilities (**nroff/troff**), not with the UNIX editors.

3.2.2.4 Screen Refresh. Another confusing difference between **vi** and other full-screen editing systems is the manner in which the screen is managed and refreshed when entering data and cursor control commands. Basically, the screen is only refreshed, that is, reformatted with new information, after a command is terminated. Thus, if you have entered several words and decide to modify them, backspacing does not refresh the screen by blanking out characters. They remain on the screen. Only when the command ends will extraneous characters be deleted, and the screen will reflect the last operation performed.

3.2.2.5 Command Echo. When you enter a command in the basic **vi** command mode, it will not echo on the screen. Thus, when the command to delete is entered (see below), you will not know that a command has been entered. The keys which are entered next will determine how many characters or lines will be deleted. This can initially be very confusing.

3.2.3 vi *Command Modes*

Since the entire screen is a window to be operated on, the editor interprets key sequences, control characters, etc., as commands without printing them, unless the command specifically directs **vi** to do so. Therefore, with **vi,** we can define two modes:

1. *Command Mode.* Key entries are interpreted as commands.
2. *Input Mode.* Key entries are interpreted as text and are inserted into the displayed window

For some commands, usually those requiring a variable length and complex type of argument, the cursor is positioned at the bottom of the window after entering the command, and you then enter the rest of the command.

3.2.4 *Cursor and Window Movement*

Like **ed, vi** operates on a line in the file which is designated the current line and displays a window of the file which is usually the number of lines it takes to fill up the screen. The displayed window can be scrolled, that is, moved up or down. In **vi**, the cursor indicates the current line and position.

Our first set of functions involve the movement or scrolling of the window. By entering the different scrolling operations, the position of the window changes and different sections of the file can be viewed and operated on:

ctrl-U	scroll up one half screen
ctrl-B	scroll backward one full screen
ctrl-D	scroll down one half screen
ctrl-F	scroll forward one full screen

If you enter a value before entering the half-screen scrolling sequences, the movement will be the number of lines entered. When the command is entered again without a count, the number of lines scrolled up or down will default to the previous value of the command.

10 ctrl-U   scroll up ten lines

Paging up or down multiple screens is accomplished by preceding the full page scroll commands (**ctrl-B, ctrl-F**) with values indicating the number of pages to scroll. In this case, however, subsequent page scroll commands default back to one page at a time.

3.2.5 Basic Cursor Movement

In addition to scrolling the window, the cursor can be moved around the visible window using cursor movement commands. The first group we will discuss simply places the cursor at the top, middle, or bottom of the window. The cursor can be placed in the upper left corner with the **H**(ome) command, in the middle of the window with the **M**(iddle) command, and at the bottom of the window with the **L**(ower) command. These keys do not change the position of the window, only the cursor within the window, and they must be upper case. Figure 3.11 illustrates the **H, M,** and **L** positions within the window and the operation of the window scrolling commands.

The commands which control the cursor may refer to **vi** text objects, which are basically characters, lines, words, sentences, and paragraphs. Thus, a cursor command will move or operate on the next or previous text object(s) specified, depending on the count. Table 3.1 defines these objects.

The format for a cursor movement command is:

[count] command

File:

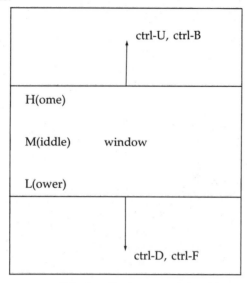

Figure 3.11. Window Positions and Scrolling

The count is always optional and, when omitted, defaults to 1.

Character cursor movement is controlled by the conveniently placed **h, j, k,** and **l** keys. They cause the cursor to move left one space, up one line, down one line, and right one space, respectively. This is illustrated in Figure 3.12.

While this is standard **vi,** different versions may be tailored to your terminal keyboard, and the cursor positioning and scrolling keys (*Home, PgUp, PgDn, rubout,* etc.) may also perform the desired action.

Other commands position the cursor at the beginning (**w**) or end (**e**) of the next word, back to the beginning of the previous word (**b**), to the beginning (**left parenthesis**) or end (**right parenthesis**) of a sentence, and to the beginning (**{**) or end (**}**) of a paragraph. The commands are listed in Table 3.2. Some examples of their use are illustrated in Figure 3.13.

TABLE 3.1
vi *Text Objects*

Object	Description
Characters	
Words	Strings separated by space, tab, newline, or punctuation
Line	Text up to the next newline character
Sentences	Strings ending in .,?, !, followed by two spaces
Paragraph	Series of lines terminated by a blank line (nroff/troff delimiters are also recognized)

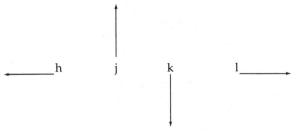

Figure 3.12. Cursor Movement

3.2.6 Inserting Text

To insert text you have to place **vi** in the insert mode. All insertions are relative to the current line. After entering one of the **vi** insert commands, characters entered will become part of the text. The escape (ESC) key returns you to the command mode. The insert commands are similar to the **ed** command with some variations and extensions.

The first two types of input mode commands are **i** and **I**. Lower case **i** inserts before the location of the cursor. **I** positions the cursor at the beginning of the current line. Any text entered will become part of the file.

The append commands, **a** and **A,** operate in the same way as **i** and **I,** except that text is entered after the cursor position or, in the case of **A,** at the end of the current line.

A third insertion command pair is **O** and **o** which open up the line before and after the current line, respectively. In both cases the insert mode is entered, and you can enter any number of new lines. Insertion modes are illustrated in Figure 3.14.

3.2.7 Deleting Text

Text is deleted by character or by reference to the text objects described above (lines, words, sentences, and paragraphs). For example, to delete

TABLE 3.2
Cusor Movement Commands

Command	Description
w	Beginning of the next word
b	Beginning of the previous word
e	End of the next word
(	Beginning of a sentence
)	End of a sentence
{	Beginning of a paragraph
}	End of a paragraph

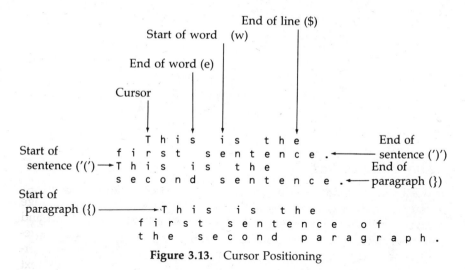

Figure 3.13. Cursor Positioning

individual characters, the **x** command is used. With a count, **x** characters are deleted to the right of the cursor. The more general **d** command is used to delete text objects and takes the type of object as an argument. Objects which can be deleted include lines, words, sentences, and paragraphs. To delete the next word, you enter **dw.**

A count can also be used when deleting multiple text objects. The count can be associated either with the delete command or with the text object. Therefore, the following two commands delete three paragraphs:

```
3d}
d3}
```

Table 3.3 lists some of the **d** command options.

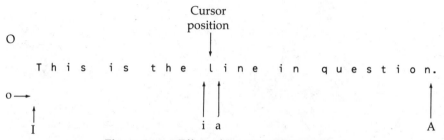

Figure 3.14. Effect of Insertion Commands

TABLE 3.3
Delete Command Options

Command	Description
dw	Delete word
d)	Delete to end of sentence
d}	Delete to end of paragraph
dd	Delete lines

3.2.8 Modifying Text

Text is changed using the change and replace **vi** commands. The change command, **c,** replaces the object. Objects include words, sentences, and paragraphs. When the **c** command is entered, **vi** will display a $ to delimit the range of the change and place **vi** in the input mode. After entering the desired text, you leave the input mode by pressing ESC. The text part of the command may contain several lines. This is illustrated in Figure 3.15.

The replace command is used in a similar fashion to the change command, except the range of the insert is either one character (**r**) or a number of lines (**R**).

3.2.9 Searching for Text

The **vi** and **ex** editors use the same pattern searching commands as **ed.** The / and **?** commands can be used to search for regular expressions forward in the file and backwards in the file, respectively. The **vi** editor responds to

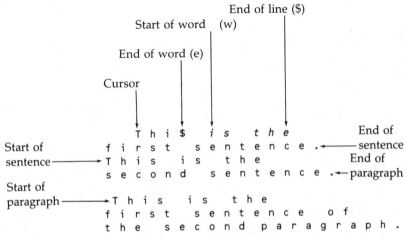

Figure 3.15a. Change Word: **cw**

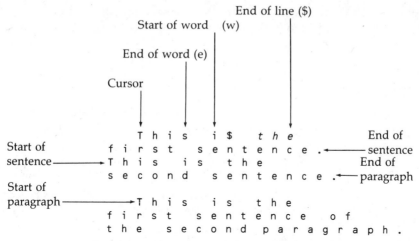

Figure 3.15b. Change two Words: **2cw**

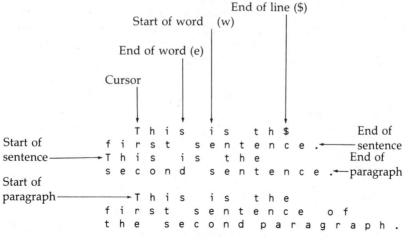

Figure 3.15c. Change Line: **c$**

a search command by positioning the cursor at the bottom of the window and waiting for the rest of the search criteria string to be entered. For example, to search forward from the cursor position for lines beginning with ABC, you enter:

```
/^ABC/<cr>
```

The **vi** editor has other search commands for finding characters on the current line (**f,F**) and positioning just before the found character (**t,T**). The repeat search command, **n,** repeats the last search command entered. **N** will reverse the direction of the last search. Search commands are summarized in Table 3.4.

3.2.10 ex escape mode

As indicated earlier, **vi** and **ex** are really the same editor. This relationship is seen when you use the **ex** command **:** in **vi,** which sets up a command line at the bottom of your screen and accepts a full range of **ed**-like commands from the **ex** command mode of **vi.** The **ex** editor from University of California, Berkeley, is an expanded version of the **ed** editor. While all the **ed** subcommands are valid in **ex,** the use of **ed** subcommands in **ex** is actually an abbreviation of the longer, more meaningful mnemonic name. Table 3.5 gives the **ex** commands and their abbreviated **ed** counterparts.

After an **ex** command is executed, as illustrated in Figure 3.16, the cursor returns to its original position in the **vi** command mode. All modified text is based on the original cursor position.

From **vi,** if you use the **Q** command, you will be placed into the **ex** command mode, and all subsequent commands will keep you in the **ex** editor. To flip back to **vi,** simply enter **vi** without any arguments from the **ex,:** prompt (see below). Since **ex** is an editor in its own right, it is possible to enter it directly from the shell with arguments similar to **ed** and **vi.**

The **ex** operation is similar to **ed** and uses the same commands, manner in which line addresses are computed, and format for creating regular expressions.

3.2.11 Search and Replace

To perform search and replace operations in **vi,** you escape to **ex** (using the **:** command) and use the substitute command, **s,** in the same way it is

TABLE 3.4
vi Search Commands

Command	Description
/RE/	Search for regular expression forward
?RE?	Search for regular expression backward
f*char*	Search for character forward
F*char*	Search for character backward
;	Repeat last character search
,	Reverse last direction of last character search
n	Repeat last search command
N	Repeat last search command in reverse

TABLE 3.5
ex *Commands and Their* **ed** *Counterparts*

ex	ed and ex Abbreviation
append	a
change	c
copy	t
delete	d
ex	e
file	f
global	g
insert	i
join	j
mark	k
list	l
move	m
next	n
print	p
quit	q
read	r
substitute	s
write	w

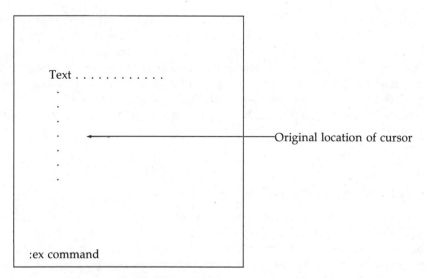

Figure 3.16. Issuing ex Commands

done in **ed.** In this way, you can reference lines by using absolute and relative line references as well as patterns. Furthermore, **ex** supports additional regular expression symbols for more complex patterns, including the ability change from upper-to-lower or lower-to-upper cases and to search for the beginnings and ends of words. For example, to search for a character at the beginning of a word, the \< pattern matching sequence is used:

```
:p
this is a test of earching for a word beginning
:s/\<e/se/p
this is a test of searching for a word beginning
```

In the example, the "e" in "test" is not matched, but the "e" in "earching" is matched. The substitution replaces the starting "e" with "se."

To indicate conversion to upper or lower case in search replacement strings \U and \L are used. For example, to capitalize a word in the example above:

```
: s/word/\Uword/p
this is a test of searching for a WORD beginning
```

This is more appropriately used with regular expressions. To capitalize the beginning of each word:

```
:s/\<./\u&/g
This Is A Test Of Searching For A Word Beginning
```

In this example, the search argument is \<.. This is interpreted as any first character (.) At the beginning of a word (\<). The target string \u& changes every first character to upper case. & is a shorthand for the search argument. Thus, the search string matched (first character of a word) is changed to upper case. The last part of the command, **g,** causes the changes to occur on all matched strings on the current line.

Table 3.6 summarizes the additional pattern matching and replacement symbols.

3.2.12 Cut and Paste with **vi**

One way to perform cut and paste operations within **vi** is to use the **ex** escape mode and the **m** and **t** (move and copy) commands from **ed.** This requires that you first determine the relative line positions by using the = command in the **ex** escape mode (entering .= returns the position of the

TABLE 3.6
ex *Expanded Pattern Matching Characters*

Command	Description
\<	Match beginning of word
\>	Match end of word
\l	Convert following character to lower case
\u	Convert following character to upper case
\L	Convert following characters to lower case
\U	Convert following characters to Upper case
\e	Delimit case conversion
\E	Delimit case conversion

current line). You then specify the from/to address range of the block and the line number of the target location:

> :10,20m30   moves lines 10–20 after line 30
>
> :10,20t30   copies lines 10–20 after line 30

A second technique marks the text, similar to **ed,** and then executes the move or copy in the **ex** escape mode. The **vi** command **m** (**k** as in **ed** if you use the **ex** escape mode) marks the line where the cursor is positioned with the single letter specified. Thus, to mark a block of text, position the cursor at the beginning and give it a single letter name (e.g., **b** for beginning). Then position the cursor at the end of the text and mark the line with another name (e.g., **e** for end). Now, move to the spot where the text is to be copied or moved and use the **m** or **t** command in **ex** escape mode:

```
:'b,'em.
```

In this example, the text demarcated by **b** and **e** are moved to the current line position.

Marked text can be referenced in other ways. The name reference is a text block delimiter in the same way that the close parenthesis delimits sentences. Operations which use the built-in text markers will work with the named references. For example, to move to the text marked 'b, simply enter 'b as a command. Lines of text also can be deleted in this way.

Perhaps the most direct way to move text does not involve using the ex escape mode at all. Instead, a special set of work areas (called buffers) is used. This is discussed next.

3.2.13 Named Buffers

Each time you delete a block of text, the deleted lines go into an unnamed work area called a buffer. The unnamed buffer can be referenced simply with the **P** and **p** commands, which place the lines before and after the current line, respectively. Thus to perform a simple cut and paste:

1. Mark the end of the block to cut.
2. Position the cursor at the beginning of the block.
3. Delete the block. For example, if you named the block x: **dx**
4. Position the cursor at the location you wish to paste the block.
5. Use the **p** command to deposit the contents of the unnamed buffer.

If you are managing several blocks of text at the same time, it is possible to yank text into a named buffer. The double-quote is used to reference named buffers which can have names from a to z. The **y** command preceded by a buffer name yanks lines into the named buffer:

> **"ay**　　yanks 1 line into buffer **a**
> **5"ay**　　yanks 5 lines into buffer **a**

To paste the text, you would use the **p** command with the named buffer:

> **"ap**　　puts the named buffer **a** into the text at the current cursor
> location

3.2.14 Recovering from Mistakes: **undo**

If you have made a change by mistake, and want to reverse it, the undo command, **u,** will reverse the action of the last editing command. Suppose you deleted five lines by mistake. Entering the **vi** or **ex** command **u** will restore them. Entering **u** again will delete them. The range of the undo will include more than one change to a line or changes to multiple lines. Unfortunately, you cannot undo changes to the file system, so undo will not work if you have already saved changes with write (**w**).

3.2.15 vi and ex Communication with the Shell: Filtering Text

At times, you will want to leave an editing session temporarily, execute one or more UNIX commands, then return to the current editing session. If you want to enter a single command, you enter an exclamation point followed by the command in the **ex** escape mode:

```
:!ls
```

To temporarily leave the editor and execute a series of commands at the shell level, you would use the **ex, sh** command:

```
:sh
$
```

You return to the **vi** (or **ex**) by terminating the shell with a *ctrl-D*. In this mode, you can enter any shell command, even a new editing session. The exact manner in which this works is discussed further in later chapters. Furthermore, the read and write shell interfaces from **ed,** which can be used to read in the output of commands or write lines to commands, are available from **ex** or the escape mode of **vi**.

More interestingly, it is possible to run UNIX commands against a set of lines in the file and have the output of the filter replace the original lines. The **vi** filter command **!** is used for this. To sort the telephone directory, for example, we specify the cursor command with the end of paragraph indicator which will sort lines up to the first blank line:

```
!}sort
```

This is illustrated in Figure 3.17.

Cursor position

```
Smith Robert 212 555-1234
Jones William 914 555-2345
Blake Michael 312 555-3456
Browne Peter 203 555-4567
vanWormer Judy 914 555-9876
Condliffe Jane 212 555-8901
Sugarman David 212 555-5678
Loxley Robert 212 555-1365
                .
                .
                .
```

```
!}sort
```

Figure 3.17a. Indicating the Filter

```
Blake Michael 312 555-3456
Browne Peter 203 555-4567
Condliffe Jane 212 555-8901
Jones William 914 555-2345
Loxley Robert 212 555-1365
Smith Robert 212 555-1234
Sugarman David 212 555-5678
vanWormer Judy 914 555-9876
```

.
.
.

Figure 3.17b.   After Entering the **sort** Command

3.2.16 *Leaving* vi

You leave **vi** either by causing **vi** to save the changes using the **ZZ** command, or by not saving the changes and escaping to **ex** using the **Q** or **:** command. Since all **ex** commands are available, you can quit without saving the changes, **quit!,** or enter any other **ex** command, including write, **w.**

3.2.17 vi/ex *Environment Options*

When operating with **ex**, there are a wide variety of options you can set which control the current execution of the editor. Table 3.7 lists the most important ones.

Options are set with the **ex, set** command. If you enter **set** with the **all** argument, the currently set options will be displayed. While this is illustrated in Figure 3.18a, you will have to refer to your system documentation for complete descriptions of all the options displayed. Some options are set on or off, others are set to values. For those options which turn a feature on, there is a counter option preceded by "no" which turns it off. For example, where **number** causes all line displays to list the relative line number, **nonumber** inhibits it. In a development environment, the most useful of these options are **autoprint, number, autoindent,** and **nomagic.** The options described below are illustrated in Figures 3.18a-c.

In many of our earlier illustrations, we used the **ed** or **ex p** option so that the result of an operation would also be displayed. By setting **autoprint,** results of commands like substitute (**s**) are automatically printed. The **number** option causes the relative line number to display whenever lines print. Furthermore, in the insert modes, the line number of the line to be inserted is displayed. This is illustrated in Figures 3.18b and 3.18c.

TABLE 3.7
Selected ex and vi Options

Option		Description
autoindent	(noautoindent)	Set on (off) automatic indentation
autoprint	(autoprint)	Set on (off) automatic verify
autowrite	(noautowrite)	Set on (off) automatic save
ignorecase	(noignorecase)	Set on (off) case recognition in pattern matching
magic	(nomagic)	Set on (off) special character recognition in pattern matching
number	(nonumber)	Set on (off) automatic number display during insert modes (a, i)
shiftwidth=value		Set value for back shifting when autoindent set
term=value		Set terminal type
terse	(noterse)	Set on (off) terse messages
tabstop=value		Set tab width value
wrapscan	(nowrapscan)	Set on (off) line wrap on long lines

If you are writing programs and want the physical structure of the text to reflect the logical structure of the program, you indent lines accordingly. Instead of tabbing to the appropriate point for each line entered, the **autoindent** option causes the next line in the append, insert, or change mode to position at the last indented position after a carriage return. To unindent one tab position, you enter a *ctrl-D* on a line by itself. This is illustrated in Figure 3.18c. (For C programs, see **cb** in Chapter 9).

C programs use all kinds of special characters as part of the language syntax: []*/\ etc. These are also regular expression symbols with special meaning, and they would have to be quoted if used in a regular expression context in **ex** or **vi**. The **nomagic** option turns off most of the regular expression symbol meaning, leaving only ∧ (beginning of a line) and $ (end of a line). This is a very significant convenience! For example, suppose the text had the following C program declaration for an integer pointer variable:

```
int ivar;
```

```
:set all
noautoindent        open                                      tabstop=8
autoprint           optimize                                  taglenth=0
noautowrite         paragraphs=lPLPPPQPP Llpp1pipbp           tags=tags
/usr/lib/tags
nobeautify          prompt                                    term=du
directory=/tmp      noreadonly                                noterse
noedcompatible      redraw                                    timeout
noerrorbells        remap                                     ttytype=du
hardtabs=8          report=5                                  warn
noignorecase        scroll=8                                  window=16
nolisp              sections=NHSHH HUnhsh                     wrapscan
nolist              shell=/bin/csh                            wrapmargin=5
magic               shiftwidth=3                              nowriteany
mesg                showmatch
number              slowopen
```

Figure 3.18a.   Sample Option Settings

```
:set number
:1,8p

1       Smith Robert 212 555-1234
2       Jones William 914 555-2345
3       Blake Michael 312 555-3456
4       Browne Peter 203 555-4567
5       vanWormer Judy 914 555-9876
6       Condliffe Jane 212 555-8901
7       Sugarman David 212 555-5678
8       Loxley Robert 212 555-1365
```

Figure 3.18b.   List with the Number Option Set

Start of insert:

```
1      #include <stdio.h>
2      -
```

After one indent:

```
       .
       .
       .
2      main()
3      {
4                  printf(".....;
5                  -
```

Backward indent:

```
       .
       .
       .
2      main()
3      {
4                  printf(".....;
5                  printf(''.....;(ctrl-D
6      -
```

Figure 3.18c. Autoindent

Suppose the statement is missing an * indicating a pointer variable. It is necessary to quote the special characters:

```
s/ivar/\*ivar;/
```

The above statement is difficult to interpret, and statements with a lot of quoting are prone to error (consider C comments with / and *). By turning off **magic,** the substitute command becomes much easier:

```
:set nomagic,autoprint
:s/ivar/*ivar/
:int *ivar
```

Note that with autoprint set, the **p** command on the **s** command is not necessary.

3.2.18 The ex/vi Profile

Since you will want to enter some of the options during each editing session, **ex** has two methods for reading options from the environment. In the first method, you place in a file, *.exrc,* the **set** command for all the options you want set. This file must be in your home directory. A second method involves setting the environment variable, EXINIT, in your user profile:

C-shell:

```
setenv EXINIT "set nomagic autoprint, . . . "
export EXINIT
```

Bourne

```
EXINIT="set nomagic autoprint  . . . "
export EXINIT
```

Chapters 4, 7 and 8 discuss both the file system and profiles in some detail, and you may want to come back to this section after reading those chapters.

3.2.19 The **vi** *and* **ex** *Commands*

usage: **ex, vi** [options] files

When entering **ex** or **vi,** you can specify a number of options and more than one file to be edited. The **-x** option is used for editing encrypted files, and the **-R** option sets the **vi** or **ex** to read only.

Many times, you will want to perform an editing operation on a collection of files. This can be done by specifying a file list on the command line (you can use wildcard characters). Then you can go from file to file by using the **ex** escape mode next (**n**) command which sequences through the file list. The **ex** mode **rew** command rewinds the file list to the beginning.

3.3 Further Exploration

While we have not covered all of **vi** and **ex,** we have described its most important elements. On most UNIX systems, some type of full screen editor will be provided which possesses most of the capabilities of **vi.** See which features your system supports.

1. Create and modify a telephone index using **vi** and **ex.**
2. Which keyboard keys are supported by your system (PgUp, PgDn, Home, cursor arrows, etc.)?
3. When in **ed, vi,** or **ex,** escape to the shell and run the **ps** (process status) command. Return to the editor by terminating the shell.

3.4 Manual References

ed	basic editor
ex	Berkeley editor
grep	pattern matching filter
more	file scanner with vi option
ps	process status
sed	stream editor
vi	visual editor
view	visual editor in read-only mode

4

The UNIX File System

In this chapter we explore the UNIX file system. Our discussion will be divided into a description of the file system from the user's perspective and a discussion of files from a systems, or implementation, point of view. The former represents the logical file system, from which you will create, access, and manipulate data and programs. For new users this section should be read carefully.

The discussion of implementation focuses on the physical file system and describes how files are stored at the system level. As a command or shell-level user, you may not need to understand how files are actually implemented and you can skim this section. Programmers and those who may have administrative responsibility for the system need a conceptual understanding of file system internals and may want to come back to this section later on.

Here are the key concepts discussed in this chapter:

UNIX File Types
Directories
Hierarchical File Structure
Path Names
File Types
Basic File Operations

File Security and Protection
Physical File Structure
   Superblock
   Inodes
   File Allocation

4.1 The Logical File System

This section discusses the UNIX file system from the logical or shell-level perspective. Understanding how the UNIX file system works and how to use the basic features of the shell (see Chapter 2) are sufficient to begin to use the UNIX system to its full advantage. Users of MS-DOS will see many similarities.

The UNIX system has three types of files: *ordinary, directory,* and *special* files.

4.1.1 Ordinary Files

Ordinary files are simply a sequence of bytes which may contain source programs, object programs, shell programs (command sequences), data, etc. For these types of files, there are no special identifying characteristics which distinguish one type of file from another. The program which processes the file will determine any internal organization which may be required.

4.1.2 Directory Files

Directory files contain the names of other files and pointers to system information about the files.

4.1.3 Special Files

Special files represent physical devices and the programs which operate them. In the UNIX operating system, all I/O devices are treated as files, which simplifies their management from both the user and the systems points of view. Thus, output to a printer is treated as output to a particular special file.

The entire collection of ordinary, directory, and special files, organized into a hierarchical structure, constitute a file system.

4.2 The File System Hierarchy

The UNIX file system is organized into a *hierarchy,* or tree, as shown in Figure 4.1. Tree nodes which have no branches coming out of them represent special or ordinary files. Thus, nodes F1 through F11 are either special or ordinary files.

Nodes with branches are called *directories.* As mentioned earlier, directories are files that contain the names of other files. Nodes D1 through D6 in Figure 4.1 are directory files.

Figure 4.2 illustrates a typical UNIX file system. The top of the hierarchy is called the root directory and has the name /. You can check which files are in the root directory on your system by using the **ls** command with the / file parameter:

```
$ ls /
bin
dev
etc
usr
$
```

In this example, all the files are directory files, which contain filenames of lower parts of the hierarchy. The directory names in the root directory are distributed with your UNIX system. Table 4.1 gives the contents of some of the standard UNIX directories which are at the root level.

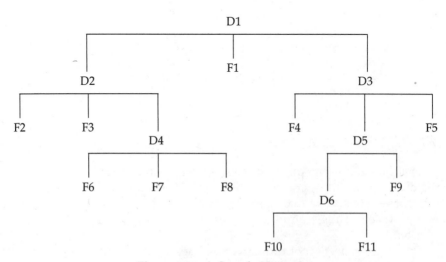

Figure 4.1. A Sample Hierarchy

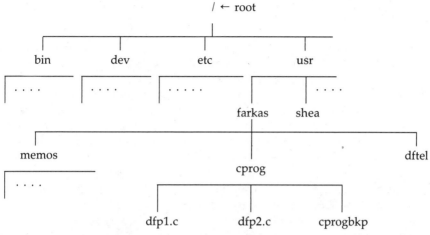

Figure 4.2. UNIX File Hierarchy

4.3 *Home Directory*

When you log in, UNIX will automatically establish one directory (designated when your user-id was established) as a home directory. This directory is displayed when you use the **ls** command without any parameters. By convention, your home directory is part of the file system hierarchy starting at the *usr* node. Some systems leave the */usr* directory for vendor distributed libraries and create another directory for users (e.g. */csusr* for the Computer Science department). Referring to Figure 4.2, the *usr* directory contains two files, *farkas* and *shea,* which are home directories to the two users. When farkas does an **ls** command from his home directory, filenames from the *farkas* directory will be displayed:

```
$ ls
cprog
memos
dftel
$
```

Try listing out the files in your home directory.

TABLE 4.1

Directory	Contents
bin	UNIX commands
dev	Special files for devices
etc	Administrative programs and commands
lib	System libraries
usr	Individual user directories
tmp	System temporary file area

4.4 File and Path Names

A filename consists of up to fourteen ASCII characters. While a filename may consist of any character, some subsystems require that files have an extension, usually a period (.) followed by a single character, to identify the type of file it is. For example, *.c* indicates a C program to the C compiler. Table 4.2 shows some of the common file extensions and their meanings. It is important to remember, however, that in UNIX there are no extensions, only characters in a name. A subsystem or utility will interpret the extension when it is required.

In UNIX, the entire file system hierarchy is accessible to you. For example, we have already listed the contents of the root directory by using the **ls** / command. The parameter to **ls** was a directory filename. Each file in the UNIX file system is unique because it is identified by all of the directory names in the path to the name.

The full name of the directory file, *farkas,* is */usr/farkas*. In this case, the first slash (/) indicates that we are starting at the root. Since each name following is a directory name, each name must be separated from the others with a slash. The last name in the list can be any type of file. The full pathname of the file *dfla.c* is */usr/farkas/cprog/dfla.c*. Therefore, while names within a directory must be unique, files in different directories can have identical names.

Any file in the system becomes potentially accessible when the user enters its fully qualified pathname. While access may be limited (see permissions below), the user, farkas, can inspect any other directory or file. From your home directory, take a look at what is in the */bin, /dev,* and */etc* directories. To help you get started, we will illustrate these ideas by finding the games on your system and playing one:

First, use the **ls** command to list out the *usr* directory:

```
$ ls /usr
```

TABLE 4.2
File Extensions

Extension	Meaning
.c	C program
.o	Object file
.p	Pascal Program
.f	Fortran program
.l	Load module
.a	Library

The list displayed should include the directory games. To list it out, you must give the fully qualified pathname:

```
$ ls /usr/games
```

Select a game and enter its name to play it. Remember, you must give the full pathname; otherwise, UNIX will look for the game in your home directory. For example:

```
$ /usr/games/fortune
```

The game fortune acts like a fortune cookie. Try it a few times. If your system doesn't have a game directory (too bad!), use **ls** to see all the basic UNIX commands supported:

```
$ ls /bin
```

4.5 The Current or Working Directory

When you log in and issue the **ls** command, the files in your home directory are displayed. This is called your *current* or *working directory*. The **pwd** command prints the full pathname of that directory. In our sample file system, farkas would see the files in the directory */usr/farkas*, and shea would see those in */usr/shea*.

It would be very inconvenient if every reference to files other than the home directory required the full pathname. Fortunately, this is not the case. The change directory command, **cd,** changes what the system considers the current working directory. The user, farkas, can change the current directory to the C program directory in either of two ways. First, he could enter the full path name:

```
$ cd /usr/farkas/cprog
```

Another way to accomplish the same result would be to omit the path components up to the current working directory:

```
$ cd cprog
```

The second entry appends the directory specified to the current working directory to form the full path name. Unless the root is specified as the first directory in the path, the path of the current working directory is placed at the beginning of the filename specified. This convention is true for all commands which have file parameters. Thus, it is easier to reference files in the current directory as well as anywhere in the file system.

4.6 Special Directories: ., ..

Every directory has two special directory file entries which are not displayed by a simple **ls** (try **ls -a**). A single period (.) refers to the current directory. A double period (..) refers to the parent directory. These directory names, illustrated in Figure 4.3, can be used anywhere it would make sense to use a directory reference. Referring again to Figure 4.2, if the current directory is memos, there are two ways to list the contents of the cprog directory without changing the current directory. You may use either the full path name:

```
$  ls /usr/farkas/cprog
```

or the parent directory reference:

```
$  ls ../cprog
```

Suppose you wanted to copy a file from the cprog directory to the memos directory. You would use the copy, **cp,** command. If the memos directory is current, there are two ways to accomplish this. Either use the full path names:

```
$ cp /usr/farkas/cprog/dfla.c /usr/farkas/memos/dfla.c
```

or the current and parent directory references:

```
$ cp ../cprog/dfla.c .
```

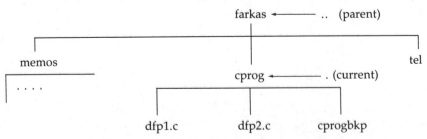

Figure 4.3. UNIX File Hierarchy (cprog current)

In this example, the target of **cp** is the current directory (.). **cp** is discussed fully in the next section. Note that the current and parent directory references are a shorthand for the full path names of these directories.

In the case of the parent reference, one can go up several levels. For example, with memos as current, one can list the contents of the *shea* directory using .. for each upward reference. In this case, we would use the shorthand notation repeatedly, the first for *farkas* and the second for *usr*:

```
$ ls ../../shea
```

Explore some of the directories on your system in this way. This will help solidify the understanding of the file system, as well as give you a sense of what it contains.

4.7 Basic File Manipulation

While we have seen a number of file manipulation commands in our discussion of different UNIX features, this section describes the basic commands to create, copy, move, delete, rename, and share files. In the discussion below, commands are given with their syntax, followed by some examples using the file system shown in Figure 4.2. The current directory is */usr/farkas/cprog*.

4.7.1 Creating and Deleting Directories: **mkdir, rmdir**

The syntax for the **mkdir** command (to make a directory) and the **rmdir** command (to remove a directory) is as follows:

mkdir   filename
rmdir   filename

As we have seen, files are in directories, and other than standard directories which are distributed with your system, you will want to create your own and, on occasion, to delete them. You use **mkdir** and **rmdir** to create and delete directories, respectively. The only restriction on **rmdir** is that the directory to be deleted must be empty.

For example, to create a directory for C object code:

```
$ mkdir cprogobj
```

To delete a directory:

```
$ rmdir cprogobj
```

4.7.2 *Copying Files:* **cp**

The **cp** command is used to copy one or more files to another file or directory. The basic syntax is as follows:

    cp file1 [file2 ...] target

If the target is a file, then one file is copied to the target file. If the target is a directory name, then one or more files are copied to the named directory. It is not possible to copy directories, that is, *file1* cannot be a directory name.

    One common usage of **cp** is to create backup copies of files. You can create a single copy:

```
$ cp dfla.c dfla.bkp
```

or place a collection of files into a backup directory:

```
$ cp dfla.c dfny.c cprogbkp
```

or

```
$ cp *.c cprogbkp
```

Remember, we can use wildcard characters to reduce typing.

4.7.3 *Moving and Renaming Files*

The **mv** command operates in the same way as the **cp** command, except that after **mv** is used, the original filename no longer exists. It uses the following syntax:

    mv file1 [file2 ...] target

Within the same directory, the effect of a move is that the file is renamed. For example, to rename *dfla.c* you enter:

```
$ mv dfla.c dfla.bkp
```

To move files between directories we can also use wildcard character expressions. In the example below, all the C programs are to be moved to the *cprogbkp* directory:

```
$ mv *.c cprogbkp
```

4.7.4 Deleting Files: rm

The **rm** command deletes files. Its basic syntax is as follows:

rm [options] file1 ...

The command line options include **-i,** which requires the user to verify each file deletion. Another option, **-r,** deletes all the files in the directory and then deletes the directory. This option will work recursively to delete an entire subtree of the directory structure.

Consider the following examples:

```
$ rm dfla.c
$ rm *.c
$ rm *
```

The last entry deletes all the files in the directory and therefore must be used with extreme caution. Some UNIX versions protect against this and will ask if you are sure you want to remove all the files. By always indicating the **-i** option, you will protect your files.

To remove a directory, its files, and its subdirectories recursively, you would use the following command:

```
$ rm -r cprogbkp
```

In this situation you want to be particularly careful. While you can prevent complete disaster (see Section 4.8 File Protection), the following command would wipe out your entire system:

```
$ rm -r /
```

4.7.5 Sharing Files: ln

The link command, **ln,** permits the sharing of files by creating a new name for an existing file or directory. It is used with the following syntax:

ln file1 [file2 ...] target

For example, to make the C program file dfla.c in the current directory (*cprog*) available in the *cprogbkp* directory, you enter:

```
$ ln dfla.c cprogbkp
```

An **ls** of *cprogbkp* will show *dfla.c* in the directory. However, unlike the **cp** command, this name refers to the original file in the cprog directory. Furthermore, the new name doesn't need to be the same:

```
$ ln dfla.c cprogbkp/newla.c
```

As another example, consider linking all the files in the memos directory to the current (*cprog*) directory:

```
$ ln ../memos/* .
```

Also note the use of parent and current directory references rather than full pathnames.

Try some examples on your own system. Create some files by using **cp,** rename them with **mv,** delete some with **rm,** and create links to other directories with **ln.** What happens when you remove a linked file? Is it removed from both directories? (Hint: do an **ls -l** in each directory, before and after, and see which value changes for the file.)

4.7.6 *Listing Directory Contents:* **ls**

One final note about the basic file manipulation: The **ls** command may be used with different options to provide considerably more information about a file than its name. Figure 4.4 shows that the **ls** command with the -l option displays the user name, group name, protection information, file size, and access dates. We will be describing some of this information in

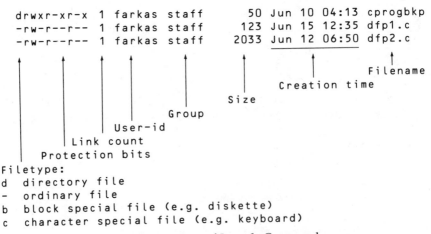

Figure 4.4. Output of Long **ls** Command

greater detail later in the chapter, but try using this option on your own files and on some of the system directories:

```
$  ls  -l
$  ls  -l  /bin
```

Other options to **ls** can display the files in different orders or list all files beginning with a period. Table 4.3 summarizes the commonly used options of **ls.**

4.8 File Protection

Up until now, we have indicated that the entire file system is available to you from your home directory. While this is true, file protection attributes associated with all types of files will restrict your access to different parts of the system. For example, ordinary users should not have the ability to remove all the root files or directories. Furthermore, you may want to restrict the access by others to your own files.

4.8.1 Classes of Users and Modes of Protection

From your perspective, UNIX divides the world into three classes of users: you (the owner of files), your work group, and all others. There are three types of access made available to each class: read, write, and execute.

Read access permits a user to see a file. Our telephone index may offer read access to the owner and the group, but not to everyone else. Write access permits a user to modify a file. You might give write permission on the telephone index to yourself but not to the group or to others. Execute access permits a user to execute a file (providing, of course, that it makes

TABLE 4.3
1s Command Options

Option	Action
–l	Long listing
–t	Sort by last modification first
–a	Include filenames beginning with .
–s	Include the size in blocks
–r	Reverse the order of the sort
–u	Sort by last access first

sense to execute it). Programs are an example of files which must have the execute attribute before they can be invoked from the command line.

These permissions are kept in a nine-bit user protection mode string which is displayed when the **-l** option of the **ls** command is used. Permission is indicated by an **r** for read, **w** for write, and **x** for execute. The absence of permission is indicated by a dash (-). Referring back to Figure 4.4, the output of the **ls** command for C source programs shows read/write access to the owner and read access to the group and to others.

When the file is a directory, the read, write, and execute protections have special meaning:

read	permission to list the contents
write	permission to create or delete files
execute	permission to access lower levels

Note the permissions in Figure 4.4 for the cprog directory.

4.8.2 Establishing and Changing Protection Modes

When an ordinary file is created, the owner is given read/write permission by default, and the group and others are given read-only access. (See below for a discussion of the default and its setting.) It is often desirable to change the mode. For example, you may want to turn off the write mode to ensure that you don't inadvertently change a file. Or you may want to give members of your group the ability to modify a file. The change mode command, **chmod,** changes the protection mode bits. In the symbolic form of the command, you indicate for which class of user the new protection will be in effect:

u	user (owner)
g	group
o	others
a	all

You then add (+) or take away (−) the desired permissions.

Programs and shell scripts (see Chapter 7) must have the execute permission bit set before they are directly executed. Suppose we have a shell script which manages the telephone directory called *tel* (see Chapter 7 for a working prototype). Furthermore, we will assume its default permissions have been set to: **-rw-r--r--.** The following examples show how it changes by use of the **chmod** command.

You can add execute access only to the owner.

```
chmod u+x tel  --> rwxr--r--
```

You also can add execute access to all classes of users:

```
chmod a+x tel  --> rwxr-xr-x
```

or simply,

```
chmod +x tel
```

To take away read access from the group and other users, do the following:

```
chmod go-r tel  --> rwx------
```

The = operator assigns or sets the permission. The other permissions are reset (-).

```
chmod ugo=+r tel  --> r--r--r--
```

Multiple specifications are separated by commas.

```
chmod +x,o=-r tel  --> rwxr-x--x
```

There is also a nonsymbolic mode in which you give three octal digits whose binary representation is the nine-bit protection mode.

```
chmod 666 tel  --> 110 110 110 --> rw-rw-rw-
```

4.8.3 The Permission Default: umask

Files are given a default permission setting when they are created:

```
rw-rw-rw-
```

This default is modified by the *umask* setting, which turns off permissions in the default. Login shells are given umask value of 022, which selectively turns off group and other write permission:

```
rw-rw-rw-  ----> rw-r--r--
```

Note that execute permission must explicitly be set.

For example, to turn off all group and other permissions by default you would enter:

```
$ umask 077
```

which masks all group and other bits:

```
rw-------
```

4.8.4 Run Time Protection: Set User ID

Consider the case where a program accesses a data file which must be kept confidential. It would seem that the user running the program must have at least read access to the data for the program to run. This isn't always desirable, since the department running the programs may be different than the department responsible for the integrity of the data. The set-user-ID and set-group-ID bits are a UNIX system facility that addresses this problem. In order to protect the situation described above, groups and others are not given any access to the data file.

```
$ chmod 600 datafile
```

For the program, set-user-ID bit is set to one. The three bits (1 octal digit) preceding the permissions contain the user- and group-ID bits. In the example below, binary **100** or octal **4** sets the set-usr-ID bit to one (010 sets the group-ID):

```
$ chmod 4711 program
```

In the work situation, the department running the program does not have access either to the program code or to the data, since they are both read/write protected. When the program begins executing, it will inherit the protection environment of its owner, which in this case includes the owner of the data file. Thus, the data and program are protected from other departments.

4.9 The Physical File System

The implementation of the UNIX file system is very straightforward and provides a large degree of flexibility. If you are installing and maintaining

your own file systems, it is important to understand how they are organized.

For an active UNIX system, there is initially one file system on a single
disk drive, on-line to the user. Figure 4.5 is a diagram of the UNIX file
system which consists of a collection of fixed-size blocks. Block sizes depend on the UNIX version and are typically 512 or 1024 bytes long. The
first block of a file system, block 0, is unused. The second block, block 1,
is called the *superblock* and contains all the information about the active
file system. The next series of blocks contains file descriptions called *inodes*.
Following the inode list are the data blocks of the file system. Lastly, there
is a swap area used by the process scheduling algorithms. Table 4.4 lists
some of the important fields of the superblock, and Table 4.5 lists the contents of an inode.

4.9.1 File Operations

Every file in the system is represented by an inode. The relative position
of the inode in the inode list is the inode number of the file. The **ls** command displays inode information, and with the **-i** option **ls** will also display
the inode number. In this way, it is not necessary for directories to contain

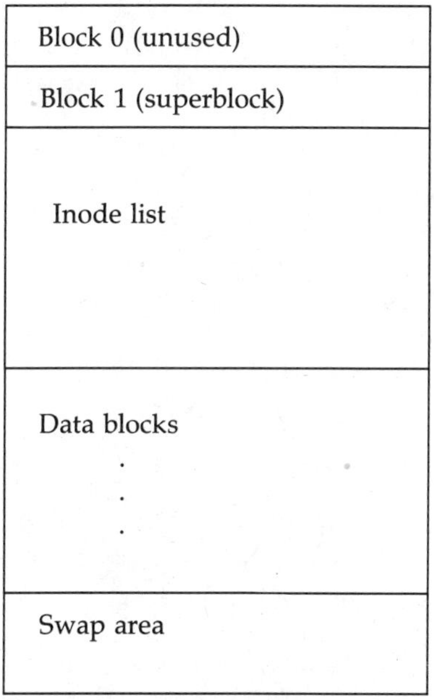

Figure 4.5. Layout of the File
System

TABLE 4.4
Superblock Information

Length of the inode list
Size of the file system
Number of free blocks
Number of free inodes
File system name

any information about a file other than a name and a pointer to the file information, the inode. Figure 4.6 shows the relationship between directories and files. This makes several of the file operations we discussed earlier much easier to understand.

cp -1. Create a directory entry for the new file.
   2. Allocate a free inode.
   3. Allocate space for the new file.
   4. Copy the old file to the new file.
mv-1. Create a directory entry for the new file.
   2. Copy the inode number to the new entry.
   3. Delete the directory entry of the old file.
ln -1. Create a directory entry for the new file.
   2. Copy the same inode number as the linked file.
   3. Add one to the link count of the file in the inode (physical removal of a file occurs when the link count is 0).

The concept of a directory as a file, and the dot notation for current/parent directories, becomes clearer. As shown in Figure 4.6, the inode entry for the . file , 10, refers to the entry for *cprog*. The inode for .., 12, refers

TABLE 4.5
Inode Information

Protection mode
Type of file
Number of links
Owner and group id
Size of the file
Pointers to the file
Time last accessed
Time last modified
Time created

cprog *Directory*			*Inode List*	
i#	file		i#	file
10	.		1	
12	. .		2	
5	d f p 1 . c		3	
7	d f p 2 . c		4	
9	c p r o g b k p		5	d f p 1 . c
			6	
			7	d f p 2 . c
			8	
			9	c p r o g b k p
			10	c p r o g
			11	
			12	f a r k a s

Figure 4.6. Relationship of Directory to Inode List

to the parent, *farkas*. Thus, the directory concept that creates the logical hierarchical view is elegantly implemented by the physical file system.

4.9.2 File Allocation

A UNIX ordinary file is a sequentially organized set of blocks referenced through pointers in the inode. Each inode contains 13 pointers to the file. The first 10 pointers are direct to data blocks. The next three provide indirect access through additional levels of pointers. In Figure 4.7, the file allocation pointers in the inode are illustrated.

After a file grows beyond 10 data blocks, an eleventh data block is allocated which, rather than contain data, will contain pointers to data, providing a single level of indirect access. If the file continues to grow beyond the number of blocks that can be referenced from the file pointer block, a second level of indirection is introduced. The twelfth inode data block points to a block which contains pointers to another set of pointer blocks. If necessary, this can even be expanded to a third level of data pointer blocks. If a block of addresses contains 256 pointers, then the maximum file size is quite large (try to figure it out).

This organization has several advantages. Most files are small, so no additional accesses to the disk are required for most files, since the data is directly accessible from the pointers in the inode. Furthermore, inodes of open files are held in memory. The system is therefore fairer to small files which are using less file system resources.

Another advantage is that all bytes are accessed through the block pointers. This can be used to provide random access processing. For exam-

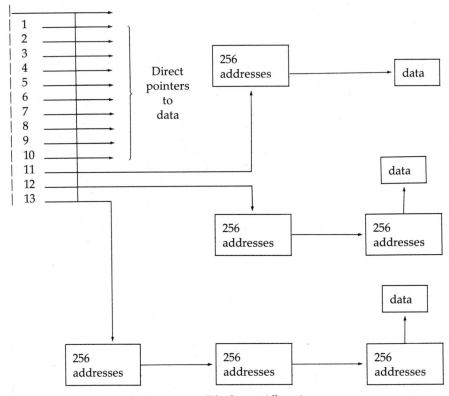

Figure 4.7. File Space Allocation

ple, if you have 80 byte records, the tenth data record begins at byte 720 (assume byte numbering from 0).

The major disadvantage is that since the files are not physically contiguous (the data may be scattered all over the disk), sequential processing performance will degrade as the file system ages and grows. Another disadvantage for large files is that there will be additional disk accesses for block pointer retrieval.

4.10 Further Exploration

The UNIX file system is comprehensive but not difficult to understand. In the next chapter, we will look at the basic file utilities and tools which come with your system. For now, explore the file system and practice with the basic commands:

1. List the different files in the root directories.
2. Create a directory in your home directory.
3. Copy files from one of the root directories.
4. Link a file in the new directory to one in your home directory.
5. Delete a linked file and check the link count. When are linked files actually removed from the system?
6. Investigate the permissions on the files in the root directories.
7. Change the permissions of files in your own directory.

4.11 Manual References

cd	change the current directory
chmod	change protection mode
cp	copy files
filesystems	file system description
fortune	fortune cookie game
fs	file system layout
ln	link files
li	list directory contents
ls	list directory contents
mkdir	create a directory
mv	move files
pwd	print working directory
rm	remove files
rmdir	remove a directory
umask	set permission default mask

5

Filters: File Manipulation Tools and Utilities

The UNIX system is distributed with very powerful utilities, tools, called filters which can be simply used to manipulate files, records, and fields. Utilizing I/O redirection and pipes, you can create complex command sequences more easily than on most other systems. The tools can be broadly categorized by their function:

Comparison Utilities
Printing Utilities
Database Utilities
Record and Field Selection
Translation and Transformation Filters

Some of the filters we will discuss are not on all the versions of UNIX. For example, some may only be distributed with XENIX, or Berkeley 4.2, and not be available on AT&T System V. Check your documentation or try entering the command. You will know soon enough whether it is available on your system. Don't worry, however. Most of the filters and utilities below are standard on all UNIX systems.

The sections in this chapter are organized alphabetically by command name so that the chapter can be used as both a tutorial and a reference. While the filters have a variety of options and features, we will cover the basic usage of the commands and the more important options. Table 5.1 lists most of the utilities which are standard on most UNIX systems.

Figure 5.1 shows two files of names and numbers which we will use in our examples. These are drawn from the telephone directory created in Chapter 2. Each command section is preceded by a general form of the command which gives its syntax and usage:

usage: command name arguments

If an argument is optional, it is placed in square brackets.

TABLE 5.1
Utilities and Filters by Type

COMPARISON	
cmp	Compare two files
comm	Show sorted file differences
diff	Show file differences
diff3	Compare 3 files
diffmk	Mark file differences

RECORD SELECTION AND MANIPULATION	
awk	Pattern matching and processing
cut	Field selection
dd	Copy file
head	List top of file
paste	Record manipulation
sed	Pattern matching and editing
tail	List end of file
tr	Translate characters
uniq	Discard duplicate records

PRINTING	
cat	Concatenate and print
nl	Line numbering utility
pr	Formatted print utility
print	Print spool utility
lpr	Print spool utility

MISCELLANEOUS	
sort	Sort merge utility

tel1	tel2
Smith Robert 212 555-1234	Driver Martha 212 555-7890
Jones William 914 555-2345	Condliffe Jane 212 555-8901
Blake Michael 312 555-3456	Steffens Pieta 212 555-9012
Browne Peter 203 555-4567	Jones William 914 555-2345
vanWormer Judy 914 555 9876	Weber Vanessa 312 555-0123
Condliffe Jane 212 555-8901	Roberts Judy 415 555-0987
Sugarman David 212 555-5678	Blake Michael 201 555-3456
Loxley Robert 212 555-1365	

Figure 5.1. *tel1* and *tel2*

5.1 *awk*

usage: **awk** [-options] [awk program] [awk file] [file(s)]

The **awk** command is a comprehensive report writing utility which uses the pattern matching techniques we developed earlier to select lines from a file. Other elements of the language can be used to select fields, print them out in different formats, perform arithmetic, and produce summaries and totals.

5.1.1 awk *Variables and Basic Usage*

Each component or word of a line is assigned a variable name—$0, $1, $2, etc.—where $0 refers to the entire line and each of the other variables refers to fields separated by one or more blanks or tab characters. For example, in our telephone directory, each line is divided into four fields:

$0	Smith Robert 212 555-1234
$1	Smith
$2	Robert
$3	212
$4	555–1234

In addition to its options, if any, **awk** is invoked with two arguments, an **awk** program, and a file from which the program selects lines and performs the associated operations. As with other filters, standard input can be used instead of a file. The **awk** program statements consist of two parts, a selection criterion and an action. Selection criteria are similar to the search criteria used in the editors we discussed in Chapter 3. Actions are statements which manipulate the information on selected lines by printing it, using it in arithmetic, and incorporating other file manipulation operations. The general format of an **awk** program is:

selection criteria { actions }
selection criteria { actions }

awk is invoked with one of two options. The **-e** option, which defaults, indicates that the **awk** program is to be taken from the command line. The **-f** option indicates that the next argument is a file which contains the **awk** program. In UNIX jargon, when commands to any utility are listed in a file, the file is called a *script*.

One simple use of **awk** is printing out the contents of a file. In Figure 5.2a, the **awk** print action is performed for each line which matches the selection criteria. If there are no selection criteria, the action is performed for each line in the file. The **awk** text is enclosed in single quotes to inhibit the shell from expanding any special characters which are part of the **awk** syntax.

The **awk** program in Figure 5.2b also prints each line, but it uses the symbolic notation $0. It also introduces the special variable NR, which contains the current record number that **awk** is processing. This example gives a line number listing of the file.

We take this one step further in the example shown in Figure 5.2c, where we use the field references to print out the file with line numbers,

```
$awk '{print}' tel1

Smith  Robert  212 555-1234
Jones  William 914 555-2345
Blake  Michael 312 555-3456
             .
             .
             .
$
```

Figure 5.2a. Simple **awk**

```
$awk '{print NR, $0}' tel1

1 Smith  Robert  212 555-1234
2 Jones  William 914 555-2345
3 Blake  Michael 312 555-3456
             .
             .
             .
$
```

Figure 5.2b. Simple **awk** with Line Number

```
$awk '{print NR,$2,$1,$3,$4}' tel1

1 Robert Smith 212 555-1234
2 William Jones 914 555-2345
3 Michael Blake 312 555-3456
                .
                .
                .
$
```

Figure 5.2c. Simple **awk** with Field Arguments

first name first rather than last name first. If you have your telephone directory, try printing a listing with only last names and telephone numbers.

5.1.2 awk *Line Selection*

In order to select lines, it is necessary to determine a line range in terms either of the line number variable NR or of start and end patterns. You can also specify selection criteria in the form of comparison with fields on the line. To print lines 3 through 7, the selection criteria part of the **awk** command would contain a program with the range specified as follows:

```
$awk 'NR==3,NR==7 {print}' tel1
```

In the above command line, we see a range consisting of two criteria separated by commas. The double equal sign is similar to the C language equality relation symbol. The relational operators for **awk** are summarized in Table 5.2a. Start and end patterns use a regular expression similar to the ones used in the **ed** or **ex.** The lines selected extend from the first line containing the pattern through the line containing the second pattern:

```
$awk '/first/,/last/ {print}' file
```

This example prints all the lines from the line containing "first" through the line containing "last." If there are only one pattern, only those lines

TABLE 5.2a
awk *Relational Operators*

==	Equal
!=	Not equal
<	Less than
<=	Less than or equal
>	Greater than
>=	Greater than or equal

TABLE 5.2b
awk *Advanced Actions*

print	Print
printf	Formatted print
if	Conditional statement
while	Loop statement
for	Loop statement

TABLE 5.2c
Advanced Features

Variables
Built-in mathematical and string functions
Arrays

which match are selected. You can also compare fields to regular expression patterns. The tilde, ~, tests for a match. With an exclamation point, !~, the test is for no match. In Figure 5.3a, an **awk** program is created which searches for lines which begin with B, utilizing the regular expression special character for beginning of a line, ^. In addition, the action prints the selected lines with line numbers and first name first. *new*

Two other important selection criteria are the keywords BEGIN and END, which cause the actions to occur before and after any line selection has taken place. Figure 5.3b shows an **awk** program with a heading printed using BEGIN, a total line with END. In this example, since there is more than one line to the **awk** program, we use the **-f** option and give a filename, or script, which contains it.

5.1.3 Advanced Actions

It is possible to go beyond the basic usage of the **awk** utility and incorporate actions whose syntax begins to look like C programs. The **awk** utility supports integer and real arithmetic, sequence control statements, and formatted printing. Furthermore, unlike our previous examples, it is possible to associate different selection criteria and actions for different lines. The example in Figure 5.4a uses the **printf** action with syntax similar to the

```
$awk $1~/^B/{print NR, $2,$1,$3,$4} tel1

3 Michael Blake 312 555-3456
4 Peter Browne 203 555-4567
$
```

Figure 5.3a. Selecting by Field Comparison

awk script *awkex*:

before selection

```
BEGIN {print "Telephone Directory:\n"}
      {print $1,$4}
```

after selection

```
END   {print "\nTotal Entries: ", (NR)}
```

awk execution:

```
$awk -f awkex tel1

Telephone Directory:

Smith 555-1234
Jones 555-2345
Blake 555-3456
Browne 555-4567
vanWormer 555-9876
Condliffe 555-8901
Sugarman 555-5678
Loxley 555-1365


Total Entries: 8
$
```

Figure 5.3b. awk with a File Option

C **printf** function to produce a formatted listing. In this case the %-15s specification indicates a field 15 characters wide and left justified. In our last example, illustrated in Figure 5.4b, an augmented telephone directory file containing the number of hours worked in the last field ($5) is used to compute and print the sum and average of all the hours of all the entries in the directory.

5.1.4 Further Exploration

The **awk** program is a complete report writer and can be used with some of the other utilities to easily and efficiently perform standard file and database operations. Try some of the following exercises:

1. Modify *awkex* in Figure 5.4b to select records with more than 25 hours ($5 > 25).

```
$awk '{printf("%-15s%-15s%-15s%-15s\n",$1,$2,$3,$4)}' tel1

Smith          Robert         212                           555-1234
Jones          William        914                           555-2345
Blake          Michael        312                           555-3456
      .
      .
      .
$
```

Figure 5.4a. Formatted Report with **awk**

awk script *awkex*:

```
BEGIN {print "Telephone Directory\n"}
      {sum = sum + $5}
      {print NR,$0}
END   {print "\n total hours: " sum "average hours: " sum/NR}
```

awk execution:

```
$awk -f awkex tel1
Telephone Directory
1 Smith Robert 212 555-1234 25
2 Jones William 914 555 2345 35
3 Blake Michael 312 555 3456 42
            .
            .
            .
total hours:2633 average hours: 292.556
$
```

Figure 5.4b. Report and Calculations with **awk** Program

2. Print out the telephone directory with the last name and number only.

5.2 *Concatenate and Print:* ***cat***

usage: **cat** [files]

We have seen the **cat** command in earlier chapters and used it for printing out the unformatted contents of a file. The command collects the file arguments and writes the concatenated result to standard output. If there are no file arguments, **cat** reads from standard input. For example, to create a file you enter **cat** with no arguments, but you direct standard output to the new file:

```
$cat > newfile
---
---
ctrl-D
$
```

Figure 5.5 illustrates the concatenation and printing of our two telephone directory files. If we wanted to create a new file, *tel3*, which contained the contents of both *tel1* and *tel2*, we would redirect the output to the new file:

```
$cat tel1 tel2 > tel3
```

```
$cat tel1 tel2
Smith Robert 212 555-1234
Jones William 914 555-2345
Blake Michael 312 555-3456
Browne Peter 203 555-4567
vanWormer Judy 914 555-9876
Condliffe Jane 212 555-8901
Sugarman David 212 555-5678
Loxley Robert 212 555-1365
Driver Martha 212 555-7890
Condliffe Jane 212 555-8901
Steffens Pieta 212 555-9012
Jones William 914 555-2345
Weber Vanessa 312 555-0123
Roberts Judy 415 555-0987
Blake Michael 201 555-3456
$
```

Figure 5.5. Concatenate and Print: **cat**

5.3 *File Comparison: cmp*

usage: **cmp** [options] file1 file2

The **cmp** command is used to compare two files and print to standard output the location in the first file argument where the files differ and, with the proper option, the value of the differing bytes. If the files are identical, no message is printed. In Figure 5.6, there are two copies of our original *tel1* and *tel2*, *t1* and *t2*. The *t2* file has its fifth line deleted. In the **cmp** output, the exact line and character displacement of the first discrepancy is displayed. The **-l** option would cause all the differing bytes to be displayed.

Files to Compare

t1	t2
Smith Robert 212 555-1234	Smith Robert 212 555-1234
Jones William 914 555-2345	Jones William 914 555-2345
Blake Michael 312 555-3456	Blake Michael 312 555-3456
Browne Peter 203 555-4567	Browne Peter 203 555-4567
vanWormer Judy 914 555-9876	Condliffe Jane 212 555-8901
Condliffe Jane 212 555-8901	Sugarman David 212 555-5678
Sugarman David 212 555-5678	Loxley Robert 212 555-1365
Loxley Robert 212 555-1365	

cmp execution:

```
$cmp t1 t2
tel1 t1 differ: char 107, line 5
$
```

Figure 5.6. Compare Files With One Line Missing: **cmp**

5.4 *File Comparison:* comm

usage: **comm** [options] file1 file2

This file comparison command, **comm,** displays lines from two sorted files in three columns indicating which lines are in the first file but not the second, in the second but not the first, and lines common to both. Options 1,2,3 can be used to suppress the printing of the *file1* only, *file2* only, and data common to both columns, respectively. The two sorted files are shown in Figure 5.7a. The output of **comm** is shown in Figure 5.7b. Figure 5.7c illustrates the use of the options to suppress output of one or more columns. In this case, by specifying **-3**, the *file1* only and *file2* only columns are displayed.

Sorted Files
   tel1

                                               tel2

```
Blake Michael 312 555-3456      Blake Michael 201 555-3456
Browne Peter 203 555-4567       Condliffe Jane 212 555-8901
Condliffe Jane 212 555-8901     Driver Martha 212 555-7890
Jones William 914 555-2345      Jones William 914 555-2345
Loxley Robert 212 555-1365      Roberts Judy 415 555-0987
Smith Robert 212 555-1234       Steffens Pieta 212 555-9012
Sugarman David 212 555-5678     Weber Vanessa 312 555-0123
vanWormer Judy 914 555-9876
```

Figure 5.7a. Sorted *tel1* and *tel2*

```
$comm tel1 tel2
                Blake Michael 201 555-3456
        Blake Michael 312 555-3456
        Browne Peter 203 555-4567
                        Condiliffe Jane 212 555-8901
                Driver Martha 212 555-7890
                        Jones William 914 555-2345
        Loxley Robert 212 555-1365
                Roberts Judy 415 555-0987
        Smith Robert 212 555-1234
                Steffens Pieta 212 555-9012
        Sugarman David 212 555-5678
                Weber Vanessa 312 555-0123
        vanWormer Judy 914 555-9876
```

in tel1 only ⌐
    in tel2 only ⌐
        in tel1 and tel2 ⌐

Figure 5.7b. Comparison of Different Files

```
$comm -3 tel1 tel2

        Blake Michael 201 555-3456
Blake Michael 312 555-3456
Browne Peter 203 555-4567
        Driver Martha 212 555-7890
Loxley Robert 212 555-1365
        Roberts Judy 415 555-0987
Smith Robert 212 555-1234
        Steffens Pieta 212 555-9012
Sugarman David 212 555-5678
        Weber Vanessa 312 555-0123
vanWormer Judy 914 555-9876
$
```

Figure 5.7c. Comparison without Common Lines

5.5 *Record Manipulation:* cut

usage: **cut** [options] [files]

The **cut** filter reads a file line by line and, based on either default or defined delimiters, prints selected fields. The **-d** option is used to define the delimiter between fields. If it is omitted, the tab character is used. The character immediately following the **d** is the new delimiter. For example, if the file had records with fields separated by commas, the cut option to indicate this is **-d,.** The example in Figure 5.8 uses a blank as the delimiter. Since blank has special meaning to the shell in that it separates command arguments, it must be quoted.

The field selection option is **-f.** Similar to **awk,** individual fields of a record are the strings between the defined or default delimiter. Thus, in our telephone directory the fields are:

first	last	area	number
1	2	3	4

Figure 5.8 uses **cut** to select the last name and telephone number.

```
$cut -d" " -f1,4

Smith 555-1234
Jones 555-2345
Blake 555-3456
        .
        .
        .
$
```

Figure 5.8. **cut** with Blank Delimiter

5.6 File Comparison: *diff*

usage: **diff** [options] file1 file2

The **diff** filter displays the difference between two text files on standard output, indicating what must be done to *file1* to change it into *file2*. The format of its output resembles the **ed** editor commands for appending, deleting, and changing lines. Following each **ed**-type command are the lines from *file1*, preceded by <, and those from *file2*, preceded by >, which would be modified by the **ed**-type commands.

Looking at the example in Figure 5.9, the left column displays the output of **diff** without any options. Here, "1,5c1" indicates that one line from the second file will replace lines 1–5 of the first file. The five lines from *tel1* are then displayed (each with <). Following these, the new line from *tel2* preceded by > is listed. A similar interpretation of the next command— "7,8c3,7"—replaces lines 7–8 of *tel1* with 3–7 of *tel2*.

If the **-e** option is used, actual **ed** commands are produced which, if applied to *file1*, convert it to *file2*. To capture the **ed** commands in a file, you redirect the standard output of **diff**. This is illustrated in the righthand column and provides a convenient way to maintain successive backups of a file without having to keep complete copies. Only the **diff** script is needed. For example, if the original file is *t1*, after each successive change you would keep the **diff** **ed**-file output (e.g., *d1, d2, d3, d4*, etc.). To recon-

Standard Output `diff tel1 tel2`	`diff -e tel1 tel2` ed Script Output
`1,5c1`	`7,8c`
`< Smith Robert 212 555-1234`	`Steffens Pieta 212 555-9012`
`< Jones Wiliam 914 555-2345`	`Jones William 914 555-2345`
`< Blake Michael 312 555-3456`	`Weber Vanessa 312 555-0123`
`< Browne Peter 203 555-4567`	`Roberts Judy 415 555-0987`
`< vanWormer Judy 914 555-9876`	`Blake Michael 201 555-3456`
`---`	`.`
`< Driver Martha 212 555-7890`	`1,5c`
`7,8c3,7`	`Driver Martha 2122 555-7890`
`< Sugarman David 212 555-5678`	`.`
`< Loxley Robert 212 555-1365`	
`---`	
`> Steffens Pieta 212 555-9012`	
`> Jones William 914 555-2345`	
`> Weber Vanessa 312 555-0123`	
`> Roberts Judy 415 555-0987`	
`> Blake Michael 201 555-3456`	

Figure 5.9. diff with Standard Output and **ed** script Output

struct a previous revision, you would apply the necessary **diff** file changes to the original file up to the revision you needed. For example, to get revision 2, run **ed** on *t1* with *d1*, and then with *d2:*

t1—via **ed** and *d1*→revision 1—via **ed** and *d2*→revision 2

This can be incorporated into a shell program so that it is all done automatically. Shell programming and shell scripts are discussed in detail in Chapters 7 and 8.

5.7 *Pattern Matching:* **grep**

usage: **grep** [options] pattern [files]

As we have seen in Chapter 2, the **grep** filter can be used to select lines which match patterns specified on the command line. In our previous examples we used absolute strings, but **grep** can handle regular expressions which have the same basic format as those described in Chapter 3 and used in **awk.** Table 5.3 summarizes the special characters and their meaning. One must take special care when using patterns on the command line, since some of them are special characters and are meaningful to the shell syntax. It is therefore necessary to surround them in single quotes so as to inhibit the shell from processing them as wildcard characters.

We have already seen how **grep** can be used to match a simple pattern. However, the examples in Figure 5.10 show even more of **grep's** flexibility. The second example uses the **-v** option, which prints the lines not matched on standard output. Going back to our telephone directory example, this can be used to delete entries. In this case, by redirecting output to an updated telephone directory, the vanWormer entry is deleted. In the third example, we are searching for all lines which begin with J or C. The fourth example begins to demonstrate some of the power of pattern matching in general. In this pattern, we are looking for all occurrences of lines containing the initials S and D. With your telephone directory, try searches on other kinds of patterns.

TABLE 5.3
Regular Expression Special Symbols

.	Matches any character
*	0 or more of previous character
+	Match 1 or more of previous character
[ ]	Match any single character between square brackets
^	Match beginning of a line
$	Match end of a line
|	Separates alternative patterns

Absolute string:

```
$grep 'van' tel1
vanWormer Judy 914 555-9876
$
```

Nonmatched strings:

```
grep -v 'van' tel1
Smith Robert 212 555-1234
Jones William 914 555-2345
Blake Michael 312 555-3456
Browne Peter 203 555-4567
Condliffe Jane 212 555-8901
Sugarman David 212 555-5678
Loxley Robert 212 555-1365
```

Start of line character:

```
$grep '^[JC]' tel1
Jones William 914 555-2345
Condliffe Jane 212 555-8901
$
```

Repetition and any character:

```
$grep 'S.* D.*' tel1
Sugarman David 212 555-5678
$
```

Figure 5.10.   Sample **grep** Patterns

We haven't covered all of **grep**'s features. Your system documentation will describe other command options and two other related commands, **fgrep** and **egrep.** The former is an optimized version of **grep** which operates on fixed strings. The latter is a more general regular expression recognizer which includes all the special characters we have discussed plus the ability to backtrack and try alternatives. For example, we may want to search for the initials JW or SD; **egrep** has an alternation operator, |, which incorporates this type of extended search:

```
$egrep'J.*W.* | S.*D.*' tel1
```

In this example, the Jones and Sugarman entries will be selected.

5.8 List the Beginning of a File: *head*

usage: **head** -count file

It is often useful to be able to quickly check the beginning of a file or several files to determine their contents. On some systems this requires using a display command which begins to list the entire file. On other systems it may be necessary to go into the editor. UNIX has several commands which make this task quite simple. Using **head** without any options will list the first 10 lines of a file. If a count is present, it will display the number of lines specified in the count.

5.9 Screen Display: *more*

usage: **more** [options] [-k] [+j] [+/pattern/] file

The **more** command displays one screen of a file at a time, pausing and displaying more at the bottom of the screen. Single lines are displayed after a carriage return, and another full screen is displayed after the space bar. Options determine the characteristics of the display. For example, **-s** removes blank lines; *-k* sets the size of the window or screen displayed where *k* is an integer. The + options starts the display either at line number *j* or at the first occurrence of the pattern.

When a screen is being displayed by **more,** there are several commands which you can enter. An integer, *k*, followed by a space scrolls k lines while *ctrl-D* scrolls one half screen. An equal sign, =, displays the current line number, and an exclamation point, !, followed by a UNIX command escapes to the shell. A **v** starts up the vi editor at the current position in the file. After leaving **vi, more** resumes.

5.10 Line Numbering: *nl*

usage: **nl** [options] file

We have already seen how to obtain a line-numbered listing of a file using **awk.** The **nl** command provides a simpler way if that is all you want. Figure 5.11 shows how **nl** is used without options to list the lines of tel1. It also has several options which may be used to create formatted output.

To effectively use these options, pages are divided into three logical components—headers, bodies, and footers,—which are created by sequences of /: on lines by themselves:

/:/:/:	precedes the header
/:/:	precedes the body
/:	precedes the footer

```
$nl tell

1   Smith Robert 212 555-1234
2   Jones William 914 555-2345
3   Blake Michael 312 555-3456
.
.
.
$
```

Figure 5.11.   Line Number Filter

The **nl** options, -h, -b, and -f, refer to these sections and describe the type of line numbering desired:

a	number all the lines (defaults for body)
t	number only lines with text
n	no line numbering (defaults for header and footer)

For example, the options, *-ha -ba -fa*, requests that the entire page be numbered. Figure 5.12a shows the file with embedded lines to delimit the header, body, and footer sections. Figure 5.12b is the result of the **nl** filter on the formatted file. In this case, with no options, only the body of each page will be numbered.

Formatted file:

```
\:\:\:
Telephone Directory:

\:\:
Smith 555-1234
Jones 555-2345
Blake 555-3456
Browne 555-4567
vanWormer 555-9876
Condliffe 555-8901
Sugarman 555-5678
Loxley 555-1365
\:
Total Entries:  8
```

Figure 5.12a.   Formatted **nl**

nl standard output:

```
Telephone Directory:

1 Smith 555-12334
2 Jones 555-2345
3 Blake 555-3456
4 Browne 555-4567
5 vanWormer 555-9876
6 Condliffe 555-8901
7 Sugarman 555-5678
8 Loxley 555-1365

Total Entries:  8
```

Figure 5.12b. Standard Output of **nl**

5.11 File and Record Manipulation: *paste*

usage: **paste** [options] [files]

The **paste** filter takes lines of input from its file arguments or standard input and literally pastes them together. Its simplest usage, without any options, lists lines from different files side by side. This is illustrated in Figure 5.13a with our two telephone directories.

This filter can also be used to read standard input and print the result in separate columns. For example, in Figure 5.13b, the **ls** command standard output is piped into **paste.** Each occurrence of a dash (-) as an argument to **paste** causes one line to be read from standard input—in this case, the piped **ls** output. The result is three entries per line rather than one.

```
$paste tel1 tel2

Smith Robert 212 555-1234       Driver Martha 212 555-7890
Jones William 914 555-2345      Condliffe Jane 212 555-8901
Blake Michael 312 555-3456      Steffens Pieta 212 555-9012
Browne Peter 203 555-9876       Jones William 914 555-2345
Condliffe Jane 212 555-8901     Weber Vanessa 312 555-0123
Sugarman David 212 555-5678     Roberts Judy 415 555-0987
Loxley Robert 212 555-1365      Blake Michael 201 555-3456
$
```

Figure 5.13a. paste for Columnar Output

```
$ls | paste - - -

t1      t1.bak  t2
t3      t4      t5
tel1    tel1s   tel2
tel2s   tel3
$
```

Figure 5.13b. paste with piped Standard Input

5.12 *Formatted Print: pr*

usage: **pr** [options] [files]

The **pr** command uses the file arguments to produce a formatted listing on standard output. Options give the ability to control different aspects of the print. In Figure 5.14a, *tel1* is printed. Without options, the date, time, filename, and page number are printed as a header. The number of lines per page (66) and characters per line (72) default. By using **pr**'s different options, different characteristics can be set. For example, it is possible to get a line-numbered listing by using the **-n** option. In 5.14b, several other options are used. The line width, **-w**, is set to 72, the page length, **-l**, is set to 76, and a header, **-h,** is established.

```
$pr tel1

Aug 6 09:48 1984 tel1 Page 1

Smith Robert 212 555-1234
Jones William 914 555-2345
Blake Michael 312 555-3456
Browne Peter 203 555-4567
vanWormer Judy 914 555-9876
Condliffe Jane 212 555-8901
Sugarman David 212 555-5678
Loxley Robert 212 555-1365
        .
        .
        .
$
```

Figure 5.14a. Simple Formated Print: **pr**

```
$pr  -w72 -l76 -h "Telephone Index" tel1

Aug 12 20:03 1984 Telephone Index Page 1

Smith Robert 212 555-1234
Jones William 914 555-2345
Blake Michael 312 555-3456
Browne Peter 203 555-4567
vanWormer Judy 914 555-9876
Condliffe Jane 212 555-8901
Sugarman David 212 555-5678
Loxley Robert 212 555-1365
    .
    .
    .
$
```

Figure 5.14b. Formatted Print with Options

5.13 Printing Files

In this section we discuss how files are physically printed. There are two mechanisms for printing files. The first involves direct specification of the special file which represents the physical printer or output device. The second method uses a special process which controls all the printing for a collection of output devices.

5.13.1 Redirecting Standard Output to the Printer

In the */dev* directory are all the special files for the devices which are supported on your system. There will be one or more files which represent the printers, usually named *lp, lp0, lp1,* depending on their number and characteristics. Output directed to the file that controls your printer will activate it and produce a listing. For example, to print the contents of our *tel1* file we simply redirect standard output to the *lp* device (*lp, lp1, lp2*):

```
$cat tel1 > /dev/lp
```

For a formatted print, you could use **pr** instead of **cat**:

```
$pr tel1 > /dev/lp
```

If it is going to be a long printout and you don't want to wait while it is printing, you can indicate background execution using the ampersand:

```
$ cat tel1 > /dev/lp &
```

Background and foreground execution is discussed fully in Chapter 7. You must be the only user on the system when printing directly to the device.

5.13.2 Print Spools

The method of redirecting standard output to the device should only be used on a single user system. If more than one user send their standard output to the device, the lines will be interleaved and the result will be unusable. UNIX systems have built-in processes which manage different kinds of resources. Since these processes are started up when the system is brought up, and they are not associated with any terminal, they are called *daemons*—in this case, *print daemons*. Access to the print daemon is through either the **lpr** or the **print** command, depending on which system you are using. These commands place the file on a list with other files to be printed called a *spool*. The print daemon prints files one at a time. In this way there is no conflict with other users.

5.13.3 Print Queuing: **print**

usage: **print** [queue] [options] [files]

Without any options, the files are arranged on the standard print queue initialized when UNIX is started. If there are alternate printing devices and print queues, the first argument to print is the symbolic name of the queue for that device. Different options control the print queue operations and allow for cancelling print requests, printing multiple copies, notifying the user when the job has been printed, providing modified printer characteristics, and displaying the status of the printer queues.

5.13.4 Print Queuing: **lpr**

usage: **lpr** [options] [files]

The **lpr** command works in a similar fashion to **print** but with less control over the print queue. Without any options, it takes the files listed on the command line and queues them for printing. The mail option, **-m,** causes a message to be sent when the file completes printing. The **-r** option removes the file after it has printed. Without any file arguments, **lpr** will take its input from standard input and may be used as a filter at the end of a pipe:

```
$ ls | pr | lpr
```

Remember, in multiuser environments, you must use the print spool commands.

5.14 The Stream Editor: *sed*

usage: **sed** [options] [sed specification] [sed file] [files]

The **sed** editor is a subset of the ed editor, providing the ability to make file modifications in a single pass over the input lines. The **sed** command line consists of a **sed** specification (**-e** option), similar to ed commands, or a file name (**-f** option) that contains the specifications. The file arguments are searched for lines that satisfy the **sed** search criteria, then the editor commands are applied.

The **sed** specifications, like **awk** and **ed,** consist of an address range followed by a **sed** action.:

start, end action

Line ranges are quite similar to those defined in ed. They can be absolute line references or context references. Figure 5.15a gives line range reference for the entire file (the -e option defaults). The editor action is to simply go to the next line, **n.** The line is passed to standard output. Most **ed** noninteractive actions and line range specifications can be used by **sed.** The examples in Figure 5.15b and 5.15c show the general use of **sed** for context search and substitution. While not shown here, the same regular expression patterns used in **awk, ed, ex** and **grep** are permissible in **sed.** In Figure 5.15b, line 5 of the file is deleted. Figure 5.15c shows a context search in which the lines from the line containing /203/ to the one containing /914/ are modified by the substitute command.

Since **sed** is a filter, the results are passed to standard output. To modify

```
$sed '1,$n' tel1

Smith Robert 212 555-1234
Jones William 914 555-2345
Blake Michael 312 555-3456
Browne Peter 203 555-4567
vanWormer Judy 914 555-9876
Condliffe Jane 212 555-8901
Sugarman David 212 555-5678
Loxley Robert 212 555-1365
$
```

Figure 5.15a.   Listing with File with **sed**

```
$sed '5d' tel1

Smith Robert 212 555-1234
Jones William 914 555-2345
Blake Michael 312 555-3456
Browne Peter 203 555-4567
Condliffe Jane 212 555-8901
Sugarman David 212 555-5678
Loxley Robert 212 555-1365
$
```

Figure 5.15b.   Search for an Absolute Line Reference

```
$sed '/203/,/914/s/555/888/' tel1

Smith Robert 212 555-1234
Jones William 914 555-2345
Blake Michael 312 555-3456
Browne Peter 203 888-4567
vanWormer Judy 914 888-9876
Condliffe Jane 212 555-8901
Sugarman David 212 555-5678
Loxley Robert 212 555-1365
$
```

Figure 5.15c. Context Search Line Range

the file being edited, you must redirect the output to a temporary file, then rename it back (**mv**) to the original:

```
$ sed '1,$s/555/777/' tel1 > t1
$ mv t1 tel1
```

In this example, all occurrences of 555 are changed to 777.

5.15 Sorting and Merging: *sort*

usage: **sort** [options] [+position] [-position] ... [files]

One of the most powerful utilities on any operating system is the **sort.** UNIX provides a **sort** program which utilizes different options to select **sort** fields, merge files, select ascending or descending order, etc. With no options, the **sort** will arrange its file arguments in ascending order using the entire line as the sort key. This is illustrated in Figure 5.16a. The **-r**

```
$sort tel1

Blake Michael 312 555-3456
Browne Peter 203 555-4567
Condliffe Jane 212 555-8901
Jones William 914 555-2345
Loxley Robert 212 555-1365
Smith Robert 212 555-1234
Sugarman David 212 555-5678
vanWormer Judy 914 555-9876
$
```

Figure 5.16a. **sort** on the Entire Record

option reverses the **sort** and arranges the output in descending order (Figure 5.16b).

Selecting **sort** fields is done by using the position parameter, specified in terms of the field number which, similar to cut, is defined by strings separated by delimiters. The format for a field specification is +*position* indicating the starting field and -*position* indicating the ending field. The blank character is the default delimiter, but it can be changed with the **-t** option.

For example, if we want to **sort** by the area code of the tel1 file, we must indicate that it is the third field. Since we are counting delimiters, we would want to say skip two fields or delimiters and end after the third delimiter. Since the default delimiter for **sort** is a blank, the **-t** option is not necessary. This is illustrated in Figure 5.16c.

```
$sort -r tel1

vanWormer Judy 914 555-9876
Sugarman David 212 555-5678
Smith Robert 212 555-1234
Loxley Robert 212 555-1365
Jones William 914 555-2345
Condliffe Jane 212 555-8901
Browne Peter 203 555-4567
Blake Michael 312 555-3456
```

Figure 5.16b. Reversed **sort** on the Entire Record

```
$sort +2 -3 tel1

Browne Peter 203 555-4567
Smith Robert 212 555-1234
Loxley Robert 212 555-1365
Sugarman David 212 555-5678
Condliffe Jane 212 555-8901
Blake Michael 312 555-3456
Jones William 914 555-2345
vanWormer Judy 914 555-9876
$
```

Figure 5.16c. **sort** on a Selected Field

Leaving out the ending field, **-3,** would cause the sort key to start at the third field (the area code) and continue through the end of the line. Multiple keys can be specified by additional start/end position pairs.

Merging is accomplished with the **-m** option on files which are already sorted:

```
$ sort -m file1 file2 > mergedfile
```

5.16 List the End of a File: *tail*

usage: **tail** [+ /-position] [options] file

The **tail** command displays the last few (10 defaults) lines of the named file. The plus sign indicates how many lines from the beginning and the minus sign indicates how many lines from the end to commence listing. You can use **tail** to see if a file is changing by checking whether lines have been appended since the last time **tail** was executed. The **-f** option causes this to occur automatically by causing **tail** to go into an infinite loop. It checks the file displaying its tail every second. If the tail has changed since the last time, you know the file is being updated. This is useful if you are expecting it to be changed by a background process and want to monitor its progress.

Figure 5.17 shows the last five lines of *tel1*.

5.17 Character Translation: *tr*

usage: **tr** [options] [string1 [string2]]

The command **tr** copies standard input to standard output, translating characters it finds in string1 by corresponding characters in string2. For

```
$ tail  -5  tel1

Browne Peter 203 555-4567
vanWormer Judy 914 555-9876
Condliffe Jane 212 555-8901
Sugarman David 212 555-5678
Loxley Robert 212 555-1365
$
```

Figure 5.17. **tail** of *tel1*

example, if we wanted to change the 5's in the telephone numbers of *tel1* to 8, we would enter:

```
tr '5' '8' <tel1

Smith  Robert  212  888-1234
Jones  William  914  888-2348
Blake  Michael  312  888-3486
        .
        .
        .
```

Like other filters, the output will go to standard output unless you redirect the output to a temporary file and rename it to the original. Character ranges are specified using square brackets. For example, to change all the upper case characters in tel1 to lower case, the following **tr** command would be used:

```
tr '[A-Z]' '[a-z]' <tel1

smith  robert  212  555-1234
jones  william  914  555-2345
blake  michael  312  555-3456
        .
        .
        .
```

An asterisk can be used to indicate repetition. Changing all the digits to x uses the * in string2:

```
tr '[0-9]' '[x*10]' <tel1

Smith  Robert  xxx  xxx-xxxx
Jones  William  xxx  xxx-xxxx
Blake  Michael  xxx  xxx-xxxx
        .
        .
        .
```

The delete, **-d,** option can be used to delete the characters specified in string1, and the **-s** option will squeeze repeated occurrences of the characters in string2 to a single character. The latter is useful when compressing intervening blanks:

```
tr -s ' ' ' ' < file1
```

or

```
tr -s ' ' < file1
```

In the first command, we are explicitly indicating no change to the blank. This can be expressed simply by not specifying string2.

5.18 Removing Duplicate Lines: *uniq*

usage: **uniq** [file]

The **uniq** filter removes duplicate lines from a sorted file. In our two files, *tel1* and *tel2*, there are some duplicate entries. When putting them together we would eliminate these entries. This can be accomplished with **uniq**. The example in Figure 5.18 shows two pipes. The output of the first is without **uniq** in which * (the * is not displayed by **uniq**) marks the duplicate entries. Duplicates are eliminated if the output of the sort is piped into **uniq**.

5.19 Counting Characters, Words, and Lines: *wc*

usage: **wc** [options] file

As we have seen in earlier chapters, the **wc** command can be used to display a count of the characters, words, and lines in a file with the **-c,**

```
cat tel1 tel2|sort >tel1         cat tel1 tel2|sort|uniq >t2

 Blake Michael 201 555-3456       Blake Michael 201 555-3456
 Blake Michael 312 555-3456       Blake Michael 312 555-3456
 Browne Peter 203 555-4567        Browne Peter 203 555-4567
*Condliffe Jane 212 555-8901     *Condliffe Jane 212 555-8901
*Condliffe Jane 212 555-8901      Driver Martha 212 555-7890
 Driver Martha 212 555-7890      *Jones William 914 555-2345
*Jones William 914 555-2345       Loxley Robert 212 555-1365
*Jones William 914 555-2345       Roberts Judy 415 555-0987
 Loxley Robert 212 555-1365       Smith Robert 212 555-1234
 Roberts Judy 415 555-0987        Steffens Pieta 212 555-9012
 Smith Robert 212 555-1234        Sugarman David 212 555-5678
 Sugarman David 212 555-5678      vanWormer Judy 914 555-9876
 Weber Vanessa 312 555-0123
 vanWormer Judy 914 555-9876
```

Figure 5.18. Discarding Duplicate Lines with **uniq**

-w, and **-l** options, respectively. The **wc** is sometimes used with other commands in a pipe. For example, to count the number of users on the system:

```
who | wc -l
```

In the above example, the **who** command will send one line for each user to the **wc** command through the pipe. The **wc** will print a count of the lines.

5.20 Case Study and Conclusion

We will conclude this chapter with a small case study that demonstrates how the use of pipes and filters can be put together to provide sophisticated functions without any real programming.

PROBLEM: Produce a telephone directory from tel1 and tel2 with the following characteristics:

1. sorted by last name
2. contains first name, last name, number
3. has a title
4. has no duplicates
5. formatted into three columns

SOLUTION:

Without pipes:

cat tel1 tel2 >t1	combine files
sort t1 > t2	sort the files
cut -d" " -f1,2,4 t3 >t4	select fields
uniq t2 > t3	remove duplicates
awk -f awktel t4 > newtel	format and print

With pipe:

```
cat tel1 tel2|sort|uniq|cut -d" "-f1,2,4|awk-f awktel > newtel
```

Figures 5.19a-e show the intermediate results of each command. Note the effect on the Black, Michael entry. What happens if **uniq** and **cut** are re-

```
cat tel1 tel2 >t1

Smith Robert 212 555-1234
Jones William 914 555-2345
   .
   .
   .
Roberts Judy 415 555-0987
Blake Michael 201 555-3456
```

Figure 5.19a. cat

```
sort t1 > t2

Blake Michael 201 555-3456
Blake Michael 312 555-3456
   .
   .
   .
Weber Vanessa 312 555-0123
vanWormer Judy 914 555-9876
```

Figure 5.19b. sort

```
cut -d" " -f1,2,4 t3 >t4

Blake Michael 555-3456
Blake Michael 555-3456
   .
   .
   .
Weber Vanessa 555-0123
vanWormer Judy 555-9876
```

Figure 5.19c. cut

```
uniq t2 > t3

Blake Michael 555-3456
Browne Peter 555-4567
   .
   .
   .
Weber Vanessa 555-0123
vanWormer Judy 555-9876
```

Figure 5.19d. uniq

```
$awk -f awktel t4 > newtel
```

with **awk** script *awkex*

```
BEGIN {print "Telephone Directory:\n"}
{printf("%-15s%-15S%-15s\n",$2,$1,$3)}
  END   {print "Total Entries: ", NR, "\n"}
```

awk execution:

```
Telephone Directory:

Michel      Blake          555-3456
Peter       Browne         555-4567
Jane        Condliffe      555-8901
Martha      Driver         555-7890
William     Jones          555-2345
Robert      Loxley         555-1365
Judy        Roberts        555-0987
Robert      Smith          555-1234
Pieta       Steffens       555-9012
David       Sugarman       555-5678
Vanessa     Weber          555-0123
Judy        vanWormer      555-9876
Total Entries:   12
```

Figure 5.19e. Case Study: Sorted, Formatted Telephone Directory

versed? If *tel1* and *tel2* contained address lines and zip codes, how would you produce name and address labels?

5.21 *Further Exploration*

This concludes our chapter on the file utilities and filters which are standard on most UNIX systems.

1. Which utilities are supported on your system?
2. Which utilities have tutorials?
3. Create an appointment file with fields for date, time, and description, produce an appointments report sorted by time within date and with date, time, and description in columns. The columns should have headings, and each appointment should be numbered.

5.22 *Manual References*

awk	pattern match and file manipulation
cat	concatenate and print
cmp	byte by byte file comparison
comm	line by line file comparison
cut	field selection filter
dd	copy file
diff	file difference utility
diff3	multiple file difference utility
diffmk	file difference utility
grep	pattern matching filter
head	list beginning of file
lpr	print spool command
more	screen display utility
nl	line numbering filter
pr	formatted print utility
print	print spool command
sed	stream editor
tail	print end of file
tr	translate file characters
uniq	remove duplicate lines filter
wc	character, line, word count utility

PART II

Advanced UNIX Topics

The chapters in this section cover various advanced features of the UNIX operating system you will need to become an experienced user. The chapters assume a basic knowledge of UNIX, the shell, and, where indicated, the C language.

The chapters describe advanced shell topics, the C-shell, programming tools and techniques, and an introduction to nroff/troff.

6

Document Formatting

In this chapter we cover the UNIX text processing utilities, **nroff** and **troff**. These are powerful document formatting systems designed for use with line printers, laser printers, and typesetting equipment. Our emphasis will be on **nroff,** since all readers will have line or dot matrix printers to produce output. The new low-cost laser printers, however, are making it possible to produce typeset-quality output. Since many **nroff** and **troff** commands are for the most part identical, readers with laser printers will be able to produce dramatic results with little effort.

The organization of this chapter is a little different than many introductory UNIX books. As a programmer, it is assumed that you will want to understand how **nroff/troff** works. For this reason, the basics are presented first. If you are not interested in how these processors work, but merely want to produce quick results, then you should skip to section (6.6) which discusses the **nroff/troff** *macro packages*. These are precoded **nroff/ troff** command sequences that perform high-level text formatting functions.

The concepts covered in this chapter include:

Page Formatting
Adjustment
Line Formatting
Macros

Registers
Conditional Expressions
Table Formatting: **tbl**
Equation Formatting: **eqn**
Text Processing Tools
Spelling Checker
Style and Diction

6.1 Document Formatting with *nroff*

Like many other concepts we have been discussing, UNIX operates in a manner that is a little different than what most users of text processing are accustomed to using (**nroff** and **troff** are similar to IBM's Script). The **nroff** system is not a word processor but what is called a *mark-up language*. This refers to the work of an editor (a person), who marks up text to indicate the typesetting information required. Rather than create documents in a "what you see is what you get" mode (wysiwyg), you embed commands in the text that affect the way it will be formatted and printed. There are products coming on the market that give you a wysiwyg interface and generate **nroff** text, which is then suitable for further processing by the UNIX utilities.

Both **nroff** and **troff** are complex, comprehensive systems which provide for a wide degree of flexibility in formatting documents. This flexibility, however, makes it difficult for most users to begin using **nroff** or **troff** effectively without a lot of trial and error. In this chapter, we will only cover those aspects of nroff which will enable you to begin formatting documents (letters, memos, reports, etc.) and which provide the framework for more sophisticated applications.

6.1.1 The **nroff** System

The **nroff** system has a number of features which, if understood conceptually, will make it much easier to use. It is not complicated once you accept the fact that it is an advanced document preparation tool rather than a word processor. These features include:

1. *Commands*. **nroff** consists of several types of commands that determine how the text following the command is to be interpreted. The basic commands appear at the beginning of a line, preceded by a dot.

2. *Spacing*. Spacing is measured in lines, inches, and printer's measures (pica), depending on context. When appropriate, lines and inches will be

interpreted interchangeably. Font sizes are expressed in pica measurements.

3. _Registers._ **nroff** has a variety of internal registers that are accessible to the user. These registers contain values which pertain to the document being processed, for example, the current line number, current page number, etc.

4. _Conditional Expressions._ These are **nroff** statements in which actions are applied only if certain conditions are met. For example, footers are printed when **nroff** detects the bottom of a page.

5. *Macros.* These are command sequences that have been predefined and that provide the mechanism for creating your own **nroff** commands. For example, if you want to skip to a new page, print a title, and center the first line of text, the commands can be incorporated into a single macro and specified repetitively throughout the document with one command. The macros may also accept parameters which add additional flexibility.

6. *Macros Packages.* Because of the level of detail required when using basic **nroff** commands, several libraries of macros are supplied with your UNIX system which facilitate setting up basic document components (headers, footers, lists, etc.). Your system will probably come with either the MM or MS macro package (or both).

7. *Preprocessor Packages.* Two important supplemental packages come with all **nroff** systems. The first is **eqn,** which is used for specifying mathematical statements containing special symbols (integral, summation, etc.). The second is **tbl,** which is used to create tables with appropriate headings, borders, and columns. Output of **eqn** and **tbl** is incorporated with other macros and nroff commands to produce the final document.

8. *Supporting Utilities.* In addition to the editors and file manipulation filters discussed in Chapter 5, UNIX provides a number of programs specifically for document preparation, including spelling and grammar checks.

The following sections apply these concepts to the creation of a simple document. We illustrate them with extracts from the Constitution of the United States and the Declaration of Independence, shown in Figure 6.1.

6.2 Invoking *nroff*

usage: *nroff* [options] files

Running **nroff** with no options or embedded commands will cause your document to be formatted according to default settings for the page length, margins, line length, line adjustment, and word placement. Figure 6.2

shows the results of running **nroff** on the Preamble to the Constitution and illustrates what some of these settings will do.

The line length defaults to 65 characters (6.5 inches) with the left margin size set to zero. Word wrap is invoked, or in **nroff** terminology the lines have been ''filled,'' and the margins have been justified left and right. Lines are single-spaced and there is no indention. While not shown in the example, the page length is set to 66 lines (11 inches).

Some of the options to **nroff** are discussed in greater detail in Section 6.9. For now, we begin by discussing the different formatting characteristics that can be set with the appropriate **nroff** command.

6.2.1 Lines

There are a number of general things one wants to do with lines, including spacing, length, and adjustment. To specify horizontal spacing, you would use the **.ls** command, which without any argument defaults to single

The Constitution

We the people of the United States, in order to form a more perfect Union, establish Justice, insure domestic Tranquility, provide for the common defense, promote the general Welfare, and secure the Blessings of Liberty to ourselves and our Posterity, do ordain and establish this Constitution for The United States of America.

Article I.

Sect. 1. All legislative powers herein granted shall be vested in a Congress of the United States, which shall consist of a Senate and House of Representatives.

Sect. 2. The House of Representatives shall be composed of Members chosen every second year by the people of the several states, and the electors in each state shall have the qualifications requisite for electors of the most numerous branch of the state legislature.

No person shall be a representative who shall not have attained to the age of twenty five years, and been seven years a citizen of the United States, and who shall not, when elected, be an inhabitant of that state in which he shall be chosen.

Figure 6.1a. Extract from the Constitution

Thomas Jefferson's draft of the Declaration of Independence consisted of two parts. The first was a general and abstract statement about the right of revolution, which has been an inspiration to many people for the past two hundred years:

> We hold these truths to be self-evident, that all men are created equal, that they are endowed by their Creator with certain unalienable Rights, that among these are Life, Liberty and the pursuit of Happiness. That to secure these rights, Governments are instituted among Men, deriving their just powers from the consent of the governed. That whenever any Form of Government becomes destructive of these ends, it is the Right of the People to alter or to abolish it. . . .

The second part was a list of grievances against George III, which justified the exercise of the rights described in the beginning of the document.

Figure 6.1b. Extract from the Declaration

```
We the people of the United States
in order to form a more perfect Union, establish
Justice, insure domestic Tranquility, provide
for the common defense, promote the general Welfare, and secure
the Blessings of Liberty to ourselves and our Posterity, do
ordain and establish this Constitution for
The United States of America.
```

Figure 6.2a. Preamble to the Constitution

```
We  the  people  of  the  United  States  in  order  to  form  a  more
perfect  Union,  establish  Justice,  insure  domestic  Tranquility,
provide  for  the  common  defense,  promote  the  general  Welfare,  and
secure  the  Blessings  of  Liberty  to  ourselves  and  our  Posterity,
do  ordain  and  establish  this  Constitution  for  The  United  States
of  America.
```

Figure 6.2b. After Processing by **nroff**

space. The argument can be specified either as units (lines) or as inches, in which case the value is specified with an **i**:

.ls	single space
.ls 1	single space
.ls 2	double space
.ls 1i	space one inch (6 lines)

The specification in units is illustrated in Figure 6.3.

In the example in Figure 6.3, the default line length is 65 or 6.5i. This can be changed with the **.ll,** line length command. Figure 6.4 shows the effects of changing both line spacing and line length:

.ll 72	72 columns
.ll 7i	7 inches

The fill option still defaults.

To indicate one time vertical space movements you use the **.sp** command and indicate the number of lines to space on insert. The action is a multiple of the global line spacing. For example, if you have double spacing in effect, **.sp 1** will space 2 lines, **.sp 2** will space 4 lines, and so on. This is illustrated in Figure 6.5.

```
.ls 1
We the people of the United States
in order to form a more perfect Union, establish
Justice, insure domestic Tranquility, provide
.ls 2
for the common defense, promote the general Welfare, and secure
the Blessings of Liberty to ourselves and our Posterity, do
ordain and establish this Constitution for
The United States of America.
```

Figure 6.3a. Text with Line Spacing Commands

```
We  the  people  of  the  United  States  in  order  to  form  a  more
perfect  Union,  establish  Justice,  insure  domestic  Tranquility,
provide  for  the  common  defense,  promote  the  general  Welfare,  and

secure  the  Blessings  of  Liberty  to  ourselves  and  our  Posterity,

do  ordain  and  establish  this  Constitution  for  The  United  States

of  America.
```

Figure 6.3b. After **nroff Processing**

```
.ll 50
.ls 2
We the people of the United States
in order to form a more perfect Union, establish
Justice, insure domestic Tranquility, provide
for the common defense, promote the general Welfare, and secure
the Blessings of Liberty to ourselves and our Posterity, do
ordain and establish this Constitution for
The United States of America.
```

Figure 6.4a. Line Length in Columns

```
We  the  people  of  the  United  States  in  order  to

form   a   more   perfect   Union,   establish   Justice,

insure   domestic   Tranquility,   provide   for   the

common  defense,  promote  the  general  Welfare,  and

secure  the  Blessings  of  Liberty  to  ourselves  and

our   Posterity,   do   ordain   and   establish   this

Constitution for The United States of America.
```

Figure 6.4b. Line Length after **nroff** Processing

```
.ll 5i
.ls 1
We the people of the United States
in order to form a more perfect Union, establish
Justice, insure domestic Tranquility, provide
for the common defense, promote the general Welfare, and secure
the Blessings of Liberty to ourselves and our Posterity, do
ordain and establish this Constitution for
The United States of America.
```

Figure 6.4c. Line Length with Inch Specification

```
We  the  people  of  the  United  States  in  order  to
form   a   more   perfect   Union,   establish   Justice,
insure   domestic   Tranquility,   provide   for   the
common  defense,  promote  the  general  Welfare,  and
secure  the  Blessings  of  Liberty  to  ourselves  and
our   Posterity,   do   ordain   and   establish   this
Constitution for The United States of America.
```

Figure 6.4d. After **nroff** Processing

6.2.2 *Margins and Indentation*

Margins are established by using the line length command in combination with the indentation command **.in** or the page offset command, **.po**. To set a left margin at column 5 and a left margin at column 70, you would set the offset to 5 and the line length to 65. This is shown in Figure 6.6.

```
.ll 50
.ls 1
The Constitution
.sp 3
We the people of the United States
in order to form a more perfect Union, establish
Justice, insure domestic Tranquility, provide
for the common defense, promote the general Welfare, and secure
the Blessings of Liberty to ourselves and our Posterity, do
ordain and establish this Constitution for
The United States of America.
.sp 2
article I.
.sp 2
Sect. 1. all legislative powers herein granted . . .
```

Figure 6.5a. Vertical Spacing

```
The Constitution



We the people of the United States in order to
form a more perfect Union, establish Justice,
insure domestic Tranquility, provide for the
common defense, promote the general Welfare, and
secure the Blessings of Liberty to ourselves and
our Posterity, do ordain and establish this
Constitution for The United States of America.


Article I.

Sect. 1. All legislative powers here in granted . . .
```

Figure 6.5b. Document with Vertical Spacing

```
.ls 1
.po 5
.ll 70
We the people of the United States
in order to form a more perfect Union, establish
Justice, insure domestic Tranquility, provide
for the common defense, promote the general Welfare, and secure
the Blessings of Liberty to ourselves and our Posterity, do
ordain and establish this Constitution for
The United States of America.
```

Figure 6.6a. Setting Margins

```
We  the  people  of  the  United  States  in  order  to  form  a  more  perfect
Union,  establish  Justice,  insure  domestic  Tranquility,  provide  for  the
common  defense,  promote  the  general  Welfare,  and  secure  the  Blessing
of  Liberty  to  ourselves  and  our  Posterity,  do  ordain  and  establish
this  Constitution  for  The  United  States  of  America.
```

Figure 6.6b. After Margin Processing

Indentation is accomplished by using a sequence of commands which set the indentation value either permanently until changed or temporarily over a range of lines. The specification of the value is made either absolute or relative to the previous setting by using plus and minus ($+/-$).

Suppose you want to indent a quotation and then resume at the previous column after the quotation. Let's further assume that the document is to be double-spaced, but the quotation is to be single-spaced. Figure 6.7 shows how this can be accomplished simply. We will use the **.in** command, which permanently sets the indentation value. In this example, both the indentation and line length values were set and reset to change left and right margins, respectively.

Another typical situation concerns indentation for paragraphs. In this case, we want to change the indentation for the initial line, then revert to the original setting. Figures 6.8 and 6.9 show two interesting uses of the

```
.ll 60
.ls 2
.fi
Thomas  Jefferson's  draft  of  the  Declaration  of  Independence
consisted  of  two  parts.  The  first  was  a  general  and  abstract
statement  about  the  right  of  revolution  which  has  been  an
inspiration  to  many  people  for  the  past  two  hundred  years:
.in 5
.ll 45
.ls 1
We  hold  these  truths  to  be  self-evident,  that  all  men  are
created  equal,  that  they  are  endowed  by  their  Creator  with
certain  unalienable  Rights,  that  among  these  are  Life,
Liberty  and  the  pursuit  of  Happiness.  That  to  secure  these
rights,  Governments  are  instituted  among  Men,  deriving  their
just  powers  from  the  consent  of  the  governed.  That  whenever
any  Form  of  Government  becomes  destructive  of  these  ends,  it
is  the  Right  of  the  People  to  alter  or  to  abolish  it  .  .  .
.ls 2
.ll 65
.in 0
The  second  part  was  a  list  of  grievances  against  George  III,
which  justified  the  exercise  of  the  rights  described  in  the
beginning  of  the  document.
```

Figure 6.7a. nroff Indentation

Thomas Jefferson's draft of the Declaration of Independence consisted of two parts. The first was a general and abstract statement about the right of revolution, which has been an inspiration to many people for the past two hundred years:

We hold these truths to be self-evident, that all men are created equal, that they are endowed by their Creator with certain unalienable Rights, that among these are Life, Liberty and the pursuit of Happiness. That to secure these rights, Governments are instituted among Men, deriving their just powers from the consent of the governed. That whenever any Form of Government becomes destructive of these ends, it is the Right of the People to alter or to abolish it . . .

The second part was a list of grievances against George III, which justified the exercise of the rights described in the beginning of the document.

Figure 6.7b. nroff Indentation Processing

temporary indentation, **.ti.** Figures 6.8a and 6.8b show traditional paragraph indentation. In Figure 6.9, we effectively unindent to bring the first line of the paragraph back 5 columns.

6.2.3 *Justification*

Justification involves the manner in which words are placed on successive lines within margins that have been set up (or defaulted). The first aspect of justification depends upon whether **nroff** fills or completes lines between margins with words from following lines. The commands that turn the fill feature on and off are **.fi** and **.nf,** respectively. These commands work in conjunction with the adjustment commands to achieve desired output results. Referring back to Figure 6.2, we see that the fill option is specified by default, as is the justification or lining up of both right and left margins. We show the use of no fill in Figure 6.10.

When the fill option is on, it is possible to turn adjustment off with the no-adjust command, na, or specify adjustment with the **.ad** command and the following arguments:

l	left justification only
r	right justification only
c	center lines
b or **n**	justify both margins

These options are illustrated in Figures 6.11 through 6.15. The complicated aspect of justification occurs when it is used with the fill/nofill options. Just remember, you usually either want to fill and adjust or nofill and noadjust. In fact, the nofill command inhibits the adjustment.

The filling of text from the next line is stopped when the line begins with an nroff text formatting command (e.g., new page, skip a line) or blank characters. In this way, paragraphs occurring naturally (by spacing) are not filled incorrectly. Should the situation arise in which you want to force the termination of the fill operation for the current line, you would use the break command, **.br.**

6.2.4 *Centering and Underlining Titles*

Centering and underlining lines of text is done with the **.ce** and **.ul** commands, respectively. The commands take a value as an argument that indicates the number of lines following to be centered or underlined. The com-

```
.ll 65
.ls 1
The Constitution
.sp 3
.in 5
.ti +2
We the people of the United States
in order to form a more perfect Union, establish
Justice, insure domestic Tranquility, provide
for the common defense, promote the general Welfare, and secure
the Blessings of Liberty to ourselves and our Posterity, do
ordain and establish this Constitution for
The United States of America.
.sp 2
Article I.
.sp 2
.ti +2
Sect. 1. All legislative powers herein granted shall be vested in a
Congress of the United States, which shall consist of a Senate and
House of Representatives.
.ti +2
.sp 1
Sect. 2. The House of Representatives shall be composed of members
chosen every second year by the people the several states, and the
electors in each state shall have the qualifications requisite
for electors of the most numberous branch of the state legislature.
.ti+2
.sp 1
No person shall be a representative who shall not have attained
to the age of twenty five years, and been seven years a citizen of the
United States, and who shall not, when elected, be an inhabitant
of that state in which he shall be chosen.
```

Figure 6.8a.   nroff with Paragraph Indentation

```
The Constitution


    We the people of the United States in order to form a
more perfect Union, establish Justice, insure domestic
Tranquility, provide for the common defense, promote the
general Welfare, and secure the Blessings of Liberty to
ourselves and our Posterity, do ordain and establish this
Constitution for The United States of America.


Article I.


    Sect.  1.  All  legislative  powers  herein  granted
shall be vested in a Congress of the United States, which
shall consist of a Senate and House of Representatives.

    Sect. 2 The House of Representatives shall be composed
of members chosen every second year by the people the
several states, and the electors in each state shall have
the qualifications requisite for electors of the most
numberous branch of the state legislature.

    No person shall be a representative who shall not have
attained to the age of twenty-five years, and been seven
years a citizen of the United States, and who shall not,
when elected, be an inhabitant of that state in which he
shall be chosen.
```

Figure 6.8b. After Normal Paragraph Indentation

mands can be used together and with other commands that cover a range of lines. In Figure 6.16, we continue to format the Constitution by centering the headings.

A special command, **.tl,** creates a three-part title with the parts justified left, centered, and justified right, respectively:

```
.tl 'left title'center title'right title'
```

If a percent sign is embedded in any of the title characters, it will translate into the current page number. Thus, to title our documents, we might include the following statement:

```
.tl 'American History'Constitution'Page %'
```

This is illustrated in Figure 6.17. Note that this will not cause the title to appear on every page but only at the place in the text where the statement appears. Furthermore, the page number is set to zero. To solve these problems and address others, we introduce some of the more sophisticated features of UNIX text processing next.

6.3 *Registers*

The nroff system contains two types of registers or variables, built-in and user-defined. Registers are set with the **.nr** command, which names a register and gives it a value. To set the page number in our previous example to 1, you would enter the following command:

```
.nr % 1
```

The general syntax for setting a register is:

.nr   registername ± value

```
.ll 65
.ls 1
The Constitution
.sp 3
.in 10
.ti -5
We the people of the United States
in order to form a more perfect Union, establish
Justice, insure domestic Tranquility, provide
for the common defense, promote the general Welfare, and secure
the Blessings of Liberty to ourselves and our Posterity, do
ordain and establish this Constitution for
The United States of America.
.sp 2
Article I.
.sp 2
.ti -5
Sect. 1. All legislative powers herein granted shall be vested in a
Congress of the United States, which shall consist of a Senate and
House of Representatives.
.ti -5
.sp 1
Sect. 2. The House of Representatives shall be composed of members
chosen every second year by the people the several states, and the
electors in each state shall have the qualifications requisite
for electors of the most numberous branch of the state legislature.
.ti -5
.sp 1
No person shall be a representative who shall not have attained
to the age of twenty-five years, and been seven years a citizen of the
United States, and who shall not, when elected, be an inhabitant
of that state in which he shall be chosen.
```

Figure 6.9a.   Before Paragraph Unindentation

The Constitution

We the people of the United States in order to form a more
    perfect Union, establish Justice, insure domestic
    Tranquility, provide for the common defense, promote
    the general Welfare, and secure the Blessings of
    Liberty to ourselves and our Posterity, do ordain and
    establish this Constitution for The United States of
    America.

    Article I.

Sect.1. All legislative powers herein granted shall be
    vested in a Congress of the United States, which shall
    consist of a Senate and House of Representatives.

Sect.2. The House of Representatives shall be composed of
    members chosen every second year by the people the
    several states, and the electors in each state shall
    have the qualifications requisite for electors of the
    most numberous branch of the state legislature.

No person shall be a representative who shall not have
    attained to the age of twenty-five years, and been
    seven years a citizen of the United States, and who
    shall not, when elected, be an inhabitant of that state
    in which he shall be chosen.

Figure 6.9b. After Paragraph Unindentation

.nf
We the people of the United States
in order to form a more perfect Union, establish
Justice, insure domestic Tranquility, provide
for the common defense, promote the general Welfare, and secure
the Blessings of Liberty to ourselves and our Posterity, do
ordain and establish this Constitution for
The United States of America.

Figure 6.10a. No Fill Option

We the people of the United States
in order to form a more perfect Union, establish
Justice, insure domestic Tranquility, provide
for the common defense, promote the general Welfare, and secure
the Blessings of Liberty to ourselves and our Posterity, do
ordain and establish this Constitution for
The United States of America.

Figure 6.10b. After No Fill Processing

```
.na
.fi
We the people of the United States
in order to form a more perfect Union, establish
Justice, insure domestic Tranquility, provide
for the common defense, promote the general Welfare, and secure
the Blessings of Liberty to ourselves and our Posterity, do
ordain and establish this Constitution for
The United States of America.
```

Figure 6.11a. Fill with No Adjustment

```
We the people of the United States in order to form a more
perfect Union, establish Justice, insure domestic Tranquility,
provide for the common defense, promote the general Welfare, and
secure the Blessings of Liberty to ourselves and our Posterity,
do ordain and establish this Constitution for The United States
of America.
```

Figure 6.11b. After Fill Processing

```
.fi
.ad l
We the people of the United States
in order to form a more perfect Union, establish
Justice, insure domestic Tranquility, provide
for the common defense, promote the general Welfare, and secure
the Blessings of Liberty to ourselves and our Posterity, do
ordain and establish this Constitution for
The United States of America.
```

Figure 6.12a. Left Adjust

```
We the people of the United States in order to form a more
perfect Union, establish Justice, insure domestic Tranquility,
provide for the common defense, promote the general Welfare, and
secure the Blessings of Liberty to ourselves and our Posterity,
do ordain and establish this Constitution for the United States
of America.
```

Figure 6.12b. After Left Adjust Processing

```
.fi
.ad r
We the people of the United States
in order to form a more perfect Union, establish
Justice, insure domestic Tranquility, provide
for the common defense, promote the general Welfare, and secure
the Blessings of Liberty to ourselves and our Posterity, do
ordain and establish this Constitution for
The United States of America.
```

Figure 6.13a. Right Adjust

```
         We the people of the United States in order to form a more
      perfect Union, establish Justice, insure domestic Tranquility,
      provide for the common defense, promote the general Welfare, and
      secure the Blessings of Liberty to ourselves and our Posterity,
      do ordain and establish this Constitution for The United States
                                                          of America.
```

Figure 6.13b. After Processing Right Adjustment

```
.fi
.ad c
We the people of the United States
in order to form a more perfect Union, establish
Justice, insure domestic Tranquility, provide
for the common defense, promote the general Welfare, and secure
the Blessings of Liberty to ourselves and our Posterity, do
ordain and establish this Constitution for
The United States of America.
```

Figure 6.14a. Centering

```
      We the people of the United States in order to form a more
      perfect Union, establish Justice, insure domestic Tranquility,
      provide for the common defense, promote the general Welfare, and
      secure the Blessings of Liberty to ourselves and our Posterity,
      do ordain and establish this Constitution for The United States
                              of America.
```

Figure 6.14b. After Processing Center

```
.fi
.ad b
We the people of the United States
in order to form a more perfect Union, establish
Justice, insure domestic Tranquility, provide
for the common defense, promote the general Welfare, and secure
the Blessings of Liberty to ourselves and our Posterity, do
ordain and establish this Constitution for
The United States of America.
```

Figure 6.15a. Right and Left Margins

```
We  the  people  of  the  United  States  in  order  to  form  a  more
perfect  Union,  establish  Justice,  insure  domestic  Tranquility,
provide  for  the  common  defense,  promote  the  general  Welfare,  and
secure  the  Blessings  of  Liberty  to  ourselves  and  our  Posterity,
do  ordain  and  establish  this  Constitution  for  The  United  States
of America.
```

Figure 6.15b. After Right and Left Justification

where register names are one or two characters long and the value modifies the previous value of the register. References to numeric register values within **nroff** statements other than **.nr** use a \n prefix. Finally, if the name of the register has two characters, the name is preceded by an open parenthesis. For example, to reference the current date stored in the year, month, and day registers (**yr, mo,** and **dy**), the following sequence would be entered:

```
\n(mo/\n(dy/\n(yr
```

which would print the date in the standard format: 10/15/87

```
.ll 65
.ls 1
.ce 1
.ul 1
The Constitution
.sp 3
.in 5
.ti +2
We the people of the United States
in order to form a more perfect Union, establish
Justice, insure domestic Tranquility, provide
for the common defense, promote the general Welfare, and secure
the Blessings of Liberty to ourselves and our Posterity, do
ordain and establish this Constitution for
The United States of America.
.sp 2
.ce 1
.ul 1
Article I.
.sp 2
.ti +2
Sect. 1. All legislative powers herein granted shall be vested in a
Congress of the United States, which shall consist of a Senate and
House of Representatives.
.ti +2
.sp 1
Sect. 2. The House of Representatives shall be composed of members
chosen every second year by the people the several states, and the
electors in each state shall have the qualifications requisite
for electors of the most numberous branch of the state legislature.
.ti +2
.sp 1
No person shall be a representative who shall not have attained
to the age of twenty-five years, and been seven years a citizen of the
United States, and who shall not, when elected, be an inhabitant
of that state in which he shall be chosen.
```

Figure 6.16a. Text to Center and Underline

<u>The Constitution</u>

We the people of the United States in order to form a more perfect Union, establish Justice, insure domestic Tranquility, provide for the common defense, promote the general Welfare, and secure the Blessings of Liberty to ourselves and our Posterity, do ordain and establish this Constitution for The United States of America.

<u>Article 1.</u>

Sect. 1. All legislative powers herein granted shall be vested in a Congress of the United States, which shall consist of a Senate and House of Representatives.

Sect. 2. The House of Representatives shall be composed of members chosen every second year by the people the several states, and the electors in each state shall have the qualifications requisite for electors of the most numberous branch of the state legislature.

No person shall be a representative who shall not have attained to the age of twenty-five years, and been seven years a citizen of the United States, and who shall not, when elected, be an inhabitant of that state in which he shall be chosen.

Figure 6.16b. After Processing Center and Underline

```
.tl 'American History'Constitution'Page %'
.ll 65
.ls 1
.ce 1
.sp 2
The Constitution
.sp 3
.in 5
.ti +2
We the people of the United States
in order to form a more perfect Union, establish
Justice, insure domestic Tranquility, provide
for the common defense, promote the general Welfare, and secure
the Blessings of Liberty to ourselves and our Posterity, do
ordain and establish this Constitution for
The United States of America.
```

Figure 6.17a. Three-Part Titles

```
American History          Constitution                  Page 0


                     The Constitution


   We the people of the United States in order to form a
more perfect Union, establish Justice, insure domestic
Tranquility, provide for the common defense, promote the
general Welfare, and secure the Blessings of Liberty to
ourselves and our Posterity, do ordain and establish this
Constitution for The United States of America.
```
Figure 6.17b. Use of the Three-Part Title

This is illustrated in Figure 6.18. We set the page register, %, with an initial value of one. Then in the second three-part title, we center the current date by referencing mo, dy, and yr. Remember, with the **.nr** command you do not use the \n notation, but for referencing a register, you do. If the register has a two-character name, it is preceded with an open parenthesis.

One last point about registers. We have been setting and referencing **nroff** built-in registers, but you can simply define your own by giving a one- or two-character name in the **.nr** command. Be careful that your name doesn't conflict with any built-in name. In Figure 6.18a section numbers are generated and incremented in a user-defined register called **sn**. First it is initialized to 0 and a default increment is set. When referenced for Sections 1 and 2, the increment is successively applied. The general format for referencing a register with an increment is:

\n+*name* -	single character name + increment
\n−*name* -	single character name − decrement
\n+*(name* -	double character name + increment
\n−*(name* -	double character name − decrement

6.4 *Conditional Expressions*

Conditional expressions cause nroff actions to occur if the expression is true. They are set with the **.if** command, which has the following format:

   .if expression text

where the expression is either a built-in condition name, a value, or a string comparison. Here we illustrate by using a condition name for even or odd page numbers. Many documents have titles which will be different for even and odd pages. This can be tested with the o (odd) and e (even) page condition names. In our continuing example, suppose we want the main title to appear on even pages and the date title to appear on odd pages. The expressions for these would be:

```
.if e .tl 'American History'Constitution'Page %'
.if o .tl ''\n(mo/\n(dy/\n(yr''
```

Multiline actions are delimited with \{ and \{ character sequences:

```
if expression \{
        ------
        ------
        ------

    \}
```

```
.nr % 1
.nr sn 0 1
.tl 'American History'Constitution'Page\n%'
.tl "\n(mo/\n(dy/\n(yr"
.ll 65
.ls 1
.ce 1
.sp 2
The Constitution
.sp 3
.in 5
.ti +2
We the people of the United States
in order to form a more perfect Union, establish
Justice, insure domestic Tranquility, provide
for the common defense, promote the general Welfare, and secure
the Blessings of Liberty to ourselves and our Posterity, do
ordain and establish this Constitution for
The United States of America.
.sp 2
.ce 1
Article I.
.sp 2
.ti +2
Sect. \n+(sn. All legislative powers herein granted shall be vested in a
Congress of the United States, which shall consist of a Senate and
House of Representatives.
.ti +2
.sp 1
Sect. \n+(sn. The House of Representatives shall be composed of members
chosen every second year by the people the several states, and the
electors in each state shall have the qualifications requisite
for electors of the most numerous branch of the state legislature.
.ti +2
.sp 1
No person shall be a representative who shall not have attained
to the age of twenty-five years, and been seven years a citizen of the
United States, and who shall not, when elected, be an inhabitant
of that state in which he shall be chosen.
```

Figure 6.18a. Setting and Referencing Registers

American History   Constitution   Page 1
                             4/21/86

                        The Constitution

We the people of the United States in order to form a
more perfect Union, establish Justice, insure domestic
Tranquility, provide for the common defense, promote the
general Welfare, and secure the Blessings of Liberty to
ourselves and our Posterity, do ordain and establish this
Constitution for The United States of America.

                         Article I.

Sect. 1. All legislative powers herein granted shall be
vested in a Congress of the United States, which shall
consist of a Senate and House of Representatives.

Sect. 2. The House of Representatives shall be composed
of members chosen every second year by the people the
several states, and the electors in each state shall have
the qualifications requisite for electors of the most
numberous branch of the state legislature.

No person shall be a representative who shall not have
attained to the age of twenty-five years, and been seven
years a citizen of the United States, and who shall not,
when elected, be an inhabitant of that state in which he
shall be chosen.

Figure 6.18b. Processing Register Values

The problem, of course, is knowing where to insert these commands, since we want them to be executed at the beginning of every page (another conditional situation). So, before we can illustrate the use of the conditional expression, we first must introduce greater flexibility into our formatting specifications.

6.5 Macros

A macro is a user-defined sequence of **nroff** commands which is given a name and may be invoked repeatedly at any point in the text; **nroff** provides a comprehensive macro facility, including the ability to pass arguments to the macro. We have seen several situations in which macros might be desirable to make the specification of the document easier.

6.5.1 Macro Definition and Specification

Macros are created inline, usually at the beginning of the document, with the **.de** (define) command. The lines which follow, up to a terminating **..** on a line by itself, constitute the body of the macro. The simplest use of a macro might be at the beginning of each paragraph. We have seen that we want to space one line and indent five positions:

```
.de PG
.sp
.ti +2
..
```

To perform the required action we simply insert our new **.PG** command. In Figure 6.19, some of the spacing on the first few paragraphs was changed with the knowledge that **.PG** would include a single blank line.

In the examples in the next several sections, you will notice that macro names are defined using upper case letters. This is an **nroff** convention which makes it easier to visually distinguish between **nroff** commands from macros.

6.5.2 Macro Traps

The nroff macros have a number of facilities that invoke macros when a specific event occurs rather than at a specific point in the input stream. For example, **nroff** keeps track of the current page line and the number of lines per page. When the page position is reset to zero, the top of page event occurs. The **.wh** command causes the named macro to be invoked whenever the specified page position is reached:

```
.wh position macro
```

By specifying position 0, the **.PT** macro will be invoked at the top of every page:

```
.wh 0 PT
```

If we consider the functions we might want executed at the top of a page, we would include a top margin, a title, and some space below the title. We first define the **PT** (page top) macro, then use the **.wh** command which sets it to be invoked at every top of page:

```
.de PT
.sp 3
.tl 'American History'Constitution'Page %'
.tl "\n(mo/\n(dy/\n(yr"
.sp 2
..
```

This is illustrated in Figure 6.20 where we set a page length of 20 to demonstrate the page break (remember, the default is 66 lines per page). To cause the first heading to print (**nroff** is already at line 0), it is necessary to invoke .**PT** explicitly.

We can now illustrate the use of conditional expressions by requiring different titles for even-numbered pages and odd-numbered pages. In Figure 6.20c, the .**PT** macro is modified to include the condition names **e** and **o,** as described above to generate titles on even and odd pages:

```
.de PT
.sp 3
.if e .tl 'American History'Constitution'Page %'
.if o .tl "\n(mo/\n(dy/\n(yr'prPage %'
.sp 2
..
```

```
.de PG
.sp 1
.ti +2
..
.nr sn 0 1
.nr % 1
.tl 'American History'Constitution'Page \n%'
.tl "\n(mo/\n(dy/\n(yr"
.ll 65
.ls 1
.ce 1
.sp 2
The Constitution
.sp 2
.in 5
.PG
We the people of the United States
in order to form a more perfect Union, establish
Justice, insure domestic Tranquility, provide
for the common defense, promote the general Welfare, and secure
the Blessings of Liberty to ourselves and our Posterity, do
ordain and establish this Constitution for
The United States of America.
.sp 2
.ce 1
Article I.
.sp 1
.PG
Sect. \n+(sn. All legislative powers herein granted shall be vested in a
Congress of the United States, which shall consist of a Senate and
House of Representatives.
.PG
Sect. \n+(sn. The House of Representatives shall be composed of members
chosen every second year by the people the several states, and the
electors in each states shall have the qualifications requisite
for electors of the most numberous branch of the state legislature.
.PG
No person shall be a representative who shall not have attained
to the age of twenty-five years, and been seven years a citizen of the
United States, and who shall not, when elected, be an inhabitant
of that state in which he shall be chosen.
```

Figure 6.19a. Simple Paragraph Macro

```
American History        Constitution              Page 1
                           4/21/86


                      The Constitution


    We the people of the United States in order to form a
more perfect Union, establish Justice, insure domestic
Tranquility, provide for the common defense, promote the
general Welfare, and secure the Blessings of Liberty to
ourselves and our Posterity, do ordain and establish this
Constitution for The United States of America.


                        Article I.


    Sect. 1. All legislative powers herein granted shall be
vested in a Congress of the United States, which shall
consist of a Senate and House of Representatives.

    Sect. 2. The House of Representatives shall be composed
of members chosen every second year by the people the
several states, and the electors in each state shall have
the qualifications requisite for electors of the most
numberous branch of the state legislature.

    No person shall be a representative who shall not have
attained to the age of twenty-five years, and been seven
years a citizen of the United States, and who shall not,
when elected, be an inhabitant of that state in which he
shall be chosen.
```

Figure 6.19b. Processing of **.PG** Macro

6.5.3 Arguments to Macros

Sometimes it is desirable to design macros that are flexible and driven by parameters. This is done by referencing up to nine position arguments that are referenced by preceding the argument number by \$. Since the backslash is the quote symbol for nroff (see Chapter 2), it must also be quoted. Let's give an example. We will rewrite the header macro **.PT** so that it can be used for formatting either the Constitution or the Declaration of Independence. In the body of the macro, the parameter reference replaces the actual heading:

```
.if e .tl'American History'\\$1'Page %'
```

In this case the backslash of \$ must be quoted. Otherwise, the substitution will take place when the macro is defined rather than when invoked.

When referencing the macro, the arguments follow the name, enclosed in double quotes:

    `.PT "Constitution"`

or

    `.PT "Declaration of Independence"`

```
.de PT
.sp 3
.tl 'American History'Constitution'Page %'
.tl "\n(mo/\n(dy/\n(yr"
.sp 2
..
.de PG
.sp 1
.ti +2
..
.wh 0 PT
.nr sn 0 1
.nr % 1
.pl 20
.ll 65
.ls 1
.PT
.ce 1
The Constitution
.sp 2
.in 5
.PG
We the people of the United States
in order to form a more perfect Union, establish
Justice, insure domestic Tranquility, provide
for the common defense, promote the general Welfare, and secure
the Blessings of Liberty to ourselves and our Posterity, do
ordain and establish this Constitution for
The United States of America.
.sp 2
.ce 1
Article I.
.sp 1
.PG
Sect. \n+(sn. All legislative powers herein granted shall be vested in a
Congress of the United States, which shall consist of a Senate and
House of Representatives.
.PG
Sect. \n+(sn. The House of Representatives shall be composed of members
chosen every second year by the people the several states, and the
electors in each state shall have the qualifications requisite
for electors of the most numerous branch of the state legislature.
.PG
No person shall be a representative who shall not have attained
to the age of twenty-five years, and been seven years a citizen of the
United States, and who shall not, when elected, be an inhabitant
of that state in which he shall be chosen.
```

Figure 6.20a. Page Top Macro

```
American History        Constitution              Page 1
                        4/21/86


                    The Constitution


    We the people of the United States in order to form a
more perfect Union, establish Justice, insure domestic
Tranquility, provide for the common defense, promote the
general Welfare, and secure the Blessings of Liberty to
ourselves and our Posterity, do ordain and establish this
Constitution for The United States of America.



American History        Constitution              Page 2
                        4/21/86


                    Article I.


    Sect. 1. All legislative powers herein granted shall be
vested in a Congress of the United States, which shall
consist of a Senate and House of Representatives.

    Sect. 2. The House of Representatives shall be composed
of members chosen every second year by the people the
several states, and the electors in each state shall have
the qualifications requisite for electors of the most
numberous branch of the state legislature.



American History        Constitution              Page 3
                        4/21/86


    No person shall be a representative who shall not have
attained to the age of twenty-five years, and been seven
years a citizen of the United States, and who shall not,
when elected, be an inhabitant of that state in which he
shall be chosen.
```

Figure 6.20b. Process of Page Top Macro

This is illustrated in Figure 6.21. There are a few other items to point out in this example. First, arguments to event-invoked macros (e.g., via **.wh**) are not evaluated. It was necessary, therefore, to invoke one level of indirection and have **.wh** invoke **.WP**, which, in turn, invokes our **.PT,** since **.wh** doesn't invoke a macro, but sets it to be invoked when a specific line number on the page is reached.

American History   Constitution   Page 1

                    The Constitution

    We the people of the United States in order to form a
more perfect Union, establish Justice, insure domestic
Tranquility, provide for the common defense, promote the
general Welfare, and secure the Blessings of Liberty to
ourselves and our Posterity, do ordain and establish this
Constitution for The United States of America.

                      Article I.

                      4/21/86   Page 2

    Sect. 1. All legislative powers herein granted shall be
vested in a Congress of the United States, which shall
consist of a Senate and House of Representatives.

    Sect. 2. The House of Representatives shall be composed
of members chosen every second year by the people the
several states, and the electors in each state shall have
the qualifications requisite for electors of the most
numberous branch of the state legislature.

    No person shall be a representative who shall not have
attained to the age of twenty-five years, and been seven
years

American History   Constitution   Page 3

a citizen of the United States, and who shall not, when
elected, be an inhabitant of that state in which he shall be
chosen.

Figure 6.20c. Processing of Even and Odd Headers

    Second, you should by now have a sense of how to organize your docu-
ment, beginning with macro definitions and initialization. It might be a
good idea to create a macro, **.IN,** which contains initializations (and include page length, line length, etc., as arguments). You can introduce comments with the **.cm** or **.** command. This is a way to document your text
and your macros.

    Last, the title ''Article I'' appears on a page by itself. This seems visually

```
.cm *
.cm * Top of Header Macro
.cm *
.de PT
.sp 3
.if o .tl 'American History'\\$1'Page %'
.if e .tl "\n(mo/\(dy/\n(yr'Page %'
.sp 2
..
.cm *
.cm *    Beginning of Paragraph Macro
.cm *
.de PG
.sp 1
.ti +2
..
.cm *
.cm * Macro set by .wh
.cm *
.de WP
.cm .PT "Constitution"
..
```

Figure 6.21a. Arguments to Macros (Macro Definition)

awkward, and we might want to insure that the subtitle is kept with its body of text. One solution uses the **.wh** command to test for the remaining space (e.g., six lines), and then a macro (**.NP**) is invoked to perform the skip to the next page processing:

```
.wh -6 NP
```

Among other top-of-page activities you would use the **.bp** command to force the skip to a new page. The macro would look like our **.PT** macro:

```
.de NP
.bp
.sp 3
.if e .tl 'American History'Constitution'Page %'
.if o .tl "\n(mo/\n(dy/\n(yr'Page %'
.sp 2
..
```

By now, you can see that creating formatted documents is not an easy task. First you design the macros to make the specification easier, then you insert the **nroff** commands and macros into the text. Fortunately, there are a number of macro packages which have already been designed and may

```
.cm *
.cm *    Start of Body of Document
.cm *
.wh 0 WP
.nr sn 0 1
.nr X 1
.pl 20
.ll 65
.ls 1
.ce 1
The Constitution
.sp 2
.in 5
.PG
We the people of the United States
in order to form a more perfect Union, establish
Justice, insure domestic Tranquility, provide
for the common defense, promote the general Welfare, and secure
the Blessings of Liberty to ourselves and our Posterity, do
ordain and establish this Constitution for
The United States of America.
.sp 2
.ce 1
Article I.
.sp 1
.PG
Sect. \n+(sn. All legislative powers herein granted shall be vested in a
Congress of the United States, which shall consist of a Senate and
House of Representatives.
.PG
Sect. \n+(sn. The House of Representatives shall be composed of members
chosen every second year by the people of the several states, and the
electors in each state shall have the qualifications requisite
for electors of the most numberous branch of the state legislature.
.PG
No person shall be a representative who shall not have attained
to the age of twenty-five years, and been seven years a citizen of the
United States, and who shall not, when elected, be an inhabitant
of that state in which he shall be chosen.
```

Figure 6.21b. Arguments to Macros (continued)

be provided with your UNIX system. We turn next to this aspect of document processing.

6.6 Macro Packages

Scanning our text for formatting the Constitution, you will notice that it is quite complicated. The use of macros can simplify this, and with careful creation of the appropriate macros, it is possible to tailor **nroff** to your own installation. This has already been done several times, and UNIX comes with one or more macro packages that can be included from the **nroff** command line.

The Constitution

We the people of the United States in order to form a
more perfect Union, establish Justice, insure domestic
Tranquility, provide for the common defense, promote the
general Welfare, and secure the Blessings of Liberty to
ourselves and our Posterity, do ordain and establish this
Constitution for The United States of America.

Article I.

4/21/86   Page 2

   Sect. 1. All legislative powers herein granted shall be
vested in a Congress of the United States, which shall
consist of a Senate and House of Representatives.

   Sect. 2. The House of Representatives shall be composed
of members chosen every second year by the people the
several states, and the electors in each state shall have
the qualifications requisite for electors of the most
numberous branch of the state legislature.

   No person shall be a representative who shall not have
attained to the age of twenty-five years, and been seven
years a citizen of the United States, and who shall not,
when

elected, be an inhabitant of that state in which he shall be
chosen.

Figure 6.21c. After Processing Macro Arguments

   The two most common macro packages are the **ms** and **mm** macros
which will provide for most of the functions you will need to create and
format documents. It is not our purpose to give complete descriptions of
each of the packages, but rather to help you understand how they work,
what they can do, and how to use your system documentation to obtain
further information. Our discussion will focus on **mm**.

6.6.1 Headers and Footers

In a manner similar to our development of the **.PT** macro, **mm** supplies a number of macros for headers and footers. Given our previous discussion, their operation is self-evident:

.PH "title spec"	header
.EH "title spec"	even page header
.OH "title spec"	odd page header
.PF "title spec"	footer
.EF "title spec"	even footer
.OF "title spec"	odd footer

The title specification is the argument to the **.tl nroff** command and must be enclosed in double quotes:

```
.PH "'left'center'right'"
```

6.6.2 Paragraphs

Paragraphs are introduced with the **.P** macro. The **Pt** register determines the type of indenting. If the value is 0 (default), there is no indenting. If the value is 1, then indenting occurs according to the value of the **Pi** register (initially set to 5). Therefore, to indent paragraphs seven positions, you would set **Pt** and **Pi** at the beginning of the document and use the **.P** command before each paragraph.

Beginning:

```
.nr Pt 1
.nr Pi 7
```

Body of Text:

```
.P
Paragraph text . . . .
```

You can see how this is similar to but more complete than our **.PG** macro created above.

6.6.3 Displays

Another set of macros in **mm** allow you to define a part of the text as a display, which means that the text will be kept together on one page. There are two types of displays: static and floating. Static displays are printed on the current page if they will fit or on the next page. In the latter case, blank lines are left on the current page. In this situation, the display appears at the location in which it occurs in the text.

In a floating display, when the text has to be moved to the next page, the current page is filled with the lines that follow the display. In this way the text doesn't have the interrupted look of the static display.

Display text is started by the **.DS** (static) macro or **.DF** (floating) macro and are terminated by the **.DE** macro. The **.DS** and **.DF** macros can take arguments which affect how text in the display is treated:

```
.DS format fill rindent
     text
.DE
```

Where the format is specified as:

O or **L**	no indent
1 or **I**	indent
2 or **C**	center each line
3 or **CB**	center block

The fill option is specified as:

O or **N**	no fill
1 or **F**	fill

The **rindent** value is a right margin indentation of the line length. Some of these options are illustrated in Figures 6.22 through 6.25, which show the effects of the arguments to **.DS**

```
.DS L F
We the people of the United States
in order to form a more perfect Union, establish
Justice, insure domestic Tranquility, provide
for the common defense, promote the general Welfare, and secure
the Blessings of Liberty to ourselves and our Posterity, do
ordain and establish this Constitution for
The United States of America.
.DE
```

Figure 6.22a. Display with Fill and No Indent

We the people of the United States in order to form a more
perfect Union, establish Justice, insure domestic
Tranquility, provide for the common defense, promote the
general Welfare, and secure the Blessings of Liberty to
ourselves and our Posterity, do ordain and establish this
Constitution for The United States of America.

Figure 6.22b. Processing with Fill and No Indent

```
.DS I F
We the people of the United States
in order to form a more perfect Union, establish
Justice, insure domestic Tranquility, provide
for the common defense, promote the general Welfare, and secure
the Blessings of Liberty to ourselves and our Posterity, do
ordain and establish this Constitution for
The United States of America.
.DE
```

Figure 6.23a. Display with Indent and Fill

We the people of the United States in order to form a
more perfect Union, establish Justice, insure domestic
Tranquility, provide for the common defense, promote
the general Welfare, and secure the Blessings of
Liberty to ourselves and our Posterity, do ordain and
establish this Constitution for The United States of
America.

Figure 6.23b. Processing Indent and Fill

```
.DS C N
We the people of the United States
in order to form a more perfect Union, establish
Justice, insure domestic Tranquility, provide
for the common defense, promote the general Welfare, and secure
the Blessings of Liberty to ourselves and our Posterity, do
ordain and establish this Constitution for
The United States of America.
.DE
```

Figure 6.24a. Display with Line Center and No Fill

```
          We the people of the United States
      in order to form a more perfect Union, establish
        Justice, insure domestic Tranquility, provide
for the common defense, promote the general Welfare, and secu
   the Blessings of Liberty to ourselves and our Posterity, do
          ordain and establish this Constitution for
              The United States of America.
```

Figure 6.24b. Processing Line Center and No Fill

```
.DS CB N
We the people of the United States
in order to form a more perfect Union, establish
Justice, insure domestic Tranquility, provide
for the common defense, promote the general Welfare, and secure
the Blessings of Liberty to ourselves and our Posterity, do
ordain and establish this Constitution for
The United States of America.
.DE
```

Figure 6.25a. Display with Block Center and No Fill

```
We the people of the United States
in order to form a more perfect Union, establish
Justice, insure domestic Tranquility, provide
for the common defense, promote the general Welfare, and sec
the Blessings of Liberty to ourselves and our Posterity, do
ordain and establish this Constitution for
The United States of America.
```

Figure 6.25b. Processing Block Center and No Fill

6.6.4 Lists

mm also provides a comprehensive list processing capability that includes numbered lists, bulletted lists, indented lists, and reference lists, among others. Lists begin with a begin-list macro of the type being designated, and they are terminated with the **.LE**, list end command. Figure 6.26 shows a dash list **.DL** in which the items are preceded by a dash. Other types of lists include bullet lists **.BL** and reference lists **.RL.**

```
.ce
Famous Documents
.sp 2
.DL 5
.LI
The Declaration of Independence
.LI
The Articles of Confederation
.LI
The Constitution of the United States
.LI
The United Nations Charter
.LI
The Old Testament
.LI
The New Testament
.LE
```

Figure 6.26a. **mm** Dash List

```
              Famous Documents

  - The Declaration of Independence

  - The Articles of Confederation

  - The Constitution of the United States

  - The United Nations Charter

  - The Old Testament

  - The New Testament
```

Figure 6.26b. Processing of **mm** Dash List

6.7 Table Preprocessor: tbl

The **tbl** preprocessor processes table formatting information and produces nroff statements to create tables. Table definitions initiated by the **.TS** statement and terminated by **.TE**. Table formatting statements can be produced either from within **nroff** or in a separate step with **tbl** used as a filter. After **tbl** processing, **nroff** must be run on the table formatting statements.

Figure 6.27a shows the **tbl** statements used to format an options table. The general format of a table specification consists of options, format statements, and data:

```
.TS
options;
format.
data
.TE
```

```
.TS
center, box, allbox;
c s
l l.
tbl Options
center   center the table
expand   expand table to line length
box    enclose table in box
allbox   enclose each item in boxes
doublebox   enclose table in two boxes
tab(x)   use x to separate data items
linesize(n)   set line size
.TE
```

Figure 6.27a. Text for Options Table

tbl Options	
center	center the table
expand	expand table to line length
box	enclose table in box
allbox	enclose each item in boxes
doublebox	enclose table in two boxes
tab(x)	use x to separate data items
linesize(n)	set line size

Figure 6.27b. Options Table

6.7.1 tbl *Options*

Options direct the global format of the table, for example, table width, centering, and enclosure within boxes. The options are placed on the line following the **.TS** macro and are separated by spaces, tabs, or commas and terminated by a semicolon:

```
.TS
center, box;
```

The table produced in Figure 6.27b lists the possible options.

6.7.2 *Format and Data*

Format specifications indicate the format of the data. Each line in the format specification represents a line of the table with each character indicating how to display the associated data item. The last line of the format specification is repeated for all subsequent data lines. The last line of the format is terminated by a period. Referring to Figure 6.27a, the first **c** indicates that there is a single data item as the first line of data and it is to be centered. The second line contains the specification to left-justify two data items per line. Since this is the last line of the format, it will be repeated for each subsequent data line.

Figure 6.28 shows a table of possible format codes. The table contains multiple-level headings. The top heading is centered (**c**), and spans both columns (**s**). The secondary headings are centered in their columns. Notice that after each heading is a solid line, single for the top heading, and double for the column headings. These are indicated by placing either an un-

```
center, box;
c s
c c
c| l.
nroff Table Preprocessor
_
Key Letter Description
=
c center within column
r right adjust
l left adjust
n numerically adjust
s span columns
  span down (rows)
```

Figure 6.28a. Text for Format Key Letters

nroff Table Preprocessor	
Key letter	Description
c	center within column
r	right adjust
l	left adjust
n	numerically adjust
s	span columns
∧	span down (rows)

Figure 6.28b. Key Letter Table

derscore (_) or equal sign (=) for a single line or double line, respectively, in the data part of the table.

Each table entry is entered on a line by itself and line components must be separated by a single *tab* character.

6.8 Equation Preprocessor: eqn

The **eqn** preprocessor package allows you to give specifications for formatting mathematical equations. Its usage is primarily for **troff** and typesetting equipment, since many of the special characters and changing font sizes and characteristics are not supported by most lineprinters and terminals. With the introduction of low-cost laser printers, using **eqn** to produce quality graphic symbols should increase substantially.

A companion utility, **neqn,** will allow you to produce line printer output suitable for checking your results, though not necessarily the ultimate desired graphical result. The **eqn** package allows you to specify mathematical symbols and fonts using simple commands in the text that will translate on output to the desired symbol. For example, **sup** superscripts the following text, **int** generates an integral sign, and **sum** produces a summation symbol.

6.9 Running nroff: Basic Options

usage: **nroff** [*-olist -nk -sk*] files

We have already introduced a number of independent **nroff** packages, and we now need to describe how all of these systems are put together. We first address the **nroff** command line, which enables us to incorporate macro packages as well as to specify some global formatting characteristics.

Sometimes you will want to select certain pages for printing. This is done with the **nroff -o** option which list pages and page ranges to print. List items are separated by a comma and consist of individual pages or page ranges denoted by a dash. For example, to specify the printing of pages 5 and 10 and pages 20 through 25:

```
nroff -o5,10,20-25 filename
```

Leaving out the beginning or ending value in a range denotes from the start of the document or through the end of the document, respectively. In the following example, the same pages as above are printed, but all pages from page 20 to the end are included:

```
nroff -o5,10,20- filename
```

The **-n** option starts page numbers at the specified page, and the **-s** option pauses after every k pages:

```
nroff -n5 -s5 filename
```

In this example pages are numbered from 5 and output pauses every fifth page. The default for the **-s** is every page (k = 1), which is suitable for single sheet printer feed situations.

The **-m** option is used to include standard macro packages. The name specified as an argument to the option is used to reference a macro library name of the form:

```
/usr/lib/tmac/tmac.name
```

Your system may have the following libraries:

```
/usr/lib/tmac/tmac.m
/usr/lib/tmac/tmac.s
```

So, to invoke **nroff** with the **ms** or **mm** macro package you enter:

```
nroff -ms files
nroff -mm files
```

In this way you can set up your own macro libraries and include them with the **nroff** execution.

6.10 Using the Preprocessors

As indicated earlier, preprocessors are filters that generate nroff statements. When invoking them, you use pipes:

```
tbl | nroff
eqn | nroff
```

If you are using a line printer or want to display the output on the terminal screen, you will have to specify certain options and use a special filter to inhibit reverse linefeeds and backspaces. For example, to produce tables:

```
tbl-TX | nroff | col -b
```

The **-TX** options forces **tbl** to use full line feeds, and the **col** filter strips the text of reverse linefeeds. The **-b** option to **col** accounts for backspaces.

6.11 *nroff* versus *troff*

Throughout this chapter we have emphasized the use of **nroff**, primarily because output can be displayed easily on terminals and lineprinters. If you have typesetting equipment, conversion to **troff** is straightforward. Most **nroff** commands and options are applicable to **troff**. The major difference is that in **troff,** you can assume wider flexibility in the specification of fonts, sizes, vertical and horizontal motions, etc.

Most **nroff** files can be processed by **troff** so that a good start to UNIX text processing is to first create the document using **nroff,** then apply troff to it later.

In addition to the basic formatters, some of the packages we discussed come in **nroff** and **troff** versions. For example, **neqn** is the **nroff** alternative to **eqn,** and **mmt** macros are the **troff** equivalent for the **MM** package.

6.12 *Other Document Processing Utilities*

UNIX comes with a number of document processing utilities in addition to the text formatters. We have discussed many of them already: **cut, paste, sed,** the editors, etc. Some of the filters are for use with **nroff**/**troff** documents.

6.12.1 **deroff**

usage: **deroff** [options] file

This utility removes **nroff**/**troff** commands from text for further processing by another filter. The **-mm** and **-ms** options are used when the document contains macro commands and they cause **deroff** to treat the processing of lists and other constructions properly. The **-w** option outputs the document one word per line. This can be very useful for creating word counts, auxilliary spelling lists, index entries, etc.

6.12.2 **diction**

usage: **diction** [options] file

diction takes a pattern file, that is, a file with a list of phrases, and displays all sentences in the document which contain the phrase. Typical phrases are those you feel you use too often. For example, the phrase "for

example" is used throughout this book, and **diction** could be used to identify the sentences in which it occurs.

6.12.3 explain

usage: **explain**

Used in conjunction with **diction, explain** reports on the phrases found
by the **diction** command. The command takes no options. It interactively
asks for phrases and suggests alternatives. Thus, you process your document first with **diction,** which highlights the phrases in a document that
could be modified, and then you use **explain** to suggest alternatives.

6.12.4 hyphen

usage: **hyphen** file

This filter lists hyphenated words from the document on standard output. It is used to check manually for correct hyphenation.

6.12.5 spell

usage: **spell** [options] [+ userfile] files

spell lists words not found in the default or user-defined word list on
standard output. You specify your own spelling list with the + *usefile* option. The **-b** option includes British spelling (e.g., centre, colour).

6.12.6 style

usage: **style** [options] files

style is a program which produces statistics about the document being
checked. The utility produces statistics in five categories:

- readability
- sentence information
- sentence types

- word usage
- sentence beginnings

Options to **style** determine the statistics produced:

a	sentence length and readability
e	sentences beginning with expletives
p	sentences with passive verbs
P	parts of speech of the words

6.13 Further Exploration

We see that with the collection of editors, formatters, macro packages, and support filters, it is possible to produce any type of document. With available hardware, it is further possible to prepare it for typesetting and establish the environment for what is currently known as _desktop publishing_.

With the use of the program management utilities **make** and SCCS (see Chapter 9), it becomes possible to create and maintain large documents with versions and revisions. As new products are introduced, this aspect of UNIX is an increasingly important application area. Explore the text processing facilities of your own system.

- ⊙ Check whether you have typesetting equipment.
- Design and produce a standard memo.
- Check the spelling of the memo.
- Check the memo's style and diction.
- Create a table of names and telephone numbers.
- Check whether your installation uses the **MS** or **MM** macro package.

6.14 Manual References

checkmm	check MM macro usage
diction	language usage utility
ed,ex,vi	editors
eqn,neqn	equation preprocessor
explain	phrase usage utility
hyphen	hyphenation filter
man	manual macro package

mm	memorandum macros
ms	manuscript macros
nroff	line printer formatter
ptx	permutted index utility
spell	spelling checker
style	language usage utility
tbl	table preprocessor
troff	typesetter formatter

7

Advanced Shell Facilities

In Chapter 2, we covered the basic features of the UNIX shell. In this chapter, more advanced features of the shell at the command level are discussed. We also explain how to write programs or *shell scripts* in the shell language. This powerful feature is usually available in much larger computing systems, and it enables you to extend the system with new functions built from existing ones. The concepts discussed in this chapter include:

The Bourne Shell
The Shell Process
the Shell Environment
Shell Special Variables
User-Defined Variables
Variable Evaluation
Shell Programming
Alternative Shells

We will first look at the Bourne shell, which comes with all UNIX systems. The C-shell, originally in the Berkeley UNIX, is distributed with many UNIX variations (e.g., XENIX) and will be described in Chapter 8. You should, however, read this entire chapter, since all systems that provide the C-shell also distribute the standard shell, and the discussion of the C-shell will concentrate on differences and enhancements over the standard shell.

If you are sitting at the terminal with a C-shell prompt (%), enter the **sh** command to invoke the standard UNIX shell ($ prompt).

7.1 The Shell Process and Environment

UNIX is a multiprogramming operating system. This means that it is able to handle more than one active program in the system at one time. In Chapter 10 we will discuss how this is implemented from the system's perspective, but to understand how the shell operates, one must describe how multiprogramming under UNIX works from a functional point of view.

When you log in, a shell (indicated by a $ for the Bourne shell or a % for the C-shell) begins running. Whenever a new program is started, it becomes one of the active processes in the system. Since most of the UNIX commands are programs, each command, while executing, is a separate process in the system. After you have issued your command, the system contains at least two processes. Your shell is one process and your command is the other. This is illustrated in Figure 7.1a. Notice how the shell process waits for the completion of the command process. In Figure 7.1b, the shell doesn't wait, and as we have indicated in Chapter 2, the & on the command line creates the second process as a background one. In this case, the shell continues. From the user's point of view, the shell displays a prompt indicating that it is ready for the next command.

Each executing process has an environment associated with it consisting of a collection of data areas, or *variables*, passed on to it from the invoking process. In our examples above, the shell is the invoking process. The information directly inherited from the parent process includes the current

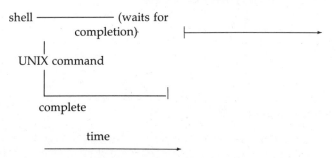

Figure 7.1a. Shell Initiates a Program and Waits

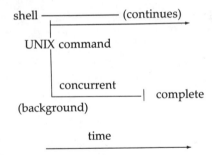

Figure 7.1b. Shell Initiates a Program and Continues (background)

directory, the open files (standard input, standard output, and standard error), and the value of some of the shell special variables discussed below. Processes cannot change the environment of its parent process, but they make use of the inherited or passed information.

In the following sections we will discuss different kinds of commands. In every case, the initiation of a command will cause the creation of new processes with new and inherited environment information. It's useful to keep this in mind as we describe the shell's advanced features.

7.1.1 Special Shell Variables

We have seen that when the shell interprets the command line, it expands wildcard character expressions into file names from the current directory. Other types of expansion also occur. If an identifier begins with a $, the shell assumes that the identifier is a variable. Variables contain character or string values that are expanded in command lines in a manner similar to wildcard character expansion for filenames. For example, the **cd** command with no arguments resets the current directory to the login or home directory. The home directory is the actual value of the shell special variable HOME (capital letters required) used by **cd**. You can display the value of your home directory with **echo:**

```
$ echo $HOME
/usr/smith
$
```

7.1.2 Setting Variables

To change or set any variable, you use an assignment statement similar to many programming languages. Consider the shell special variable containing the prompt symbol $. The variable PS1 holds the character string that is printed whenever the shell is waiting for input. To display its contents, you can use the **echo** command like we did for HOME:

```
$ echo $PS1
  $
$
```

Suppose we want to change the prompt to OK:

```
$ PS1="OK:"
$
```

From now on, the prompt would be OK instead of $:

```
OK:
```

When making assignments to variables, note that there are no blanks surrounding the equal sign. If there were, the shell would interpret PS1 as a command name and issue an error message indicating that the command PS1 is not found. Furthermore, the variable name, when being set, is not preceded by the $. The $ is used only when it is referenced (e.g., with **echo**). Table 7.1 lists the important shell environment variables.

7.1.3 User-Defined Variables

In the same manner in which the shell special variables are set and referenced, you may create and reference your own variables. For example,

---

TABLE 7.1
Shell Special Environment Variables

ENVIRONMENT VARIABLES	
$HOME	Home directory
$IFS	Blank interpretation characters
$MAIL	Mail directory
$PATH	Directory search path
$PS1	Shell primary prompt
$PS2	Shell secondary prompt

PROGRAMMING VARIABLES	
$#	Number of arguments
$?	Return code from last process
$$	Process id of the current process

suppose we want to create a variable with the name of our telephone directory:

```
$ idx=tel
```

The variable idx is created just by using it on the lefthand side of the equal sign. In the above example, it is set to the string value *tel*. Wherever the variable reference $idx is used, its value is substituted. Remember, the $ is required to cause the identifier to be evaluated as a variable. This is seen in the two examples shown in Figure 7.2. In the first example, **echo** displayed the string *idx* because the $ notation wasn't given. In the second example, *idx* was evaluated as a variable and its value was displayed.

There is a more general specification that will cause substitutions in a variety of contexts. For example, suppose you wanted to display Monday, Tuesday, etc., where the first part of the day name is in the variable *dayname* which will contain Mon, Tues, etc. Figure 7.3 illustrates the general manner in which variables are evaluated.

We see in the first example that the shell will try to evaluate the variable *daynameday*. Since this variable doesn't exist, its value is null and the empty string is printed. To tell the shell which characters compose the variable name, brackets are used. The expression ${identifier} evaluates the variable between the brackets.

7.2 Shell Scripts

Most operating systems have the capability to place several commands in a file and have all the commands executed by running the command file as if it were a program. In UNIX, a command file is called a *shell script*. By executing commands as if they were entered at the terminal, we are effectively extending the operating system and introducing new functions by combining existing ones.

For example, if you wanted to create a command that prints the date and the contents of the current directory, you create a file using an editor and include the commands which perform the desired functions.

```
1. $echo idx
   idx
   $

2. $ echo $idx
   tel
   $
```

Figure 7.2. Evaluation of Shell String Variables

1. `$dayname=Mon`
   `$echo $daynameday`

   `$`

2. `$dayname=Mon`
   `$echo ${dayname}day`
   `Monday`
   `$`

Figure 7.3. Context Evaluation of Shell String Variables

```
date
cat tel1
```

To invoke the shell script, simply enter the name of the script file. Since the default protection mode on file creation usually is not set to *execute*, you must change it before using the file. This is illustrated in Figure 7.4, which shows the protection modes before and after the **chmod** and then the result of the execution.

7.2.1 Arguments to Shell Scripts

It is sometimes desirable to change the commands being executed and tailor them to individual situations. For example, one often wants to use the same shell script on different data or files. Using our example above, *tellist* lists out only *tel1*. If we wanted to list *tel2*, it would be necessary to change the script to reference the new file.

Shell script arguments are a way of generalizing the script so that it will operate on files with different names. During the interpretation of the command line that invokes the script, arguments or parameters are established and referenced in the script, based on their position following the

```
$ls -1 tellist
-rw-r--r--    1 farkas     staff     14 Oct 3 19:40 tellist
$chmod +x tellist
$ls -1 tellist
-rwxr-xr-x    1 farkas     staff     14 Oct 3 19:40 tellist
$tellist
Wed Oct  3 19:41:11 EDT 1984
Smith Robert 212 555-1234
        .
        .
        .
```

Figure 7.4. Creation and Execution of Shell Script

command name. This is similar to the way fields were defined in **awk.** The argument's relative position is its argument number, and it can be referenced from the script by placing a dollar sign before the number. This is illustrated in Figure 7.5. If we write *tellist* with a variable instead of the explicit *tel1,* it can be used to list any file:

```
date
cat $1
```

In this example, $1 will reference the first argument on the command line. *tellist* is invoked by specifying which file to list and the argument to be substituted. Figure 7.6 shows the substitution.

As another example we can list the command name followed by the date and the file contents with the following script:

```
echo $0:
date
cat $1
```

If the script name is *tellist,* the output of the telephone list and date is preceded by the command name:

```
tellist:
    .
    .
```

Now that the script has been written to operate on a variable rather than a specific file, we can substitute any telephone index:

```
$tellist tel1
tellist:
    .
    .
    .

$tellist tel2
tellist:
    .
    .
    .
```

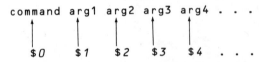

Figure 7.5. Positional Arguments

Command line:

```
$tellist tel1
```

Shell script substitutions:

```
date
cat tel1
         ↑
         |
      $1
```

Figure 7.6. Positional Parameter Substitution

7.2.2 The Profile Script

A *profile* is the collection of characteristics that determine the working environment during a UNIX session. This includes the prompt, home directory, terminal characteristics, and other functions established during login. In UNIX, you can create a script file, called *.profile*, in your login directory, that will be executed when you log in just before control is given to the terminal. Typical profiles change the default home and path directories, set any special terminal characteristics, and may change the default current directory. For example, the following functions are performed by the profile in Figure 7.7

- Set a new home directory.
- Reset the prompt to OK.
- Change the current directory to the new home directory.
- Print out the current time and date.
- Check for mail.

```
#*****************************************************************
#*
#* name: .profile
#* usage: profile file
#* desc: Run the program if the compilation is successful.
#*
#*****************************************************************
#*
HOME = /usr/farkas/cprog
PS1='ok '
cd
date
mail
```

Figure 7.7. Typical *.profile*

Referring to the example, the directory is changed by **cd** to the new home directory, the prompt symbol is set, the date is displayed, and the mail utility is invoked (see Chapter 12). Notice that the number sign # in column one treats the rest of the line as a comment. Try creating your own *.profile* file similar to the one above. You will find yourself adding to the file as you become more familiar with UNIX and want to establish your own session characteristics.

7.3 Shell Programming

This section covers shell programming with the Bourne shell. While many systems have the ability to create command sequences with parameter substitution, programming language features allow you view the operating system commands as language statements and to construct sophisticated commands that can select different functions based on arguments, repeat a function for many arguments, evaluate arguments and give diagnostic messages when necessary, etc. In short, it becomes possible to create user interfaces to meet many situations.

7.3.1 Shell Programming Commands

Throughout our discussion, we have indicated that UNIX commands are programs which are executed by the shell. In fact, there are a few commands that are not programs but are part of the shell itself. You will not find the shell programming commands in the */bin* directory like others we have seen. They are part of the shell and are used by the shell to interpret command lines. Table 7.2 lists the shell programming commands.

TABLE 7.2
Shell Programming Commands

	Shell Commands
break	Exit from a loop
case	Selection statement
continue	Exit loop iteration
exit	Exit from shell script
for	Iteration statement
if	Conditional statement
shift	Rename positional parameters
test	Evaluate conditional expressions
while	Conditional iteration statement

7.3.2 *Conditional Expressions and the* if *statement*

The shell commands **if** and **while** (see below) act upon the results of conditional expressions. Conditional expressions return values of true or false, and similar to a programming language, statements will be executed depending upon the result of the evaluation of the expression. In the shell there are two ways in which the value of a conditional expression may be set:

1. Implicit result of a command or shell script
2. Explicit result of the **test** shell command

Programs and shell scripts return values when they complete. When used in a conditional expression, the result is interpreted as false if the value is not zero. When the result is zero, it is interpreted as true. For example, to execute a program only if the C compilation is successful, you could write your own shell script, shown in Figure 7.8a, which tests for successful completion.

In the script, we see the simplest form of the **if** command:

if statement list
then
  statement list
fi

The conditional expression was the UNIX command, **cc,** operating on the first command argument. The statement list is any sequence of UNIX or shell commands. Success is determined by the return code of the last command in the statement list. In the example, the program *a. out,* (the executable output of the C compiler) is run.

We can make the script even more useful by producing a line-numbered

```
#**************************************************************
#*
#* name: myc
#* usage: myc file
#* desc: Run the program if the compilation is successful.
#*
#**************************************************************
#*
if cc $1
then
 a.out
fi
```

Figure 7.8a. Shell Conditionals: **if/fi**

```
#************************************************************
#*
#* name: myc
#* usage: myc file
#* desc: Run the program if compilation is successful.
#*       Otherwise, produce a listing on standard output.
#*
#************************************************************
#*
if cc $1
then
 a.out
else
 nl $1
fi
```

Figure 7.8b.   Shell Conditionals: **if/then/else/fi**

listing on standard output if the compilation is unsuccessful. Figure 7.8b shows the more general syntax of the **if** statement incorporating actions for both true and false situations:

> **if** conditional expression
> **then**
>   statement list
> **else**
>   statement list
> **fi**

Another approach to conditional expressions uses the **test** command, which directly evaluates its own special arguments and returns a true or false value. It is always used as part of a shell conditional statement (**if** or **while**). We will expand on our compilation script by incorporating a check of the arguments.

The script in Figure 7.9 illustrates two uses for the test command. In the first example, the value of the shell special variable $#, the number of arguments, is compared to the required number of arguments. If the number of arguments is not exactly one, an error message is displayed by the script. In the second **test** command, the existence of the argument as a file is tested. Using the test command is a rather awkward way of specifying conditional expressions. A cleaner syntax puts the text of the expression in square brackets. For example, to test the number of arguments:

```
if [$# -eq 1]
```

Note that the **exit** statement sets the return code for the script. In more complex situations, where scripts are nested, the return code can be

```
#*****************************************************************
#*
#* name: ccchk
#* usage: ccchk file
#* desc: Run the program if compilation is successful.
#*       Otherwise, produce a listing on standard output.
#*       Check for arguments.
#*   errors:
#*              ccchk01 - requires 1 argument
#*              ccchk02 - file does not exist
#*
#*****************************************************************
#*
if test $# -ne 1
then
 echo 'ccchk01 - requires 1 argument'
 exit 1
fi
if test ! -r $1
then
 echo 'ccchk02 - file does not exist'
 exit 1
fi
#*
#*               run the compile
#*
if cc $1
then
 a.out
else
 nl $1
fi
```

Figure 7.9. Shell Conditionals: **test**

checked with **if** or **while.** In the error condition of this script, it is set to 1. By default it is zero.

As shown in Table 7.3, the test command has a wide variety of options for constructing tests and generalizing shell scripts.

7.3.3 Looping: **for**

In the scripts we have already written, we operated on one file. But it is often necessary to perform the same operation on several files. This can be done in numerous ways. One way would be to repeat the commands in the script the number of times you want to perform the function. This is usually not a good choice, since it wastes space and assumes that you know how many times the function is to be performed. There are several methods for repeating the same sequence on multiple arguments.

TABLE 7.3
Test Command Arguments

Test Command Argument	Description
–r file	file is readable
–w file	file is writable
–x file	file is executable
–f file	file is ordinary
–d file	file is directory
–c file	file is character special
–b file	file is block special
–s file	file size greater than zero
s1 = s2	strings equal
s1 !– s2	strings not equal
s1	string not null
n1 –eq n2 ne, le, ge, lt, gt)	integers equal (also
–a	and operator
–o	or operator
!	not operator
(expr)	expressions

The **for** statement causes a repetition of the statements following it to occur for each argument in a list of arguments. The argument list can be specific values, wildcard expressions, or a shell special variable:

for variable in arg1 arg2 arg3 ...
do
 statement list
done

For example, if we wanted to compile and execute three programs (x.c, y.c, and z.c), we could write the script shown in Figure 7.10a. In the example, **i** is set to each value in the list following the in, and the statements between **do** and **done** are executed.

A more general usage is to make reference to all the arguments on the command line. The script in Figure 7.10b uses the **for** to compile and execute a variable number of C programs referencing the shell special variable **$***, which expands to all the arguments on the command line. The script is executed by entering the script name, *ccforall,* and a variable number of C program names as arguments:

```
ccforall x.c y.c z.c
```

```
#****************************************************************
#*
#* name: ccfor
#* usage: ccfor
#* desc: compile and run 3 C programs
#*
#****************************************************************
#*

for i in x.c. y.c z.c
do
 if cc $i
 then
 a.out
else
 nl $i
fi
done
```

Figure 7.10a. Shell Looping: **for/do/done**

7.3.4 Looping: **while**

A second type of loop, **while,** uses a conditional expression to determine whether to continue executing the loop. If the expression is true, the loop is executed again; if false, execution resumes at the statement following the loop. The general form of the conditional loop is:

> **while** conditional expression
> **do**
>   statement list
> **done**

```
#****************************************************************
#*
#* name: ccforall
#* usage: ccforall file1 file2 ...
#* desc: compile and run C programs  on the command line
#*
#****************************************************************
#*
for i in $*
do
 if cc $i
 then
 a.out
else
 nl $i
fi
done
```

Figure 7.10b. Script With General Argument Reference

We will use another special shell command, **shift,** which shifts the argument positions by one. Referring to Figure 7.11a, argument $2 becomes $1, $3 becomes $2, and so on. The highest argument set becomes null after each shift. The script in Figure 7.11b loops through the arguments compiling and executing C programs, just as in our previous example.

The text command argument is true if the string $1 is not null. Therefore, after three shifts, $1 will be null and the **while** test will fail. The execution of the script is illustrated in Figure 7.11c.

7.3.5 *The* case *Statement*

Many times, the selection process can be generalized to a collection of cases so that it is not necessary to complicate the logic with **if** statements but rather to use a **case** statement to select one of several situations. The UNIX shell uses string pattern matching, similar to the regular expressions in the editors and **grep,** to select cases. The general format of the **case** statement is:

> **case** variable in
> pattern)
> statement list; ;

Before shift:

After 1 shift:

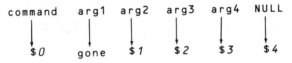

After 4 shifts:

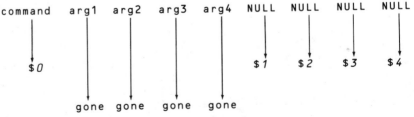

Figure 7.11a. Effect of **shift** Command

```
#*******************************************************************
#*
#* name: ccwhile
#* usage: ccwhile file1 file2 ...
#* desc: compile and run C programs  on the command line
#*
#*******************************************************************
#*
while test $1
do
 if cc $1
 then
  a.out
 else
  nl $1
 fi
 shift
done
```

Figure 7.11b. Shell Looping: **while/do/done**


```
   pattern)
      statement list; ;
   pattern)
      statement list; ;
   esac
```

For example, to create a script which recognizes C and Fortran programs with file extensions .c and .f, respectively, we could use the **case** statement illustrated in Figure 7.12. In this example, the shell script uses a **for** statement to loop through each argument on the command line. The **case** statement has patterns to determine which compiler to use. The first two cases check for any sequence of characters followed by the appropriate extension. In the last case, any string matches the * and is used as the default. If there are no matches, the next command after the case is executed.

Note that the cases are tested in the order in which they are encountered in the script. The default string must come last. Since all strings match it,


```
   ccwhile x.c y.c z.c:
```

1st time through loop $1 = x.c; $2 = y.c; $3 = z.c
2nd time through loop $1 = y.c; $2 = z.c; $3 = null
3rd time through loop $1 = z.c $2 = null; $3 = null

4th time through loop $1 = null; $2 = null; $3 = null
───────► at entrance to loop, test fails

Figure 7.11c. **shift** Effect on Arguments

```
#*******************************************************************
#*
#* name: cfcase
#* usage: cfcase file1 file2 ...
#* desc: compile and run C or Fortran 77 programs
#*
#*******************************************************************
#*
for i in $*
do
 case $i in

     *.c) cc $i;
          a.out;;

     *.f) f77 $i;
          a.out;;

     *) echo cfcase01 - invalid program type;
     exit 1 ;;
  esac
done
```

Figure 7.12. case Statement

after matching a pattern with a correct extension, control leaves the **case** statement. The other patterns are never tested.

7.3.6 *Arithmetic:* **expr**

usage: **expr** expression operation expression

While **expr** is not technically a shell programming statement, it is used when writing shell scripts. It takes string valued variables, converts them to integers for the operation, then converts the result back to strings. For example, to increment a shell variable $n by 1:

```
n=`expr $n + 1`
```

Interpreting the above, notice the use of command substitution (Chapter 2), in which the output of the **expr** command is placed in the variable n.

In addition to the basic arithmetic operators($+,-,/,*$), **expr** will also process the relational operators ($<,>,<=,>=,==,!=$).

7.3.7 Error Handling: Testing Variables

In a few of our previous scripts, we tested arguments for null or for specific values. A generalization of the variable evaluation notation provides a built-in mechanism for testing variables, setting default values, and issuing error messages. The general format for evaluation is:

{variable operator string}

The operators take effect only if the variable has not been set and determines whether the string is to be interpreted as a value or as an error message. The operators include:

-    string is a default value
=   string is a default value and assigned to the variable
?   string is an error message

For the ? operator, if the string is left out, the shell will print a default message. Figure 7.13 illustrates the use of the different operators with the **echo** command. In the first example, the value 10 is displayed since x has not been previously set. Notice the general variable reference syntax is used, {}. As shown in example 2, x is still not set. In the third example, the equal operator will cause 10 to be displayed and x will be set to 10. Lastly, in example 5, the unset variable z causes an error message to print when the ? operator is used. If no error message is supplied, a system default will be displayed. In actual practice generalized variable evaluation is used inside shell procedures when checking arguments.

```
1.  $ echo ${x-10}
    10

2.  $ echo $x

3.  $ echo ${x=10}
    10

4.  $ echo $x
    10

5.  $ echo ${z?"undefined variable"}
      z: undefined variable
    $
```

Figure 7.13. Generalized Message Handling

7.3.8 Error Handling: UNIX Signals

Other errors which can occur during the execution of any process are generated by the operating system itself. These errors include termination signals, memory faults, etc. UNIX defines 15 basic hardware and software signals, some of which you may want to respond to from within your shell script. They are assigned values from 01 through 15. While a more general discussion of signals appears in Chapter 8, Table 7.4 lists the signals of interest in the context of shell programming.

Signals sent to the shell process are responded to by terminating the process or by catching the signal and indicating some other action. The shell **trap** command is used to catch and specify alternate actions for interrupt signals:

   trap 'command list' signal-list

For example, the following **trap** catches the terminal interrupt and responds by printing a message before terminating. The **exit** command is used to exit with a return code.

```
trap 'echo Shell Terminated; exit 1' 2
```

trap is used in situations in which it is necessary to perform some housekeeping, such as the deletion of temporary files, before terminating the process. Otherwise the temporary files must be deleted manually. For example, suppose a script had created files by the name of *temp1*, *temp2*, and *temp3*, using the current PID shell variable $$. To respond to any signal by deleting them, the following **trap** command would be used:

```
trap 'rm temp?$$ ; exit 1' 1 2 3 14 15
```

Default actions are reset by specifying a null statement list:

```
trap '' 1 3 14
```

TABLE 7.4
Shell Script Signals

01	SIGHUP	hangup
02	SIGINT	terminal interrupt
03	SIGQUIT	quit
14	SIGALARM	alarm
15	SIGTERM	software termination

7.3.9 *Here Documents*

It is occasionally desirable to create a script in which the command is followed by the standard input lines that the command will use. Without some special specification mechanism, these lines will be interpreted as shell commands. This usually results in a syntax error and always yields undesired results. For example, to write a script which invokes **ed** and changes all occurrences of 'Unix' to 'UNIX' we might want to enter:

```
ed textfile
1,$s/Unix/UNIX/g
w
q
```

The difficulty is that while **ed** does not wait for standard input, the **s, w,** and **q** commands do wait to be executed by the shell upon exit of **ed.** To indicate we want to use the lines that follow as standard input, the following notation is used:

```
ed textfile <<!
1,$s/UNIX/UNIX/g
w
q
!
```

The standard input set of lines indicated in this way is called a *here* document. The sequence is initiated by double less-than symbols, < <, followed by some delimiter (e.g., !). The delimiter character may be any character as long as the input lines are followed by the same character. If the delimiter character is quoted with a backslash, the here document lines will not be expanded by the shell (variables); if it is not quoted variable evaluation will take place. Note that we could have accomplished the above **ed** example with the **sed** filter.

7.4 *Designing Shell Procedures*

When designing shell scripts, one should keep in mind that they can become as complicated as programs, and some considerations should be given to style, organization, and efficiency.

From a stylistic point of view, you should precede all scripts with a header that describes its function, arguments, usage, etc. Error messages can be numbered, which facilitates documenting them elsewhere. Commenting is accomplished with the # command, which performs no operation but treats the rest of the line as a comment. Last, indenting control structures leads to a structured and more readable appearance.

The script design should mirror the command line that invokes it. You should design the script first to interpret arguments in the UNIX format (**-letter** or **-letter arg**). After interpreting the options, arguments are evaluated and processed. Designing commands that mimic UNIX command organization will ease the integration of the command into everyday use in your installation.

You must remember that each time a command is invoked, a new process is initiated. Complex shell scripts may introduce a number of concurrent activities, and the overhead can degrade overall system performance. The ease with which new functions can be created should be exploited, since that is one of the major advantages of a UNIX development environment, but remember the drawbacks.

Figure 7.14 has a prototype shell script that interprets options to manipulate the telephone index by adding, deleting, finding, and sorting entries.

```
#******************************************************************
#*
#* name: tel
#* usage: tel [-asfs] [file]
#* desc: Print out the telephone directory according to
#*       different options.
#* options:
#*              -s sorted by last name
#*              -f find name
#*              -d delete name
#*              -a add name
#* errors:
#*          tel: telephone file does not exist
#*          tel: usage: tel [-adfs] [entry]
#*
#******************************************************************
if test ! -r telephone
then
    echo  'tel: telephone file does not exist
    exit 1
fi
case $1 in
    -a) shift
        if test  $1
        then
            if test $# -ne 4
                then
                    echo  'tel: usage: tel [-adfs] [entry]'
```

```
                else
                    last=$1
                    first =$2
                    area=$3
                    number=$4
                fi
                cat >>telephone <<!
$last $first $area $number
!
        else
            echo 'telmsg - enter: last first area number'
            read last first area number
            cat >>telephone <<!
$last $first $area $number
!
        fi
        ;;
    -d)
        echo 'deleting...'
        shift
        if test $1
        then
            grep -v "$1" telephone >tmp$$
            cp tmp$$ telephone
            rm tmp$$
        else
            echo "'tel: usage: tel [-adfs] [entry]'
        fi
        ;;
    -f)
        echo 'finding...'
        shift
        if test $1
        then
            grep  "$1" telephone
        else
            echo "'tel: usage: tel [-adfs] [entry]'
        fi
        ;;
    -s)
        echo 'sorting...'
        sort telephone
        ;;
    *)
        if test $1
        then
            grep  "$1" telephone
        else
            cat telephone
        fi
        ;;
esac
```

Figure 7.14. Prototype Script

Its design is structured and operates like many of the UNIX commands that come with the system. The script takes one of four options: **a** (add), **d** (delete), **f** (find), and **s** (sort). The file must exist and entries have four fields (last,first,area,number). **tel** with no options or arguments lists the entire telephone directory. With no options, it defaults to find and search for a pattern match (**grep**) of the first argument. There is ample room for enhancements for you to try to incorporate. For example, try to include a create option (**-c**).

7.4.1 The Shell as a Command

usage: **sh** [options] command [arguments]

We have discussed how the shell is an interactive program communicating with you through standard input and output. In fact, you can invoke the shell directly by using the **sh** command and supplying either a command or a shell script as an argument. For example, see what happens when you enter the **ls** or **pwd** command this way:

```
$ sh ls

$ sh pwd
```

Nothing different should have happened! The shell program was invoked in *batch* rather than *interactive* mode and executed the argument. The shell as a command becomes interesting when used without an argument, which invokes a new interactive shell. This can be illustrated in the following way:

- Change the prompt in the current shell by modifying the PS1 variable.
- Enter the **sh** command.
- Enter the **ps** (process status) command.
- Log off by entering *ctrl-D*.

Figure 7.15 shows the sequence of commands and standard output. Initially, the prompt was changed to OK. Invoking a new interactive shell suspended the original shell. The prompt of the new shell is $. The **ps** command shows the two shells and **ps** command running, and then when logging off, it ends the second shell and returns to the original one with the changed prompt.

The shell as a command takes several options. These options are most useful if the argument to the shell is a script, since they can be used for debugging and monitoring the progress of the script execution. If you have

```
$PS1=OK
OKsh
$ps
82      cons        sh
112     cons        sh
75      cons        ps
$⌐d
OK
```

Figure 7.15. Invoking the Shell as a Command

a syntax error, the shell will report it, but not the line number at which it occurred. The **-v** option lists each line as it is read by the shell. If there are any syntax errors, the last line listed on the terminal as a result of the **-v** option is the line in which the error occurred.

Another option is **-x**, which lists expanded lines as they are executed, providing a trace of the shell. This is useful for debugging conditional and case statements. To execute a shell script with any of the options, you enter:

sh [options] scriptname

7.4.2 The Shell Environment

We have made reference to the environment in which you are entering UNIX commands, but here we formalize this concept. All the variables, special and programer-defined, are part of the current shell environment. When a new shell is started, which occurs when shell scripts and commands are executed, a new environment is created. The new process cannot change the original environment, but variables can be passed to it. The export and read-only commands pass arguments to the new environment. With read-only, the new environment can access the variables but cannot modify them. in both cases, however, when the old environment is restored, the original contents of the variables are present.

Once a variable has been exported, it is made available to all subsequent processes:

```
export v1 v2 v3
```

All commands and shell scripts that are children to the invoking shell will be able to access these variables. For example, the login process makes the home directory available to all processes by exporting it in the following way:

```
HOME = /usr/. . . .
export HOME
```

7.5 *Alternative Shells*

As we have indicated, the Bourne shell is distributed with all UNIX systems. However, since the shell is a UNIX process that from the kernel's point of view executes like other processes, it is possible to set up alternative shells. The most common of these alternative shells is the Berkeley C-shell, which we cover in the next chapter. The C-shell is not distributed with AT&T System V, but there is an alternative to it called the Korn shell, which provides the same power and flexibility that some users need.

Other shells may be available on your system. For example, the restricted shell, **rsh,** provides limited access to UNIX commands and the overall file system. The XENIX visual shell, **vsh,** is a menu-driven interface in which you select options by pointing using the cursor or entering the option as a command.

The AT&T System V and Sun Microsystems 4.2bsd offer windowed shell environments, which provide both menus and graphically displayed concurrency. Through the use of a mouse or the cursor, experienced users can perform most, if not all, of their functions without using the more cumbersome line-oriented shell interfaces.

7.6 *Further Exploration*

In this chapter we have covered most of the standard UNIX shell advanced functions. As you gain more experience with UNIX, you will find yourself expanding its capabilities with shell scripts and with advanced command processing. Chapter 8 describes the C-shell, which, if available on your system, provides a greater ability to augment and tailor the operating environment to your specific needs.

1. Go through some of the examples of the previous chapters and try to turn them into shell scripts.
2. Do you have the restricted shell on your system? Invoke it. What are its restrictions?
3. Do you have a menu-oriented shell?
4. Do you have one of the windowed shells?
   - How do you enter and leave the windowed modes?
   - What are the top-level functions?
   - How do you expand and contract window sizes?
   - How do you switch from window to window?
   - Try creating our telephone directory from earlier chapters in this environment.

7.7 Manual References

cd	change directory
csh	C-shell
exec	execute system call
fork	fork system call
login	login a user
nice	set priority
pipe	interprocess communication
ps	display process status
sh	Bourne shell
signal	system error processing
sleep	process wait
test	conditional test
wait	interprocess communication

8

The C-Shell

As we have already indicated, the shell is a program which is started up when you log on. On some systems, an enhanced shell, originally designed for the Berkeley system, is available and can be started up when you log in. The C-shell contains all of the functions of the Bourne shell but provides additional features which make it more flexible and, in many cases, easier to use. Since the C-shell is really an expanded shell, our discussion in the following sections will concentrate on its different and expanded aspects. If you are using the C-shell, you will notice that the prompt is the percent symbol, %, instead of the $. Concepts discussed in this chapter that are specifically oriented to the C-shell include:

Aliases
History Mechanism
Foreground/Background Processing
I/O Redirection
C-Shell Programming

8.1 Abbreviating Command Line Entries: *alias*

usage: **alias** [name] [alias string]

Often you will have a standard command sequence that you will use again and again throughout a UNIX session. With the standard shell, it is necessary to enter the line in its entirety each time or else place it in a shell script. Shell script processing introduces the overhead of starting a new process, as well as the time it takes to create and test it. Furthermore, you begin to clutter up your directories with small, short-lived shell scripts which become difficult to manage (e.g., forgetting to delete when no longer needed). The C-shell **alias** command provides a quick way to extend the operating system by introducing new commands without creating shell scripts. You simply give a name to a string of words. When the shell reads the alias, it interprets the associated string of words as if it were a command line entry. For example, we can create the alias which gives a count of the files in the current directory. Note that there is no parameter substitution, only the interpretation of the original argument list to **alias**:

```
% alias 'fc ls | wc -1'
% fc
25
%
```

In the example above, we created **fc** with **ls** piped into **wc** with the number-of-lines option **-l.** The **fc alias** is then invoked, printing the number of lines in the file.

alias entered with a name but without an **alias** string prints the string associated with the **alias** name. **alias** without any arguments displays the aliases currently in effect.

You may find that as you build up a set of often-used aliases, you may want to incorporate them into your profile script (see Section 8.8).

8.2 Reusing Previous Command Line Entries: *history*

The C-shell has a *history* mechanism that keeps track of previous command line entries. Every command entry is called an *event* and is given a sequence number beginning with 1. The **history** command displays the previous events, which can be referenced by event number in subsequent command line entries.

8.2.1 *Establishing the* **history** *Event List*

The history event list is created by setting the C-shell variable *history* to a non-null numeric value which indicates the maximum number of events to remember. For example, to set the history list for five events, you enter:

```
% set history=5
```

All subsequent command lines are entered into the history list and given an event number. You can recall complete or partial command lines and incorporate them into the current command line (see section 8.3.3 for a discussion of **set**).

8.2.2 *Recalling Previous Events:* !

Figure 8.1a shows the output of the **history** command. On the left are event numbers from the point of login, but the list only contains the number of commands specified in the *history* variable. In our example, the *history* variable has been set to 5.

The exclamation point is used to refer to previous events and may appear anywhere in the current command line. References are indicated by absolute event number, relative event number, anchored search (starting from the beginning of the command line), or nonanchored search. A special notation, !!, selects the previous command. Each of these are illustrated in Figure 8.1b:

1. In this example, a reference to the **cc** command indicates that a simple repetition of the command was entered.
2. This is a relative reference to the same command using the '-3 to the third previous command.
3. In this case, the history list is searched for the most recent command, beginning with the search argument after the exclamation point.
4. This example sets up a search for the most recent command, which has the search argument embedded between two question marks.

```
% history
    39   set history=10
    40   ls -l *.c
    41   cc myfile.c
    42   grep "Smith" tel1 | sort
    43   history
%
```

Figure 8.1a. Output of **history** Command

1. Absolute Reference:

```
%  !41
   cc myfile.c
%
```

2. Relative Reference:

```
%  !-3
   cc myfile.c
%
```

3. Anchored Reference:

```
%  !cc
   cc myfile.c
%
```

4. Nonanchored Reference:

```
%  !?my?
   cc myfile.c
%
```

5. Previous Command:

```
%  !!
   history
```

Figure 8.1b. **history** Command Line References

5. In this last example, the most recent command is referenced. It is essentially a redo, or repeat command.

8.2.3 *Selecting Components of a Command Line*

The **history** command allows you to select components of a line. Each command line is divided into words, which are referenced by their relative positions starting from zero. This is similar to the reference of command arguments in shell scripts. Words are defined as strings separated by blanks, tabs, special delimiters, etc. Therefore, in a pipe, the pipe symbol, |, will count as one word.

The syntax for word selection uses a colon and word number following the history event reference. For example, to select the *tel1* file and sort it, we could select the 4th word (sort) and 2nd word (tel1) from event 42 in Figure 8.1a (remember we are counting words relative to zero.)

```
%  !42:4 !42:2
   sort tel1
        .
        .
%
```

The word modifier can have different forms indicating word ranges and actions to take on the selected words. These are summarized in Table 8.1. For example, to search *tel2* using the event list in Fig. 8.1a, you could refer to event 42 and change tel1 to tel2:

```
% !42:s/tel1/tel2/
```

While this may seem awkward at first, after a little experimentation you find the ability to refer to previous commands both efficient and handy, especially when your command entries are long or complex.

8.3 C-Shell Variables

Like the standard UNIX shell, the C-shell has the capability to establish, set, and reference variables. Like the Bourne shell, a distinction is made between shell environment and user-defined variables. Additionally, the C-shell has numeric variables that can be combined in expressions not as cumbersome as the Bourne shell **expr** command and closely resembling C language expressions.

8.3.1 Environment Variables: **setenv**

usage: **setenv** variable value

Shell environment variables such as PATH and HOME have the same meaning as we have previously described, but they are set with the shell **setenv** command. For example, to change the default home directory, you enter:

```
setenv HOME /usr/farkas/cproglib
```

TABLE 8.1
history Word modifiers

Modifier:	Description:
0,1,. . .	word number
^	word 1 (e.g. first arg)
$	last word
i-j	word i through j
h	removes trailing pathname
r	removes trailing extension
s/s1/s2/	changes string s1 to s2

For newly invoked processes, the home directory default has been changed.

8.3.2 *Shell Predefined Variables*

In addition to the environment variables, there are a collection of predefined string variables that have special meaning to the currently executing shell. Some of the variables are set by the shell with values taken from the environment (*path, home, mail,* etc.), while others govern the way the shell will operate. The most interesting of these include:

noclobber	We have indicated that improper use of I/O redirection in the standard shell can cause you to wipe out a file inadvertently: **sort** <t1 >t1. This will not sort in place, but rather will clear *t1* first, erasing its contents. If *noclobber* is set, I/O redirection to existing files will result in an error message.
history	Set the size of the history list.
ignoreeof	Prevent accidental logoffs from ctrl-D.

8.3.3 *Setting String Variables:* **set**

usage: **set** name[=value]

User-defined variables and shell predefined variables are set with the shell **set** command. Note that setting variables operates differently than in the Bourne shell set command. For example, to set a variable v1 to abc.

```
set v1=abc
```

Variables such as noclobber and ignoreeof are set without a value:

```
set noclobber
```

To remove a variable you use the **unset** command. Thus, a distinction is made between variables that have null values and those that haven't been set or established:

```
unset noclobber
```

8.3.4 String Arrays

A very interesting feature of the **set** command for string variables is the ability to create the equivalent of a string array by entering the values enclosed in braces. The following example sets the array, courses, to several subject names:

```
set courses=(math english biology politics)
```

Set without any arguments lists the value of all the **set** variables. With a variable name argument, it displays the contents of that variable.

8.3.5 Referencing String Variables

All variables—whether they are environment, predefined, or user type—are referenced in the same manner as in the Bourne shell, using the $ notation: ${variable}. If the variable is delimited by a blank, tab, newline, etc., the braces are optional. For example, if the variable day is set to mon:

```
% echo day
day
% echo $day
mon
% echo ${day}
mon
% echo $dayday

% echo ${day}day
monday
%
```

In the case of indexed string variables, a reference to the variable name will reference all of its elements:

```
% echo $courses
math english biology politics
%
```

To reference individual elements, you give the positional index enclosed in square brackets:

```
% echo $courses[3]
biology
% set courses[2]=psychology
% echo $course[2]
psychology
%
```

8.3.6 Numeric Variables and Expressions: @

The C-shell allows you to create expressions that are closer to C language than the cumbersome **expr** expressions of the Bourne shell. The @ command, in contrast to the **set** command, is used to assign the results of arithmetic expressions. While all C language operators are available, Table 8.2 lists the most common ones. You can create arithmetic expressions of arbitrary complexity, but you must be sure to separate components of the expression by blanks:

```
@ a = ($x + $y)
@ b = (($x + $y) / ($z * $q))
```

Arithmetic expressions can be combined with relational and logical operators to form relational expressions that will be used within shell sequence control commands **if** and **while,** described below:

```
$x > $y
(($x + $y) > $z) && ($a < $b)
```

8.3.7 File Attribute Expressions

While the test command is available, you can use many of the file attribute tests within relational expressions. Table 8.3 lists the basic file attribute tests you may want to make in shell scripts. For example, a relational expression that tests for x greater than y and the existence of the *f1* is written as: "($x > $y && -e f1))".

8.4 Input/Output Redirection

I/O redirection operates in the same fashion as in the Bourne shell except that, as we have indicated above, you can set the *noclobber* predefined variable to prevent inadvertent destruction of files. The exclamation point can be used to override noclobber:

```
cat t1 >! t2
```

Another convenient notation indicates the redirection of diagnostic messages (standard error). Although it was necessary in the Bourne shell to make a specific reference to its file descriptor number, 2, this common function is simplified in the C-shell by using an ampersand. When appended

TABLE 8.2
Common Expression Operators

Arithmetic Operators		Relational Operators		Logical Operators	
+	add	<	less than	&&	logical and
–	subtract	>	greater than	||	logical or
*	multiply	==	equal to	!	logical not
/	divide	<=	less than or equal to		
		>=	greater than or equal to		
		!=	not equal		

TABLE 8.3
File Attribute Tests

–r	read access
–w	write access
–x	execute access
–e	exists
–z	zero size
–f	ordinary file
–d	directory

to the output redirection symbol, >, the standard error is redirected with the standard output:

```
cmd >& t2
```

You can also mix the specifications and use them with the append format. The following overrides noclobber and appends standard error and output to the file *t2:*

```
cmd >>&! t2
```

8.5 C-Shell Programming

Writing shell scripts using the C-shell is similar to writing them using the standard shell. There is a counterpart for each control structure with slightly different formats and usage. In the following sections, we describe shell programming using the C-shell, keeping in mind our discussion in previous chapters. When we give shell script examples, we will take them from the standard shell versions of the previous chapter but rewrite them for the C-shell.

8.5.1 Arguments to Shell Scripts

Arguments processing, like the standard shell, involves referencing the positional parameters $1, $2, etc. An alternative format uses the descriptor, argv: $argv1, $argv2, etc. In the C language, argv is the pointer array to command line arguments (see Chapter 10). This generalizes to the notation for all command line variables, $argv*. In our shell script examples we will use this notation rather than the standard shell $*.

8.5.2 *Conditional Statements:* **if**

The C-shell **if** has a more elaborate structure, since it permits expressions and statements which include arithmetic variables, string variables, and commands. In its simplest format, an expression is evaluated and a simple command executed if the expression is true. The following command displays the contents of file **f1** if it exists:

```
if (-e f1) cat f1
```

Complex decisions can be made with the **if else** and **else if** commands, which have the general format shown in Figure 8.2a. The statements following the first expression that evaluated to true are executed. There can be more than one **else if.** Figure 8.2b illustrates the **if** script from the last chapter, rewritten for the C-shell.

8.5.3 *Loops:* **foreach/while**

The **foreach** and **while** operate in the same manner as the **for** and **while** in the Bourne shell. Their formats are slightly different and are illustrated in Figures 8.3a-c and 8.4a-b. The list on the **foreach** line may contain wild-card characters and variables. The **while** uses the expanded expression specification discussed above. Notice the use of standard UNIX **test and shift.** Also, to test the success or failure of command execution, the command is enclosed in brackets, which makes it an expression. The spaces separating the brackets from the command are part of the expression syntax.

8.5.4 *Premature Loop Termination:* **continue** *and* **break**

There may be times when you want to terminate the current iteration of a loop (as the result of some test within the loop) and go on to the next

```
if (expression)
    .
    .
else if (expression)
    .
    .
else
    .
    .
endif
```

Figure 8.2a.   General Format for Conditional Statement

```
#*********************************************************************
#*
#* name: ccchk
#* usage: ccchk file
#* desc: Run the program if compilation is successful.
#*        Otherwise, produce a listing on standard output.
#*        Check for arguments.
#* errors:
#*                ccchk01 - requires 1 argument
#*                ccchk02 - file does not exist
#*
#*********************************************************************
#*
if ($#argv != 1) then
  echo 'ccchk01 - requires 1 argument'
  exit 1
endif
if (! -r $1) then
  echo 'ccchk02 - file does not exist'
  exit 1
endif
#*
#*                run the compile
#*
if ({ cc $1 }) then
  a.out
else
  nl $1
endif
```

Figure 8.2b. C-Shell Conditional

iteration. In this case, you can use the **continue** statement. If you want to end the loop unconditionally, without testing the termination condition (as in the **while**) or before all the items in the **foreach** list have been exhausted, you use the **break** command. **Continue** and **break** are illustrated in Figure 8.5.

8.5.5 *Case Statement:* **switch**

As in the other control sequence statements, the C-shell case statement has greater flexibility and resembles the C language **switch** statement. The

```
foreach variablename (name 1 name2 name3 ...)
  .
  .
  .
end
```

Figure 8.3a. General Format For **foreach** Loop

```
#********************************************************************
#*
#* name: ccfor
#* usage: ccfor
#* desc: compile and run 3 C programs
#*
#********************************************************************
#*

for each i (x.c y.c z.c)
 if ({ cc $i }) then
 a.out
else
   nl $i
endif
end
```

Figure 8.3b. C-Shell **foreach** with List

```
#********************************************************************
#*
#* name: ccforall
#* usage: ccforall file1 file2 ...
#* desc: compile and run C programs on the command line
#*
#********************************************************************
#*
foreach i ($argv[*])
 if ({ cc $i }) then
 a.out
else
 n1 $i
 endif
end
```

Figure 8.3c. Script With General Argument Reference

general usage of **switch** is shown in Figure 8.6a and a script utilizing the **switch** is illustrated in Figure 8.6b.

The default case is identified with the **default** label. If you don't want subsequent cases to be tested after executing a case, the **breaksw** statement transfers control to the statement following the **switch**.

```
while (expression)
    .
    .
    .
    end
```

Figure 8.4a. General Format For **while** Loop

```
#*****************************************************************
#*
#* name: ccwhile
#* usage: ccwhile file1 file2 ...
#* desc: compile and run C programs on the command line
#*
#*****************************************************************
#*
while ({ test $1 })
 if ({ cc$1 }) then
  a.out
 else
  nl $1
 endif
 shift
end
```

Figure 8.4b. C-Shell **while**

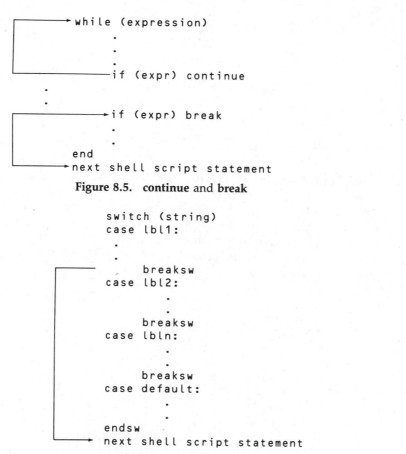

Figure 8.5. **continue** and **break**

```
switch (string)
case lbl1:
  .
  .
        breaksw
case lbl2:
        .

        .
        breaksw
case lbln:
        .

        .
        breaksw
case default:
        .

        .
endsw
  next shell script statement
```

Figure 8.6a. General Format of the Switch Statement

```
#******************************************************************
#*
#* name: cfcase
#* usage: cfcase file1 file2 ...
#* desc: compile and run C or Fortran 77 programs
#*
#******************************************************************
#*
foreach i ($argv[*])
 switch ($1)

     case *.c: cc $1
         a.out
         breaksw

     case *.f:   f77 $1
         a.out
         breaksw

     default:
         echo cfcase01 - invalid program type
         exit 1
  endsw
end
```

Figure 8.6b.   C-shell **switch** Statement

8.6 *Labels and* **gotos**

For completeness, we should mention the availability of labels and **goto** statements. Labels are strings which appear at the beginning of lines that end with colons. The **goto** statement takes as its argument a defined label and transfers control to the statement following the label. This is illustrated in Figure 8.7. We should state that shell scripts become quite complex. You should try to observe structured programming guidelines and avoid the misuse of **gotos** and labels.

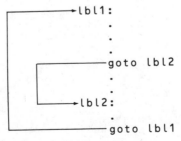

Figure 8.7.   Labels and Gotos

8.7 The C-Shell as a Command: *csh*

usage: **csh** [options] command [arguments]

The C-shell is invoked with the **csh** command with options similar to the standard UNIX shell. Table 8.4 lists the options relevant to this level of discussion.

8.8 C-Shell Profile: *.login/.cshrc*

Like the Bourne shell, you can create a shell script that will be executed when you log in. For the C-shell, the profile script is called *.login*. As we have seen, since the shell is a command, it can be invoked with a command, **csh**. When the C-shell is invoked in this way, as with the Bourne shell, .login is not reexecuted. However, if present, the script *.cshrc* is executed. It is also executed along with *.login* when the first shell starts up. Both files reside in your home directory.

8.9 Background and Foreground Processing: *fg, bg, jobs*

The initiation of background jobs operates in the same way as in the standard UNIX shell. However, Berkeley versions of the C-shell will permit you to move jobs between the foreground and the background. This is convenient when you have initiated a process and you want to move it to the background so you can perform other work.

Each time a background process is initiated, it is assigned a job number, and both the job number and process id will be displayed.

```
%  mycmd1  &
[1]  1234
%  mycmd2  &
[2]  2345
%
```

TABLE 8.4
csh *Options*

–f	do not execute *.cshrc* file
–n	read commands but do not execute
–v	expand history substitutions
–x	echo commands before execution

Job numbers are also assigned to foreground running jobs. You can stop a job with a *ctrl-Z:*

```
% mycmd3
ctrl-Z
stopped
%
```

The **jobs** command will list out all jobs in the background and all foreground jobs that have been stopped. Note that when the current job has been stopped with a *ctrl-Z,* you can execute any other UNIX command (and stop it, if you want).

```
% jobs
[1]        mycmd1
[2]   -    mycmd2
[3]   +    mycmd3
%
```

You now can access jobs with the **fg** and **bg** commands, which move jobs to the foreground and background, respectively. For example, to move job 3 to the background using the percent sign and job number:

```
% bg %3
%
```

Similarly, you can bring job 2 to the foreground and stop it with a *ctrl-Z* or let it run:

```
% fg %2
```

Since all the jobs are included in the set of processes executing from your terminal, the **ps** command (and associated options) will give all the execution details you need.

8.10 *Terminating the Shell*

There are three ways to terminate the shell. The first uses *ctrl-D.* As we have seen with the Bourne shell, it is very easy to make a mistake and inadvertently log off. Therefore, you may want to set the **ignoreeof** shell variable, which tells the shell to ignore the *ctrl-D.*

The second way to log off is by using the **logout** command. Furthermore, **logout** will search the home directory for a shell script *.logout* and, if present, execute it. This is handy when you want to perform some housekeeping each time you log off (e.g., printout of a file, backup, etc.). If you are using the C-shell, it is a good idea to set **ignoreeof** in your *.login* and *.cshrc* profile scripts, and use **logout** to terminate your session.

If you are in a non-logout shell (you have issued the **csh** command) and **ignoreeof** has been set, **logout** doesn't bring you up one level but rather terminates the session. In this case you may use **exit,** which terminates the current shell and restores the previous or invoking one.

8.11 Further Exploration

If you are fortunate enough to be using a system that has the C-shell, you should make every effort to use it. Its expanded facilities, including general expressions, login and logout profiles, C language sequence control facilities, and **alias** and **history** mechanisms, make it a powerful command interface to your personal workstation.

You can try some of the features of the C-shell on your own:

1. What variables are set when you log in?
2. Does the **fg/bg** mechanism work on your system?
3. Rewrite the *tel* script in Figure 7.14 so that it will run in the C-shell.

8.12 Manual References

cd	change directory
csh	C-shell
exec	execute system call
fork	fork system call
login	login a user
nice	set priority
pipe	interprocess communication
ps	display process status
sh	Bourne shell
signal	system error processing
sleep	process wait
test	conditional test
wait	interprocess communication

9

Program Development Tools

This chapter explores the tools available on the UNIX system for program and system development. Our point of departure assumes that you know how to write programs in the C language and it may be helpful to have a C reference handy as you read the chapter. While we use C because of its importance to UNIX, most of the tools we discuss are applicable to any language environment. The topics of particular interest to the system developer which we cover in this chapter are:

C Language
cb and **lint**
Compiling C Programs
The C Preprocessor
The Loader
Object Libraries
Performance Tools
Interactive Debugging
System Maintenance: **make,** SCCS

9.1 The C Language

C is a structured medium- to low-level language that resembles PL/1 or PASCAL. (C purists may vehemently disagree!) Because of its rich set of operations and machine-oriented data types, it permits the programmer to write programs which would normally be written in assembly language. This flexibility is incorporated directly into UNIX, since UNIX is written primarily in C. There are many advantages to this approach:

- Programs are easier to write and maintain.
- It is easier to transfer UNIX from one machine to another.
- The interfaces to the UNIX kernel may be standardized and expressed in terms of the C language.
- It is easier to transfer application programs written in C to other systems.

There are several tasks which must be accomplished during software development. UNIX provides a comprehensive set of tools to help the programmer during different phases of the system development life cycle. Table 9.1 shows the different life cycle phases and the UNIX utilities associated with each phase. The code, test, and maintenance phases are particularly applicable to UNIX development environments.

The examples in this chapter were created using the C compiler distributed with IBM's PC/IX.

9.1.1 Creating a C Program

We have already discussed the way in which text files can be created and manipulated in C. Using any of the editors available on your system (**ed, ex, vi**), you create the source file, giving a meaningful name ending in .c While UNIX has no restrictions on how files should be named, the C compiler file arguments must have a .c extension if they are C source programs.

Two useful utilities, **cb** and **lint,** are provided with UNIX to facilitate the creation of C programs.

TABLE 9.1
System Development Life Cycle Phases and Utilities

Analysis and Design:	document processing, SCCS, make
Code:	ed,ex,vi,sed,cb,lint,m4
Test:	cc,ld,ar,profile,time,size,m4
Maintainance:	make, SCCS

9.1.2 C Language Beautifier: cb

usage: **cb** Cprogram

The **cb** command is a "C language beautifier" which reads the source code and, based on the underlying block structure of the program, formats the program with proper indenting. Consider, for example, the prototype program in Figure 9.1a, which is properly structured from a language point of view but difficult to read, since brackets and statements are placed without regard to the block structure of the program. Figure 9.1b shows the reformatted program after it has been processed by **cb.**

The **cb** command doesn't change the code; instead, it modifies the use of spaces, tabs, and new lines to make the code more readable and thus easier to maintain.

9.1.3 C Language Program Checker: lint

usage: **lint** [options] Cprograms

Another important utility is **lint,** a C language program checker which provides compile-time information about C programs. While the compiled version of the C program may execute correctly, **lint** reports on code sequences with potential problems, such as portability, unreachable sequences, and outdated usage. The areas that **lint** checks for are listed in Table 9.2.

Portability checks include those involving statements based on the underlying characteristics of the machine or operating system. One example is using *-1*, a common value for end of file, in the code rather than a predefined symbol:

nonportable:

```
    .
    .
    int c;
    .
    .
    while (c=getchar() ! < 0)
    .
```

portable:

```
    .
    .
    int c;
    .
    .
    while (c=getchar() != EOF)
    .
```

```
main( )
{
declaration;
declaration;
stmt01;
stmt02;
{stmt03;stmt04;{stmt05;stmt06;}stmt07;stmt08;
{stmt09;stmt10;stmt11;{stmt12;}stmt13;
stmt14;stmt15;}
stmt16;stmt17;}
stmt18;}
}
```

Figure 9.1a. Ugly C Program Prototype

```
main( )
{
  declaration;
  declaration;
  stmt01;
  stmt02;
  {
   stmt03;
   stmt04;
   {
    stmt05;
    stmt06;                    }
   stmt07;
   stmt08;
   {
    stmt09;
    stmt10;
    stmt11;
    {
     stmt12;
     stmt13;
     stmt14;
     stmt15;
    }
    stmt16;
    stmt17;                    }
   stmt18; }
}
```

Figure 9.1b. C Program Prototype After **cb**.

EOF will be defined in the standard I/O file for your system as the end of the file symbol.

Figures 9.2 a-c illustrate some other code sequences that are picked up by **lint** and not by the C compiler. For example, unreferenced variables are picked up by **lint,** as well as variables which are used before they are set. The variable *grades* and *x* (declared in lines 5 and 6) are never referenced

TABLE 9.2
lint diagnostic categories

Portability
Unused variables and functions
Unreachable code sequences
Variable set/used information
Stronger type checking
Unconventional code sequences

```
1   main( )
2           {
3           int y,z;
4           long s,t;
5           char grades[25];                        /* unreferenced     */
6           extern x;
7
8           goto bypass;                            /* forced bypass    */
9
10          printf("Unreachable statement.\n");     /* unreachable      */
11
12          bypass:
13
14                  z =- y;                         /* ambiguous usage  */
15                  z = s;                          /* long into int    */
16
17                  goto midloop;                   /* branch into loop */
18
19                  while (z ( y)
20                      {
21                      printf("start of loop\n");
22
23                  midloop:                        /* middle of loop   */
24
25                          printf("middle of loop\n");
26
27                      }
28
29
30
31          }
32
33  int intfcn(a)
34          int a;
35          {
36          }
```

Figure 9.2a. C Source Program to Demonstrate **lint**

"lntest.c", line 10: warning: statement not reached
"lntest.c", line 14: warning: oldfashioned assignment operator "lntest.c",
line 19: warning: loop not entered at top

Figure 9.2b. Output of the C Compiler (PC/IX)

```
lntest.c
===============
(14)    warning: oldfashioned assignment operator
(14)    warning: y may be used before set
(14)    warning: z may be used before set
(15)    warning: s may be used before set
(19)    warning: loop not entered at top
(4)     warning: t unused in function main
(5)     warning: grades unused in function main
warning: argument unused in function:
     (34)   a in intfcn
warning: conversion from long may lose accuracy
     (15)
warning: statement not reached
     (10)


===============
name defined but never used
     intfcn       lntest.c(35)
name declared but never used or defined
     x       lntest.c?(6)
function returns value which is always ignored
     printf
```

Figure 9.2c. Output of **lint**

or used. In line 14, y is assigned to z. Since it has never been set, it is flagged by **lint**. Furthermore, the mismatched type assignment of long integer to short is noted (line 15).

Unreachable code (line 10), branching into the middle of a loop (line 19), and old fashioned operator usage (line 14) are flagged by both the C compiler and **lint**. Since not all C compilers will produce the same diagnostic warnings, it is a good idea always to run **lint** to check your programs.

Many times you will not want **lint** to flag situations that you feel are correct as is. In such cases, **lint** checking and diagnostics can be turned off in two ways. The easiest method is to globally turn off a specific type of checking, using one of the **lint** command line options. For example, to turn off long-integer to short-integer conversion checking, you use the **-a** option. A second method is to turn off **lint** checking selectively, using statements in the C source that appear as comments to the C compiler but are directives to **lint**. When read by **lint,** the indicated checking is turned off. The range of the directive is the function in which it appears. Table 9.3 lists the directives and their meanings.

9.1.4 Compiling a C Program

usage: **cc** [options] [files]

C programs are compiled using the **cc** command. The source file must have a name which ends in *.c*. For example, to compile a program called *cprog.c,*

TABLE 9.3
lint *Directives and Their Meanings*

/* NOTREACHED */	suppress unreachable code messages
/* NOSTRICT */	suppress strict type checking
/* ARGSUSED */	suppress unused argument checking
/* VARARGSn */	check the first n arguments to a function which takes a variable number of arguments
/* LINTLIBRARY */	suppress unused function messages

you enter **cc** *cprog.c*. Without any options, and assuming the source code contains a main procedure, the C compiler will compile your program and create two files:

cprog.o	the object code
a.out	an executable load module

If there were syntax errors, you would get error messages and the *a.out* file wouldn't be created. To run the program, enter the name *a.out* as if it were a command. Consider the program in Figure 9.3 which simply prints

```
/*****************************************************************
*
*
*       Name: main( )
*
*       Function:
*
*               Main program to print hard coded name and address
*
*       Arguments:      none
*
*       Subroutines:    none
*
*****************************************************************/


#include <stdio.h>
main( )
{
 printf("John Rogers\n");
 printf("123 E. 4th St\n");
 printf("New York, N. Y.   01012\n");
}
```

Figure 9.3. C Program to Print out a Name and Address

out your name and address on three separate lines. The following sequence would compile and run the program:

```
$cc naprog.c
$a.out
```

9.1.5 Modular Programs

The organization of the C language permits and encourages program modularization. As a result, you may have more than one module to put together before execution. Figures 9.4a and 9.4b show a modification of the name and address program. In this case, the name and address is read in from the standard input rather than being hard-coded in the program itself. A subroutine created in a separate file reads in the name and address. To compile these programs and execute them, you enter:

```
cc namain.c naread.c
```

```
/**************************************************************
*
*
*        Name: main( )
*
*        Function:
*
*                Main program to print out one name and address
*
*        Arguments:       none
*
*        Subroutines:     naread(name, addr1, addr2)
*
**************************************************************/
#include <stdio.h>
#define MAX 25
main()
 {
 char name[MAX],addr1[MAX],addr2[MAX];

 naread(name,addr1,addr2);

 printf("%s\n",name);
 printf("%s\n",addr1);
 printf("%s\n",addr2);
 }
```

Figure 9.4a. Main Name and Address C Program: main()

```
/***********************************************************
*
*
*        Name: naread( )
*
*        Function:
*
*                 Read standard input for name and address information
*
*        Arguments:        n            name character array
*                          a1           address line 1 char array
*                          a2           address line 2 char array
*
*        Subroutines:      none
*
***********************************************************/
#define MAX 25

naread(n,a1,a2)
char n[MAX],a1[MAX],a2[MAX];

{
  printf("enter name:\n");
  gets(n);
  printf("enter addr1:\n");
  gets(a1);
  printf("enter addr2:\n");
  gets(a2);
}
```

Figure 9.4b. Name and Address Subroutine: naread()

The **cc** command will, by default, compile programs link them, and create the executable load module, *a.out*. This is illustrated in Figure 9.4c.

The **cc** command reads and creates files with a variety of extensions. If the file to be compiled contains C source code, it must have a *.c* extension; if it is an assembly language program, it must have a *.s* extension; and

```
$ cc namain.c naread.c
namain:
naread:
$ a.out
enter name:
John Rogers
enter addr1:
123 East 4th Street
enter addr2:
New York, N.Y. 10012
John Rogers
123 East 4th Street
New York, N. Y. 10012
$
```

Figure 9.4c. Execution Name and Address Program

lastly, if it is already an object module to be passed on with the compiled programs to the loader, it will have a *.o* extension. For example, suppose *namain.c* has already been compiled. To re-create the name and address program, you give the object file name on the **cc** command line:

```
cc namain.o naread.c
```

This passes both object modules, the existing one and the one created to the loader. Table 9.4 summarizes the file extensions and their relationships to the **cc** command.

9.1.6 Getting a Listing of the Compiler

As we have already seen, UNIX commands seem quite reluctant to give any information beyond bare essentials. Usually one can combine different utilities to provide listings and reports of any desired complexity. This terseness is prominent with **cc** and the C compiler. You will notice that there is no option to produce a listing, cross-reference, object module load map, etc. To produce listings which resemble other languages, you have to combine several utilities and shell features. For example, one way to get a line number listing uses the **nl** command with options to number all lines (including blank ones):

```
nl -ba naread.c > naread.l
```

In this example, we are creating our own standard extension, *.l,* for source listings. When there are syntax messages, the output of the compiler gives line numbers followed by the message. We can produce a listing with line numbers and error messages by combining the **nl** filter with redirected I/O:

```
nl -ba namain.c > namain.l
cc namain.c 2>> namain.l
```

Here we redirect I/O by appending standard error (file descriptor 2) to *namain.l.* This is a generalization of the I/O redirection with explicit file

TABLE 9.4
cc *Command File Extensions*

.a	object library
.c	C source program
.o	object module
.s	assembly language program
.i	output of preprocessor

descriptor specification. Without a file descriptor value, file number 1 (standard output) defaults. With a cross-reference listing of a program produced by the **xref** command, we can get a listing with line numbers, compiler syntax errors, **lint** output, and a cross-reference listing for the name and address program:

```
nl namain.c > namain.l
cc namain.c 2>> namain.l
lint namain.c >> namain.l
xref namain.c >> namain.l
```

In this example, the load phase of **cc** (see 9.1.9 below) will flag the subroutine, naread, as an unresolved reference. The listing file, *namain.l*, will contain a line-numbered listing followed by any **cc** command diagnostics and the output of **xref** (see Figure 9.5). If your version of UNIX does not support the **nl** filter, the **-n** option to the **pr** command or even a one-line **awk** program can be used to generate the line-numbered listing.

9.1.7 *The C Compiler Options*

The **cc** command actually does more than just compile a program. It invokes a preprocessor, compiles the source, assembles it, and invokes the loader. Options to **cc** control the operation of these phases. Some of the options are passed to the preprocessor, some to the compiler, and still others to the loader. Table 9.5 summarizes the **cc** command options. The sections that follow describe the operation of the preprocessor and loader.

9.1.8 *The C Preprocessor:* **cpp**

usage: **cpp** [options] [Cprograms]

The C language preprocessor interprets statements in your source program and expands it to include other files, define macro sequences and generate source code, and conditionally compile different sections of code. Table 9.6 summarizes the C preprocessor statements and their functions. In Figure 9.6a, the original source program is shown with the #include and #define statements. Figure 9.6b shows the output of the preprocessor with these statements expanded.

9.1.9 *Standard Code Libraries: Include Files*

Include files are used for standard code and data definitions. Many of the UNIX system file layout declarations are provided with your system, and

```
 1 /****************************************************************
 2 *
 3 *
 4 *          Name:  main()
 5 *
 6 *          Function:
 7 *
 8 *                   Main program to print out one name and address
 9 *
10 *          Arguments:      none
11 *
12 *          Subroutines:    naread(name, addr1, addr2)
13 *
14 ****************************************************************/
15
16 #include <stdio.h>
17 #define MAX 25
18 main( )
19   {
20   char name[MAX],addr1[MAX],addr2[MAX];
21
22   naread(name,addr1,addr2);
23
24          printf("%s\n",name);
25          printf("%s\n",addr1);
26          printf("%s\n",addr2);
27   }

1d: Undefined -
 _end
 _naread
```

```
MAX          namain.c         17  20  20  20

addr1           namain.c        20  22  25
addr2           namain.c        20  22  26

h      namain.c         16

main()          namain.c          +18

name         namain.c         20  22  24
naread()        namain.c           22

printf()        namain.c          24  25  26

stdio        namain.c         16
```

Figure 9.5. **xref** for Name and Address: main()

TABLE 9.5
cc Command Options

COMPILER RELATED OPTIONS:	
–p	profile the object code
–O	invoke the optimizer
–S	create assembly language source in files with a .s extension
PREPROCESSOR-RELATED OPTIONS	
–E	run the preprocessor only. output to standard
–P	run the preprocessor only. output to file with .i extension
–C	do not strip comments
–I*dir*	select directory to search for include files
LOADER OPTIONS	
–lx	select object library libx.a
–L*dir*	select object library directory

in the development of applications, you will want to create standard code sequences of your own.

The method of finding include files is determined by how the file name is specified in the source program and options on the **cc** command line. In a C program, include files are specified in the #include statement by enclosing the filename either in double quotes or in greater-than/less-than symbols. If the include file name begins with a slash, indicating a directory name, the fully qualified name is used. However, if the name is enclosed in double quotes, then the current directory is searched first for a file with a matching name. If it is not found, then the standard include directory is searched (usually */usr/include*). If the include file name is enclosed in < >, then only the standard directory is searched.

On the command line, the **-I** option sets directory paths to be searched after the current directory for those include file names enclosed in quotes. For example, to search a local include directory, the command line would be specified:

```
cc -I/usr/local/include newprog.c
```

TABLE 9.6
Preprocessor Statements

#include	include source from include file
#define	define constants and text substitution
#if,#else,#endif	conditional compilation
#ifdef,#ifndef	test for symbol definition
#undef	remove symbol definition

In *newprog.c,* all lines containing include file references enclosed in quotes would first search the local directory, */usr/local/include,* for the include files.

9.1.10 *The Loader:* ld

usage: **ld** [options] files

After compiling the program, if there are no syntax errors, the loader is invoked by the **cc** command, but **ld** may also be invoked as a command. The loader takes the output of a compiler, object files with an *.o* extension, and performs two basic actions:

- Resolves external references between modules.
- Resolves external function references by searching default and specified libraries.

```
/ ***********************************************************
*
*
*        Name: main()
*
*        Function:
*
*                Main program to print out one name and address
*
*        Arguments:        none
*
*        Subroutines:      naread(name, addr1, addr2)
*
************************************************************ /
#include <stdio.h>
#define MAX 25
main()
 {
 char name[MAX],addr1[MAX],addr2[MAX];

 naread(name,addr1,addr2);

 printf("%s\n",name);
 printf("%s\n",addr1);
 printf("%s\n",addr2);
 }
```

Figure 9.6a. Main Label Function before Preprocessor

```
extern struct _iobuf {

char *_ptr;
int _cnt;

char *_base;
char _flag;
char _file;
} _iob[20];


struct _iobuf *fopen();
struct _iobuf *fdopen();
struct _iobuf *freopen();
long ftell();
char *fgets();
char *gets();

main()
 {
 char name[25],addr1[25],addr2[25];

 naread(name,addr1,addr2);

 printf("%s\n",name);
 printf("%s\n",addr1);
 printf("%s\n",addr2);
 }
```

Figure 9.6b. Label Program with **include** File: *stdio.h*

Many of the options specified on the **cc** command line are passed directly to **ld** to perform the following functions:

-o*name*   Rename *a.out*

-l*x*   Select standard library where x is defined as: *libx.a*

-L*dir*   Search directory for library files specified in the -l option

To compile a program, *newprog.c,* and use the directory, */usr/new,* and a subroutine library called *libn.a,* the **cc** command would be specified as follows:

```
cc newprog.c -ln -L/usr/new -onewcmd
```

Instead of naming the executable load module *a.out,* it will be called *newcmd,* and it can be executed like any other command.

```
$newcmd arg1 arg2 ...
```

9.2 Object Module Libraries: ar

usage: **ar** key [position] archive files

In our discussion above, we referred to two types of libraries: source libraries containing code to be included in the compiled program, and object libraries, which are searched when the executable module is created. The archive command, **ar,** is used to create and manage object libraries.

The basic function of **ar** is to collect files of any type into a single file with a *.a* extension. If the files in the archive are object files (*.o* extension), then the file is an object module library. All distributed subroutine libraries are archive-type libraries.

9.2.1 Creating the Library

Suppose the current directory contains object files we wish to incorporate into a new library called *mylib.a.* The following **ar** command will perform this function:

```
ar cv mylib.a *.o
```

In this example, the **c** option or *key* (no preceding dash) tells **ar** to add the named files to *mylib.a.* The **c** option actually defaults and may be omitted. The **v** key provides a verbose description as the operation takes place. Here we used the wildcard expression **.o* to select all the object files, but we could have listed individual files or used any other type of wildcard expression.

Figures 9.7a-c illustrate the use of **ar** to create a library. The key, *t*, displays the archive file table of contents.

```
ls -l *.o
-rw-r--r--  1 farkas  staff      466 Sep 13 20:21 p1.o
-rw-r--r--  1 farkas  staff      634 Sep 13 20:21 p2.o
-rw-r--r--  1 farkas  staff     1080 Sep 13 20:21 p3.o
-rw-r--r--  1 farkas  staff     1526 Sep 13 20:22 p4.o
-rw-r--r--  1 farkas  staff     1080 Sep 13 20:22 p5.o
```

Figure 9.7a. Object Files for the Archive

```
ar qv mylib.a *.o
ar: creating mylib.a
q - p1.o
q - p2.o
q - p3.o
q - p4.o
q - p5.o
```

Figure 9.7b. Creation of the Archive *mylib.a*

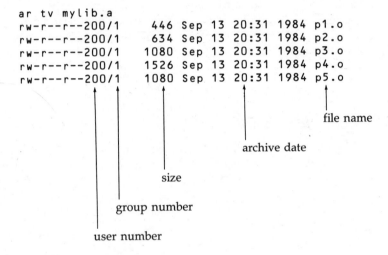

```
ar tv mylib.a
rw-r--r--200/1     446 Sep 13 20:31 1984 p1.o
rw-r--r--200/1     634 Sep 13 20:31 1984 p2.o
rw-r--r--200/1    1080 Sep 13 20:31 1984 p3.o
rw-r--r--200/1    1526 Sep 13 20:31 1984 p4.o
rw-r--r--200/1    1080 Sep 13 20:31 1984 p5.o
```

file name

archive date

size

group number

user number

protection mode

Figure 9.7c. Table of contents of *mylib.a*

9.2.2 *Updating the Library*

In addition to creating a library, we will want to modify it by adding, re-placing and deleting members. The **r** key replaces library members. If the name doesn't exist in the archive, it is added. For example,

```
ar r mylib.a p4.o
```

replaces *p4.o* in the archive with *p4.o* from the current directory.

The **d** option deletes the named file from the archive. To directly retrieve an archived file, the **x** key extracts the named file and places the archive version in the current directory. This is different than the loader operation, which extracts an archived file to incorporate an executable object module (e.g., *a.out*). In this situation, **ld** doesn't make a copy of the file in the current directory. This is illustrated in Figure 9.7d. Other archive options are summarized in Table 9.7.

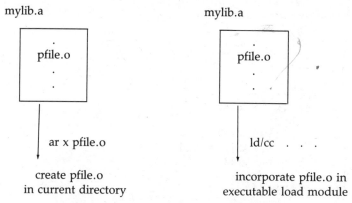

Figure 9.7d. Extraction for an Archive File

9.3 Performance Tools: *time, size, prof*

Once the program has been written and compiled, there are a number of utilities you can use to measure the performance of the finished system. The **time** command gives the execution time of program displaying its elapsed time, cpu time, and time spent in system calls. It can be applied to most programs, including UNIX commands.

Consider the program in Figure 9.8a, which consists of two functions. The first, **main,** loops MAX times, initializing a series of n by n arrays with random numbers; n starts out as 1 (1 by 1 array) and is incremented each time through the outermost loop up to MAX (set to 5 for our example). After each array initialization, the function **printarray** is called to print it. If the program is compiled without any options, *a.out* will contain the executable load module. To display its execution time you enter:

```
time a.out
```

TABLE 9.7
ar *keys*

d	delete
r	replace
q	append
t	print table of contents
p	print the names files
x	extract the named files
v	verbose messages

```
1  #include <stdio.h>
2  #define MAX 5
3  static int i,j;
4  static int rarray[MAX][MAX];
5  main()
6  {
7   int k;
8   for (k=1;k<=MAX;k++)
9   {
10   for (i=0;i<=k-1;i++)
11    for (j=0;j<=k-1;j++)
12     rarray[i][j] = rand();
13
14   printarray(k);
15                    printf("\n");
16  }
17 }
18
19 printarray(l)
20 int l;
21 {
22            printf("%-3dx%-3d Array:\n\n",1,1);
23  for (i=0;i<=l-1;i++)
24  {
25   for (j=0;j<=l-1;j++)
26    printf("%-6d ",rarray[i][j]);
27
28                    printf("\n");
29  }
30 }
```

Figure 9.8a. Array Initialization Program

The program will execute and, after printing out the array initializations, the time command will display the elapsed, user code, and system code times in seconds. Figure 9.8b shows the command execution and timing information.

The size of the program can also be displayed with the **size** command, which gives the sizes of the text, initialized data, and uninitialized data segments respectively:

```
size a.out
a.out: 3404 + 318 + 1032 = 4754
```

The third performance monitoring tool, **prof,** provides a profile of the execution behavior of the program, including subroutines and system routines used, time spent in each routine, number of calls, etc. This can be

```
1   ×1    Array:

16838

2   ×2    Array:

5758    10113
17515   31051

        .
        .
        .

        .
5   ×5    Array:

30524   28505   28394   22102   24851
19067   12754   11653   6561    27096
13628   15188   32085   4143    6967
31406   24165   13403   25562   24834
31353   920     10444   24803   7962


real        3.3
user        0.6
sys         2.3
```

Figure 9.8b. Execution and **time**

used to isolate bottlenecks in a program. In order to use the execution profile facility, you must compile the program with the **-p** option on the **cc**
command. This causes the compiler to generate code which will collect
information in a file, called mon.out, during program execution. Once the
program has finished, you use **prof** to create a report of the data collected
in mon.out. Figure 9.9 illustrates a report on the array initialization program:

```
$cc -p namain.c naread.c
$a.out
$prof
```

For each function the **prof** report gives a cumulative total and percentage of time spent. For the user subroutines, **prof** displays the number of
times it was called, plus the time in milliseconds spent in the function. The
prof report is given in decreasing percentage time order, and by using the
-l option, it can be displayed in order by symbol.

```
     name  %time   cumsecs   #call   ms/call
      csv   81.5     3.94
 __print    7.6      4.30
 _isatty    4.5      4.52
 -strlen    2.0      4.62
 __flsbuf   1.4      4.68
    lrem    0.8      4.72
   aldiv    0.6      4.75
  _fltpr    0.4      4.77
 _fclose    0.3      4.79
   _main    0.3      4.81       1      16.68
   _rand    0.3      4.82
    lmul    0.3      4.84
 __cleanu   0.0      4.84
   _brk     0.0      4.84
             .
             .
             .
             .
  mcount    0.0      4.84
   start    0.0      4.84
```

Figure 9.9. Profile of Array Initialization Program

9.4 *Debugging Tools:* **adb**

usage: **adb** [objectfile] [corefile]

There are a number of debugging tools available on your UNIX system that will help you find and remedy program bugs. Perhaps the most important of these tools is the debugger, **adb.**

9.4.1 *Symbolic Debugging*

On UNIX systems using **adb,** symbolic debugging can be performed in three ways:

1. Interactive debugging
2. Examination of core image dumps
3. Examination of important system files

We will concentrate on interactive debugging, which utilizes most **adb** subcommands.

The output of the compiler contains a symbol table containing local variables, global variables, and externally defined symbols. Thus, all the data areas and function entry points are available symbolically. The **adb** subcommands specify an address and an implied or explicit activity, **adb** addresses reference program data areas, memory locations, and external symbols. The **adb** actions include displaying and modifying address contents, setting breakpoints, and changing the sequence of instruction execution.

We next look at these activities from a functional point of view, using the array initialization program in Figure 9.8a as an example. The examples in the following sections were run on an IBM PC/XT, using PC/IX.

9.4.2 Invoking adb

The **adb** command can be invoked by specifying an object module, a core image dump, or both. If no arguments are given, the default output of the C compiler, *a.out*, is taken as the load module to be debugged. If present, the core image from a dump is also made available:

adb	debug a.out, core image
adb myprog	debug myprog
adb myprog core	debug myprog and its core image
adb – core	debug core image only

9.4.3 Core Image Dumps

In response to some UNIX system interrupt signals (see Chapter 10) or the abort function call, the kernel will create a core image dump of the executing program. The dump is placed in the current directory in a file called *core*. **adb** can be used symbolically to reference the value of the registers when the dump was taken, the text portion of the program, and the data portion. It is usually not necessary to understand the actual format of a core dump; however, the interested reader may look in the standard user manual under *core* for format information.

9.4.4 adb Subcommands

adb has a variety of subcommands that are used to inspect object files and core image dumps and to monitor the execution of a program. The general format of a command includes a reference to a location, a repetition factor, a command type, a command, a display format, and, for some commands, additional arguments:

address, count commandtype command format [arguments]

The important command types are:

?	display from the object file
/	display from the core image file
:	monitor execution of an executing program
$	miscellaneous **adb** request

In the sections below, we will introduce commands from each of the above types.

9.4.5 Inspecting Data Areas

The general format of **adb** subcommands used to display information is:

```
address?format
```

or

```
address/format
```

where

?	looks at the object file
/	looks at the core image

Similar to **ed** and **ex, adb** maintains a current address pointer, the dot, which represents the location in the object or core image file that the last **adb** command referenced. The value of . is initially zero. Other possible addresses include:

function names
global variables
local variables
hex, octal and decimal integers representing absolute and relative offsets

The output or display formats you use will depend on the type of data being displayed:

b	hex byte
o	octal word
x	hex word
d	decimal word
i	machine instruction

Looking at the sample program, we can check the static global variables i and j. They have initial values of zero. We are looking at the objectfile (?):

```
i?d                          (display i as an integer)
_etext+0x20:    0
j?d                          (display j as an integer)
_etext+0x22:    0
i?x                          (display i in hex)
_etext+0x20:    0x0
j?x                          (display j in hex)
_etext+0x22:    0x0
```

The first component above is the address, a hex offset of the global symbol address __ etext where the variables are located. The second component is the value at that location. Keep in mind that, because there are different types of storage allocations (e.g., static, automatic, register), machines, C compilers, and versions of **adb,** variable displays may vary. In general, static global variables are referenced by giving their symbol as the address in a command. To access an automatic variable, you enter a composite name, function.variable, that indicates which function the variable is in.

We can also look at the machine code, and step through instruction by instruction by entering carriage returns:

```
main?i
~main:          mov      ax, #0x146a
(cr)
~main+0x3:      call     mcount
(cr)
~main+0x6:      J        ~main+0x7a
(cr)
~main+0x8:      mov      *-6(bp), #0x1
```

Naturally you must understand the machine and assembly langauge of the underlying machine for this to make sense. In this example we are looking at PC/IX on the IBM/PC. The first column is the address relative to the function and external symbol main. The next two columns are the machine language instructions and their arguments. Each carriage return causes **adb** to display the next address.

9.4.6 Controlling Execution

To control program execution, you use commands of the format:

address, count:cmd

Because C labels will not be available to **adb,** addresses are usually program function entry points. The program execution subcommands are:

:r	begin execution
:b	set a breakpoint
:s	single step (one instruction is executed)
:c	resume execution after a breakpoint
:d	turn off breakpoint at address
:k	terminate process
:x	turn off all breakpoints

9.4.7 Starting and Terminating Execution

Execution starts with the **:r** command, which indicates any arguments to the program:

:r	start execution with no arguments
:r arg1 arg2	start execution with arguments
:r arg1 <i1 > o2	start execution with arguments and redirected I/O

To terminate execution without leaving **adb**, you use the **:k** command. To leave **adb**, the **$q** or a *ctrl-D* will allow you to exit and return to the shell.

9.4.8 Setting Breakpoints

An address in a program at which **adb** will interrupt the program just prior to executing an instruction is called a *breakpoint*. You use the **:b** command to set breakpoints. For example, to set a breakpoint at the beginning of printarray you enter:

```
printarray:b
```

When the program reaches the entry point to the function, it will stop. At this point you can enter commands to look at the arguments passed. The special command **$b** prints out all breakpoints in effect:

```
$b
breakpoints
count    bkpt                command
1        ~printar+0x2
```

Actually, it is possible to establish actions beyond just stopping at breakpoints. The first field in the breakpoint display shows how many times the instruction is executed before **adb** interrupts execution. This is useful in a looping situation, for instance, where you don't want to stop at each iteration but at every 10th or 100th. In our example, by leaving the count out, it defaults to 1.

The second field is the address of the breakpoint. The address consists of the symbolic name of the location, ~printar. The name is truncated since function names are unique to the first seven characters. The offset to the first instruction in printarray() is given in hex, 0x2.

The last field is a command to execute when **adb** interrupts execution. We have indicated no command, but if we wanted to stop at every tenth iteration of printarray and display the value of k, we would have to set the breakpoint with both a count and a command:

```
printarry,10:bprintarray.l?d
```

In summary, the general form for a breakpoint is:

```
address,count:brequest1;request2;...
```

9.4.9 Resuming Execution

Execution is resumed using the **:c** command. Without an address, the program resumes at the current instruction; with an address, however, it will resume anywhere you want. For example, to reexecute or bypass a code sequence, you specify a different resume point.

> **:c**   starts execution
> **newfcn:c**   start execution at newfcn

9.4.10 Modifying Data Areas

Another useful feature of **adb** is the ability to change memory locations. The write subcommand, **w,** is used to indicate a new value to be written at the address specified. Assume we have stopped at the breakpoint at the entry to printarray. After inspecting **l,** the dimension of the array to be printed, we decide to change it. Figure 9.10 illustrates the command sequence and program execution.

If, during the debugging processes, you want to patch the program or change an instruction, you can do that with the **w** subcommand. Since the changes are at the machine level, however, you must know the underlying machine language of your computer. Furthermore, changes are made to the run-time environment, not to the source code. After exiting **adb,** it is necessary to re-edit the program, fixing the source errors and then recompiling the program.

```
$adb a.out
printarray:b
:r
a.out: running
breakpoint          ~printar+0x2:     push      *1(bp)
:c
a   x1    Array:

16838
:c
a.out: running

3   x3    Array:

5627    23010   7419
16212   4086    2749
12767   9084    12060
breakpoint          ~printar+0x2:     push      *1(bp)
printarray.1?d
0xff46:              4
printarray.1?w 1
0xff46:              04        =         01
printarray.1?d
0xff46:              1
a.out: running
1   x1    Array:

32225
:k
$q
$
```

Figure 9.10. Execution of **adb** with Modifying Variables

9.4.11 Advanced Usage

Although this ends our discussion of **adb,** it only touches the surface regarding **adb**'s capability. Two other types of debugging activities performed by **adb** are:

1. *Debugging with a Core Image.* This is similar to our previous discussion, except that program execution is not resumed. Data areas, subroutine call trace data, etc., may be inspected while you uncover the cause of the dump.

2. *Examining UNIX Files.* By utilizing the file format description for UNIX objects found in the formats section of your UNIX manual, you can construct output formats to display formatted information. For example, to

print out the contents of a directory, you would specify a directory file as input to **adb:**

```
adb directory_name
```

Address modifiers may be used to select entries, and advanced character formatting may be used to display them:

```
0, 4?u8t14cn

1234      .
 231      ..
 223      File1
 143      File2
```

The formatting and printing characters shown above are used to print directory entries containing inode numbers (first word) and directory names (next 14 characters). The command interpretation is:

0	address of start of file
4	repeat commands 4 times
?	use main file
u	print inode value as unsigned integer
8t	space 8 positions
14c	print 14 characters
n	go to a new line

9.5 Maintenance Tools: *make, SCCS*

UNIX provides two utilities for the maintenance of object and source programs: **make** is used to construct an executable module from its component parts, and SCCS is a collection of commands used to maintain version and release control for source modules.

9.5.1 Program Maintenance: **make**

The **make** command reads a file, called a *makefile*, that contains information describing the structure of a system. Entries in the makefile describe a component, its subcomponents, and the commands necessary to create the component. In the example below, c1 is composed of subcomponents s1, s2, and s3. In order to create c1, you must run **cmd1** on s1 and s2, and then **cmd2** on s3:

```
component: sub1 sub2 sub3
command1 sub1 sub2
command2 sub3
```

Figure 9.11 is a label program which reads a filename from standard input, then produces mailing labels from records in the file. The program consists of three separate modules. Figure 9.12 gives the makefile that describes the creation structure or model of the program. In Figure 9.13, we see that the makefile actually describes the dependencies of the individual components.

By testing the last modification dates of each element, **make** determines which components of the dependency tree must be reconstructed. For example, if labeler.c has a modification date later than labeler.o, **make** will recompile labeler.c to recreate labeler.o, then recreate label. This solves the problem of systems with old versions of modules running after the source has been modified.

9.5.2 make *Macros*

Makefiles can become very complex as the structure of your system increases. In order to simplify the specification of the makefile, a macro facility is provided that allows for simple text substitution. The general format for a macro is:

```
macroname = text
```

Using our label program example, we can create a macro for all the object modules:

```
obj = labelmn.o labelpr.o labeler.o
```

Macro references are made by preceding the macro name, enclosed in parenthesis, by $. Figure 9.14 illustrates a makefile utilizing the **obj** macro.

9.5.3 *The* make *Command*

usage: **make** [options] [makefiles]

The **make** command with no options or makefile specifications will check and construct a system based on the description in the default file, called makefile. To see the command execution sequence without actually running the commands, you can use the **-n** option. This is useful for complex makefiles where you may want to see what is going to happen before it does. Whenever it encounters a UNIX command error (e.g. compiler syntax errors), **make** terminates its operation. The **-i** option tells **make** to con-

```
/*****************************************************************
*
*
*          Name: main()
*
*          Function:
*
*                    The main program communicates with standard input and
*                    output to get the file name of a name and address file.
*                    Errors are printed by the labeler function and labels by
*                    labelpr function. Main passes the names of the input
*                    output files to labelpr.
*
*          Arguments:      Filename of name and address file
*
*          Subroutines:    labelpr(InputFile, OutputFile)
*                          labeler(ErrorCode)
*
*          Error Codes:
*                          1          missing file argument
*                          2          can't open input file
*
*****************************************************************/
#include <stdio.h>
main(argc,argv)
int argc;
char *argv[];

{
 FILE *faddr,*faddrout;

 if (argc (= 1)
   {
   labeler(1);
   return(-1);
   }
 printf("ARG1: %s\n",argv[1]);
 faddr = fopen(argv[1],"r");
 if (faddr == NULL)
   {
   labeler(2);
   return(-2);
   }
 faddrout = fopen(strcat(argv[1],".l"),"w");
 printf("Printing labels for file:%-15s\n",argv[1]);

 labelpr(faddr,faddrout);
 return(0);
}
```

Figure 9.11a.   Main Label Program: labelmn.c

```
/***************************************************************
*
*
*        Name: labelpr()
*
*        Function:
*
*                labelpr reads records from the input file and writes label
*                records on the output file. Each record has names and
*                addresses separated by commas. The string function,
*                strtok(), is used to extract each label component.
*
*        Arguments:        file descriptors to the input and output files:
*                          flbl     input file
*                          flflo    output file
*
*        Subroutines:    none
*
***************************************************************/

#include <stdio.h>
#define RECLEN 80
labelpr (flbl,flblo)
FILE *flbl,*flblo;
{
 char nabuffer [RECLEN],*aline,*strtok();
 while (fgets(nabuffer,RECLEN, flbl) != NULL;
 {
  alpine = strtok(nabuffer,":");
  fputs(aline,flblo);
  fputc('>n'.flblo);
  while ( (aline = strtok(0,":")) != NULL)
   {
   fputs(aline,flblo):
   fputc('>n',flblo);
   }
 }
}
```

Figure 9.11b. Label Program Print Routine: labelpr.c

tinue despite errors encountered in the makefile creation process. Other **make** options are listed in Table 9.8.

9.6 *Source Code Control System*

The Source Code Control System (SCCS) is a collection of commands used to manage source modules and keep track of versions and releases. We will look at the basic commands for creating an SCCS file, retrieving a module, and storing a new version.

```
/ *****************************************************************
*
*
*         Name: labeler()
*
*         Function:
*
*                   labeler() prints program error messages which are in an
*                   initialized string array of messages. The function
*                   receives the error number as an argument which is used
*                   as an index into the message array.
*
*         Arguments:       Error Code
*
*         Subroutines:     none
*
*         Error Codes:
*
*                   1          missing file argument
*                   2          can't open input file
*
******************************************************************/
#include <stdio.h>
#define MAXMSG 10
labeler (ecode)
int ecode;
{
 static char *emessages[MAXMSG] =
    {
    "MLBL01 - Requires at least 1 file arg",
    "MLBL02 - Unable to open file argument"
    };

 printf("%s\n",emessages[ecode]);
}
```

Figure 9.11c. Label Program Error Routine: labeler.c

```
label:  labelmn.o labelpr.o labeler.o
 cc labelmn.o labelpr.o labeler.o

labelmn.o:
 cc labelmn.c

labelpr.o:
 cc labelpr.c

labeler.o:
 cc labeler.c
```

Figure 9.12. Label Program *makefile*

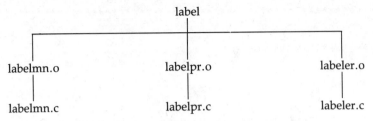

Figure 9.13. Label Program Dependency Tree

9.6.1 SCCS Functions

There are three main operations used to maintain source modules:

admin   create SCCS file
get   retrieve module version
delta   store modification

Each module is stored in its own SCCS file with a name beginning with s. For example, to maintain the label program source code, we could use three files: *s. labelmn, s.labelpr,* and *s.labeler.* Figure 9.15 shows the stages a module goes through during SCCS processing.

9.6.2 Create an SCCS File: admin

usage: **admin** [options] sccsfile

To create files, you use the **admin** command:

```
admin     -ilabelmn.c   s.labelmn
admin     -ilabelpr.c   s.labelpr
admin     -ilabeler.c   s.labeler

          obj = labelmn.o labelpr.o labeler.o

          label:   $(obj)
          cc $(obj)

          labelmn.o:
          cc labelmn.c

          labelpr.o:
          cc labelpr.c

          labeler.o:
          cc labeler.c
```

Figure 9.14. *makefile* Using Macros

TABLE 9.8
make *Command Options*

–i	ignore error codes by commands
–s	don't print commands as executed
–n	no execute, display commands that would be executed
–t	touch the makefile (sets current date)
–q	return whether file is (return code 0) or is not (return code non-0) up-to-date
–p	print out macro definitions
–d	print detailed file information

The **-i** option indicates the file from which the original text will be taken. The file argument is the name of the SCCS file. Once the source has been saved in the SCCS file, you can remove the original file from the current directory.

9.6.3 Retrieve an SCCS Module: **get**

usage: **get** [options] sccsfile

The **get** command retrieves the source files, creating a file by the original name in the current directory. If the purpose of the retrieval is to make changes which ultimately will be stored under a new version number, you must use the **-e** option. If you don't anticipate needing an update, no options are required during retrieval:

> **get** s.labelmn   no update intended
> **get** -e s.labelmn   for update with **delta**

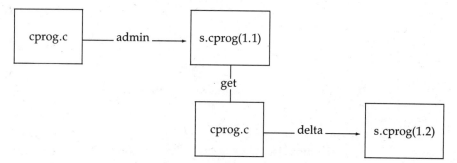

Figure 9.15. SCCS Process

9.6.4 *Create a New SCCS Version:* delta

usage: **delta** [options] sccsfile

The **delta** command returns a source file with an updated version number. The file to be returned must have been retrieved by **get** with the **-e** option. SCCS deltas are stored as a sequence of **ed** scripts which, when applied to the original file, can reconstruct any previous version. This is similar to the output of the **diff** command discussed in Chapter 5. After entering **delta,** it prompts for a comment describing the change. The **-p** option shows the editor file differences. Suppose we add a print "Label Program Done" message just before the return in the labelmn (Figure 9.11a). Figure 9.16 outlines **get** and **delta** processing.

9.6.5 *SCCS Versions*

SCCS maintains both versions and releases, and it supports more than one release at a time. The release and version number of an SCCS file is called its S(ccs) IDentification. The SID has two components—release.version. The **admin** command creates release 1, version 1 of the source file, 1.1. Subsequent deltas update the version number.

The **get** command uses the **-r** option both to indicate which version to retrieve and to update the release number. For example, to retrieve a specific version, you enter:

```
get -e -r1.3 s.file
```

```
get -e s. labelmn.c
1.1
new delta 1.2
26 lines

----> make changes using ed,ex, or vi  to labelmn.c

delta -p s.labelmn.c
Type comments, terminated with EOF or a blank line:
Addition of end of processing message
1.2
24a25
>        printf("Label Processing Done");
1 inserted
0 deleted
26 unchanged
```

Figure 9.16. **get** *and* **delta** *Processing*

This retrieves for update version 1.3 of file. To change the release:

```
get -e -r2 s.file
```

In this case, since release 2 doesn't exist, the latest version will be retrieved, but the delta will create SID 2.1

9.6.6 Other SCCS Commands

We have not covered all the SCCS features and there are a number of commands for comparing and combining deltas, displaying delta information, and generally maintaining the SCCS files. Table 9.9 lists the SCCS commands.

9.6.7 General Usage of make and SCCS

While we are concentrating on program development and maintenance, it should be emphasized that **make** and SCCS operate on any type of files, not just C programs. For example, when writing a manuscript or system documentation, chapters with revisions can be controlled with SCCS. The document can be described in a makefile, and **make** can pull all the current versions, put it together, run the appropriate text processing software, and produce the final product. Because of the flexibility of both **make** and SCCS, they are important utilities distributed with UNIX.

TABLE 9.9
SCCS commands

admin	create and SCCS file
cdc	change delta commentary
comb	combine deltas
delta	store an SCCS file version
get	retrieve an SCCS file version
prs	print an SCCS file
help	help messages
rmdel	remove a delta
sccsdiff	compare versions
unget	undo a previous get
val	validate an SCCS file

9.7 Further Exploration

This chapter has described the important and popular program development tools. Many of the commands and utilities have features which we have not described. They can be found in tutorial form in your user documentation. Try some of the following exercises:

1. Run the **cc** command on your own program (or one of the examples in the book), set an option to create a file of the preprocessor output, and display the output on the screen. Can you run the preprocessor by itself? What command would you use?

2. Run some of your own programs through **cb.** Are they more beautiful? Can you suggest improvements to **cb**? Do you agree with the placement of brackets?

3. Write a C program (several functions) to manage the telephone directory developed in earlier chapters. Your program should incorporate the features of the prototype script in Chapter 7:

- Create the source with an editor.
- **cb** and **lint** each module.
- Compile the system (**cc**).
- Debug with **adb.**
- Place the object modules in a library.
- Create a **make** file for the system.
- Manage revisions with SCCS.

9.8 Manual References

a.out	executable output of the C compiler	**help**	help for SCCS system messages
adb	interactive debugger	**ld**	system loader
admin	create an SCCS file	**lint**	check C source language programs
ar	archive		
as	assembler	**make**	maintain programming systems
cb	C source language beautifier		
		monitor	profile data file
cc	C compiler	**prof**	display profile data (from monitor)
cdc	change delta commentary of SCCS file		
		prs	print an SCCS file
core	core image dump file	**rmdel**	remove a delta from an SCCS file
cpp	C language preprocessor		
cref	cross-reference utility	**sccsdiff**	compare SCCS files
delta	install a change to an SCCS file	**unget**	undo SCCS retrieve
		xref	cross-reference for C programs
get	retrieve an SCCS file		

10

UNIX Programming Interface

In order to develop application or systems software, it is necessary to understand how the operating system works and how one communicates with it. In all operating systems, there are a set of predefined system calls that interface directly with the operating system resource management routines. Chapter 10 introduces this interface and its use through the basic system programming activities. Specific topics to be emphasized include:

> System Calls and Functions
> I/O Devices
> File I/O
> Standard I/O
> Formatted I/O
> Multiprogramming
> Interprocess Communication
> Operating System Signals

10.1 System Calls

The UNIX system has a collection of predefined system calls that interface with the resource management functions of the kernel. Thus, there are calls that provide services to the programmer for memory management, device management, file management, and process management. Table 10.1 lists some of the system calls in each of these areas.

Since system calls are entry points in the UNIX kernel, they are invoked as if they were subroutines to the calling program. Thus, the general format of a system call is:

```
scall(arg1, arg2,...)     /* no value returned */
```

or

```
var1 = scall(arg1, arg2,...) /* value returned */
```

Your UNIX manual will describe the purpose of the call, the type of arguments, and the value, if any, that the call returns. This is done by giving the first few lines of the function definition in C, in which the arguments are declared. For example, **chdir** is a system call that changes the current working directory. Its argument is a directory and returns 0 if the operation is successful, -1 if it fails:

```
int chdir(path)
char *path;
```

For **chdir,** we see that it is an integer function (returns an integer value) with one argument, **path,** which is a pointer to a string of characters—in this case, to the path name of the directory.

TABLE 10.1
Types of System Calls

MEMORY MANAGEMENT	
brk	change data segment space allocation
PROCESS MANAGEMENT	
kill	terminate processes
fork	initiate processes
I/O DEVICE MANAGEMENT	
ioctl	I/O device control
INFORMATION (FILE) MANAGEMENT	
open	open files
close	close files

10.2 *Functions and Subroutines*

In the C language, all subprograms or procedures are *functions* declared with a type for returning values. Functions that return no value have the *void* data type. In general programming language terminology, however, if a procedure does not return a value, it is called a *subroutine*. We usually speak of the routines in operating system libraries as subroutines even though some of them return values. To avoid confusion, we will use the term *function* for both types of procedures and specify whether the routine returns a value or not.

Every UNIX system has a collection of function libraries which provide commonly used generic services, *algorithms*, which are not part of the C language. For example, the math library contains trigonometric and other mathematical functions; the C standard library includes functions for processing character strings. Table 10.2 lists and gives examples of the different types of subroutines that come with the UNIX system.

UNIX system functions, like system calls, are described in the UNIX manual, which gives the first few lines of C code, indicating their arguments, data types, and type of value returned, if any. For example, the **sin** function (described under **trig** in the manual) is shown:

```
double sin(x)
double x;
```

TABLE 10.2
Types of Functions

INPUT AND OUTPUT	
fopen,fclose	open and close files
fread,fwrite	read and write files
fscan,fprint	formatted read and write
STRING FUNCTIONS	
strcmp	string comparison
strcat	string concatenation
CHARACTER CLASS FUNCTIONS	
isalpha	compare for alpha
islower	compare for lower case
toascii	convert interger to ASCII
MEMORY MANAGEMENT FUNCTIONS	
malloc	allocate storage
free	free storage
MATHEMATICAL FUNCTIONS	
sin,cos	trigonometric functions
rand	pseudo random number generation
abs	absolute value

This tells us that in any call to sin, both the argument and the value returned are double integers:

```
    .
    .
double s,t;
    .
    .
s = sin(t);
```

In the remaining sections, as we introduce different programming techniques, we will describe the C system calls and functions that perform the associated activities.

10.3 Input and Output Processing

This section describes how to do input and output at the programming level. While simplicity, redirection, and device independence distinguish I/O UNIX from other operating systems, like them, files are accessed through system calls that can be invoked either directly (low level I/O) or indirectly through a comprehensive set of function calls.

10.3.1 Low Level I/O

Low Level I/O is accomplished with six basic system calls: **open, close, creat, read, write** and **lseek**. The **creat** and **open** calls return *file descriptors,* which are integer-valued indices, into a table of opened files. Standard input, output, and error are assigned 0, 1, and 2, respectively, when the shell is initiated and, as are all open file descriptors, they are passed as part of the shell environment to any subprocess. Therefore, you can access the standard files (terminal and screen) without any special open and close processing.

1. *Creating Files.* At the basic I/O level, files are referenced via their descriptors. For example, to create a new file or overwrite an existing one, you would use the **creat** system call:

```
fd = creat(path, mode)
```

where the C system call header is:

```
int creat (path, mode)
char *path;
int mode;
```

For this system call, fd is the integer value of the return from **creat,** a file descriptor; **path** points to the path name of the file to be created, and **mode** represents its protection attributes.

2. *Opening and Closing Files.* If the file already exists, you would use the open system call:

```
fd = open(path,oflag,mode)
```

where the C system call header is :

```
#include <fcntl.h>
int open(path,oflag,mode)
char *path;
int oflag,mode;
```

The include file *fcntl.h*, contains definitions of file attributes that may be specified by the **oflag** argument of the call. For example, read-only is O_RDONLY. **Path** and **mode** are the same as in **creat.** Arguments to **open** can also be used to create files that don't already exist.

To close a file:

```
int close(fildes)
int fildes;
```

3. *Accessing Files.* **read** reads a file:

```
read(fildes, buf, nbyte)
```

where the C system call header is:

```
int read(fildes, buf, nbyte)
int fildes;
char *buf;
unsigned nbyte;
```

For **read, fildes** is the file descriptor, **buf** is a pointer to the input buffer, and **nbyte** is the number of bytes to be read.

The **write** call operates analogously to **read.** The C function header is:

```
int write(fildes,buf,nbytes)
int fildes;
char *buf;
unsigned nbyte;
```

4. *Random Access.* The sixth call, **lseek,** is used to set a byte pointer into the file. No I/O is performed, but **lseek** enables any byte in the file to be accessed randomly.

```
long lseek(fildes,offset,whence)
```

fildes is the file descriptor and **offset** is the number of bytes from some base point in the file. The base is specified by **whence:**

0	beginning of the file
1	current position in the file
2	end of file

10.3.2 *Standard Input and Output*

As you can see, basic I/O can become quite detailed. The alternative is to use a comprehensive set of standard I/O library routines that use the system calls at a slightly higher level. There are really two types of standard I/O routines. The first provides access to files, and the second provides connections to the keyboard and terminal—standard input, output, and error.

10.3.2.1 *Standard Include Library.* Before you can use the standard I/O routines, you must include the standard I/O definitions, which define functions that return values and constants such as the EOF symbol. The include file, *stdio.h,* contains these definitions, and it must be present in modules performing I/O. The main program in Figure 10.1a has the C preprocessor statement, #include <stdio.h>, at line 26.

10.3.2.2 *File I/O.* File I/O processing involves steps similar to basic I/O processing, but it uses the standard I/O function calls:

1. *Opening the file.*

```
fopen:
```

```
FILE *fopen(filename, type)
char *filename, *type;
```

The open process establishes the runtime characteristics of access to the file, which is specified by the 'type' argument:

"r"	read only
"w"	create

"**a**"   append
"**r+**"   update (read and write)
"**w+**"   create for update
"**a+**"   append for update

The file is positioned at the first byte if the open is successful and returns a file pointer, which is used during file access operations. An unsuccessful open returns a NULL file pointer.

Figures 10.1a–c have the three C subroutines from the mailing label system of Chapter 9. The program reads a file of records containing name and address lines separated by a colon. Processing includes opening the input file, creating an output label file, breaking down input records into name and address lines, and producing the label file. In Figure 10.1a the input and output files are opened in lines 40 and 46. The arguments to **fopen** include command line arguments (see below) and "**r**" and "**w**" access types.

2. *Accessing files.* Files are referenced through their file pointers (note the difference between file pointers and standard I/O, and file descriptors and basic I/O), which have been returned by the open function call. Subsequent function calls to the file will take as arguments the file pointer and pointers to fields involved in the I/O transfer. Furthermore, these functions incorporate common generic features which the basic I/O calls don't have.

For example, if the data to be accessed is a line from a text file, then **fgets** and **fputs** may be used. Looking at Figure 10.1b, **fgets** is illustrated in line 27 of *labelpr* which reads a record and places it as a string in the character array aline. In line 30, **fputs** writes out the string in the array, aline.

3. *Random Access.* As indicated above, UNIX I/O is sequential. This means that UNIX maintains a current byte pointer, and after each read or write, the byte pointer is updated to a position beyond the last byte accessed.

While UNIX does not support the sophisticated access methods of larger operating systems, it does provide the facility for building different file access techniques. Key to this is some mechanism for random access (regardless of how inefficient). Simply, since UNIX is maintaining a byte pointer for reference during the next I/O operation, changing the value of the byte pointer essentially implements random access to any point in the file.

The **fseek** function changes the value of the byte pointer:

```
int fseek(stream, offset, ptrname)
FILE *stream;
long offset;
int ptrname;
```

```
1     /*****************************************************************
2     *
3     *
4     *         Name: main()
5     *
6     *         Function:
7     *
8     *             The main program communicates with standard input and
9     *             output to get the filename of a name and address file.
10    *             Errors are printed by the labeler function and labels by
11    *             labelpr function. Main passes the names of the input
12    *             output files to labelpr.
13    *
14    *         Arguments:        Filename of name and address file
15    *
16    *         Subroutines:      labelpr(InputFile, OutputFile)
17    *                           labeler(ErrorCode)
18    *
19    *         Error Codes:
20    *
21    *                           1         missing file argument
22    *                           2         can't open input file
23    *
24    *****************************************************************/
25
26    #include <stdio.h>
27    main(argc,argv)
28    int argc;
29    char *argv[];
30
31    {
32            FILE *faddr,*faddrout;
33
34            if (argc <= 1)
35                    {
36                    labeler(1);
37                    return(-1);
38                    }
39            printf("ARG1: %S\n",argv[1]);
40            faddr = fopen(argv[1], "r");
41            if (faddr == NULL)
42                    {
43                    labeler(2);
44                    return(-2);
45                    }
46            faddrout = fopen(strcat (argv[1],".1","w");
47            printf("Printing labels for file: %-15s\n",argv[1]);
48
49            labelpr(faddr,faddrout);
50            fclose(faddr);
51            fclose(faddout);
52            return(0);
53
```

Figure 10.1a. Main Label Program: labelmn.c

```
1    /*******************************************************************
2    *
3    *
4    *        Name: labelpr()
5    *
6    *        Function:
7    *
8    *            labelpr reads records from the input file and writes label
9    *            records on the output file. Each record has names and
10   *            addresses separated by commas. The string function,
11   *            strtok(), is used to extract each label component.
12   *
13   *        Arguments:        Filedescriptors to the input and output files:
14   *                              flbl    input file
15   *                              flblo   output file
16   *
17   *        Subroutines:    none
18   *
19   *******************************************************************/
20
21   #include <stdio.h>
22   #define RECLEN 80
23   labelpr(flbl,flblo)
24   FILE *flbl,*flblo;
25   {
26           char nabuffer[RECLEN],*aline,*strtok();
27           while (fgets(nabuffer,RECLEN,glbl) != NULL)
28           {
29                   aline = strtok(nabuffer,":");
30                   fputs(aline,flblo);
31                   fputc('\\n',flblo);
32                   while ( (aline = strtok(0,":")) != NULL)
33                           {
34                           fputs(aline,flblo);
35                           fputc('\\n',flblo);
36                           }
37           }
38
39   }
```

Figure 10.1b.   Label Program Print Routine: labelpr.c

where:

stream	file pointer
offset	value of offset
ptrname	offset base
0	beginning of the file
1	current position in the file
2	end of file

To position at the fifth record of 80 byte records, the following function call sets the byte pointer:

```
fseek(fd1,320,0)
```

```
1    /*************************************************************
2    *
3    *         Name: labeler()
4    *
5    *         Function:
6    *
7    *             labeler() prints program error messages that are in an
8    *             initialized string array of messages. The function receives
9    *             the error number as an argument used as an index into
10   *             the message array.
11   *
12   *         Arguments:          Error Code
13   *
14   *         Subroutines:        none
15   *
16   *         Error Codes:
17   *
18   *                     1           missing file argument
19   *                     2           can't open input file
20   *
21   *************************************************************/
22
23   #include <stdio.h>
24   define MAXMSG 10
25   labeler(ecode)
26   int ecode;
27   {
28           static char *emessages[MAXMSG] =
29                           {
30                           "MLBL01 - Requires at least 1 file arg",
31                           "MLBL02 - Unable to open file argument"
32                           };
33
34           printf("%s\\n",emessages[ecode]);
35   }
36
```

Figure 10.1c. Label Program Error Routine: labeler.c

where:

fd1 is the file descriptor
320 is 4*80 or the first byte of the fifth record
0 sets the offset base at the beginning

4. *Closing a file.* **fclose** closes open files:

```
int fclose(stream)
FILE *stream;
```

Zero is returned if the close is successful, and EOF if not. In Figure 10.1a, **fclose** is illustrated at line 50.

10.3.3 *Standard I/O Connections*

Input and output to the standard I/O files (terminal keyboard and screen) is a simplification of general I/O. This is because, in the environment of a running program, the I/O descriptors have already been established. A wide variety of standard I/O functions are in the C subroutine library for performing standard input and output. In the program example, at line 34 in Figure 10.1c, the **printf** function displays an error message on standard output. Table 10.3 lists the standard I/O functions.

10.3.4 Formatted Input and Output

While you must refer to a C language manual to study input and output programming in more detail, we will discuss formatted input and output here because of the relationship of the C format specification to other UNIX utilities (**awk, date,** etc.).

The format of the **printf** (formatted output) and **scanf** (formatted input) functions involves a specification followed by a variable list:

```
printf("specification",variable list)
scanf("specification", variable list)
```

The specification consists of normal characters that are transferred to standard output (or from standard input, in the case of **scanf**) and special specification sequences that begin with a percent sign. Furthermore, specifications can be modified to include field width and justification information. For example, %–15s indicates a string conversion left justified in a field with 15 positions. Table 10.4 lists the editing characters for **printf** and **scanf.**

Figure 10.2 illustrates the use of the formatting characters with **printf** and **scanf.** In the program at line 24, **scanf** requires pointers to its data arguments (the array name *vstring* is already a pointer). Also, notice the use of the newline sequence, \n, in the **printf** statements. Other sequences for tabbing, backspace, etc., may be interspersed freely in the specification. Table 10.5 lists the special control characters that **printf** will recognize for output formatting.

TABLE 10.3
Standard Input and Output Functions

getchar	read a character
putchar	write a character
gets	get a string
puts	put a string
printf	formatted print
scanf	formatted input

TABLE 10.4
printf *and* **scanf** *Specification Characters*

c	a single character
s	a character string
d	an integer
e	float displayed in scientific notation
f	float displayed with decimal point
o	octal digits
x	hex digits

```
1    /*****************************************************************
2    *
3    *
4    *        Name: main()
5    *
6    *        Function:
7    *
8    *                Main program to illustrate use of formatted I/O with
9    *                scanf and printf
10   *
11   *        Arguments:      none
12   *
13   *        Subroutines:    none
14   *
15   ****************************************************************/
16
17   #include <stdio.h>
18   main()
19   {
20     char vchar;
21     char vstring[25];
22     int vinteger;
23
24     scanf("%c%s%d",&vchar,vstring,&vinteger);
25
26     printf("This is a char: %c\n",vchar);
27     printf("This is a string: %s\n",vstring);
28     printf("This is an integer: %d\n",vinteger);
29
30   }
```

Figure 10.2a. C Program Formatting with **printf** and **scanf**

Standard input:

a smith 1024

Standard output:

```
This is a char: a
This is a string: smith
This is an integer: 1024
```

Figure 10.2b. Standard Output of **printf**

TABLE 10.5
Format Control Characters

\b	backspace
\c	print without newline
\f	form feed
\n	new line
\r	carriage return
\t	tab
\value	any three-digit octal value

10.4 Multitasking

Multitasking operating systems can manage the concurrent execution of several programs. This involves keeping track of each program or process in the system through its life cycle: creation, execution, termination. In this section and in 10.5, we explain process activity and the associated commands, system calls, and subroutines. As a case study, we use the operation of the UNIX user interface itself, the shell.

10.4.1 Process Management

Processes are created when one process, called the *parent*, issues the system call, **fork,** which causes a duplicate copy, the *child*, of the parent process to be created. This may at first seem strange, but primarily it involves adding new entries to the kernel's process table. Code (which, if shared, requires no new storage allocation) and data areas are duplicated. Instead of a single process, there are now two processes which look exactly the same (see Figures 10.3a and 10.3b).

While everything looks the same in each process, the return value from the system call **fork** will be different for p1, the parent, and p2, the child. It is the process ID (PID) that identifies the new active process within the UNIX system. The PID is used by the kernel to access process data from the system tables. The parent receives the new PID of its child, while zero

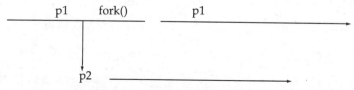

Figure 10.3a. Process Execution Timeline

```
      p1:                                    p2:
.                                        .
int pid;                                 int pid;
.                                        .
.                                        .
pid = fork();                            pid = fork();
if (pid == 0)                            if (pid == 0)

    /*   child activity    */            /*  CHILD RESUMES HERE    */

else                                     else

   /* PARENT RESUMES HERE   */            /*    parent activity   */
```

Figure 10.3b. Processes after **fork**

is returned to p2. A prototype of the p1 and p2 code is shown in Figure 10.3b. The variable name, pid, is arbitrary. Parents that spawn many children may require multiple variables to keep track, e.g., *pid1*, *pid2*, etc.

Since the values of *pid* in p1 and p2 will be different, after the execution of the **fork,** each program will be doing different processing. Because it is the parent, p1 will do the 'else' code and p2, as the child, will do the 'if' code.

The child usually issues one of a set of **exec** calls, which causes it to be overlayed by a new program. For example, if p2 runs the UNIX program **ls** to get a directory listing of C source programs, the code of p1/p2 will be as displayed in Figure 10.4a. Figure 10.4b shows the execution timeline. In the example, we use **execl,** which accepts its arguments as a list of pointers to character strings. The list is terminated by the null character string.

If p1 is the shell, we see the manner in which commands are initiated. Note, however, that there are two concurrent processes. The shell is continuing to execute, illustrating how background processing is accom-

```
      p1:                                    p2:
.                                        .
int pid;                                 int pid;
.                                        .
.                                        .
pid = fork();                            pid = fork();
if (pid == 0)                            if (pid == 0)

   execl("\bin\ls","*.c",NULL);             execl("\bin\ls","*.c",NULL);

else                                     else

   /* parent  activity */                   /*    parent activity */
```

Figure 10.4a. p2 Executes 'ls *.c'

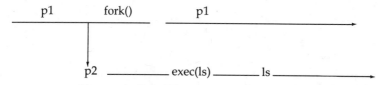

Figure 10.4b. p2 Executing 'ls *.c' Timeline

plished. Execution of **ls** with the & notation tells the shell to continue while the command executes.

We take this one step further by introducing the **wait** system call, which causes the invoking process to wait for the termination of one of its children. In our example, if p1 waits, then we have a situation similar to standard shell processing. Figures 10.5a and 10.5b illustrate this, using the shell as p1.

In summary, UNIX supports multitasking in which the programmer can initiate subprocesses with the **fork** system call. You control the activities of both parent and child with **exec** and **wait** primitives. This model is how UNIX performs all process activities from the initiation of the shell at your terminal to the execution of all UNIX command and utilities.

10.4.2 Multiprogramming Commands

Up to now we have been speaking of multiprogramming operation at the programming or system call level. There are a number of shell level commands that interact with the UNIX kernel to support multiprogramming activities.

```
    shell:
.
int pid;
.
.
pid = fork();
if (pid == 0)

   execl ("\bin\ls", "*.c",NULL);

else

  wait()
 /* perform parent activity */
```

```
    shell:
.
int pid;
.
.
pid = fork();
if (pid == 0)

   execl ("\bin\ls", "*.c",NULL);

else

  wait()
 /* perform parent activity */
```

Figure 10.5a. Shell Executes **ls**

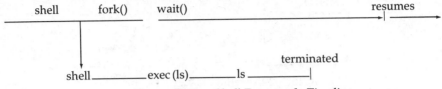

Figure 10.5b. Shell Executes **ls** Timeline

10.4.2.1 Process Status: ps

usage: **ps** [options]

The process status command displays current process activity with varying amounts of detail depending on the options given. With no options, processes are displayed which have been created as child processes by your shell (see Figure 10.6a). Notice that your shell and the **ps** command are the two processes running.

When used with the **-e** options, information is displayed about all processes in your system (See Figure 10.6b). The functions performed by **init** and **cron** are discussed in Chapter 11.

To get more information about each process, you use the **-l** option (Figure 10.6c). The **ps** display columns and their meanings are listed in Table 10.6.

```
ps
        PID TTY TIME COMMAND
         15 co  0:18 sh
         42 co  0:03 ps
```

Figure 10.6a. **ps** Command Output

```
ps -e
        PID TTY TIME COMMAND
          0  ? 11:27 swapper
          1  ?  0:02 init
         15 co  0:18 sh
         44 co  0:03 ps
         11  ?  0:03 cron
```

Figure 10.6b. **ps** Command with System Processes

```
ps -l
```

F	S	UID	PID	PPID	C	PRI	NI	ADDR	SZ	WCHAN	TTY	TIME	COMD
1	S	200	15	1	0	50	20	23200	19	15aa	co	0:19	sh
1	R	0	46	15	40	70	20	32aC0	29		co	0:03	ps

Figure 10.6c. **ps** Command with Long Listing

TABLE 10.6
ps *Display Columns*

F	process status flags (octal)
S	process state (R = running, W = waiting, S = sleeping)
UID	user id of owner
PID	process id
PPID	parent process id
C	processor utilization (for scheduling)
PRI	priority (high values indicate low priority)
NI	priority adjustment value
ADDR	memory address of process
SZ	core image size of process
WCHAN	wait information (blank indicates running)
TTY	controlling terminal (? indicates daemon)
TIME	cumulative time
COMD	command name

10.4.2.2 System Information: **pstat**

usage: **pstat** [options]

Some systems (e.g., XENIX, System V) support the **pstat** command, which displays the contents of some systemwide tables. For example, in addition to process information (process table, **-p** option), you also can ascertain data about systemwide open files with inode table, **-i,** option.

10.4.2.3 Terminating Background Processes: **kill**

usage: **kill** processid

As indicated above, when processes are initiated, they are assigned process ID numbers. The **kill** command can be used to terminate your own active processes, e.g., background processes. After determining the PID of the process to terminate (displayed by **ps**), you use it as an argument in the **kill** command. If you kill the process which represents your shell, you are effectively committing "suicide" and your login session will terminate. Try it—kill the process associated with the shell in the **ps** command listing.

10.4.2.4 Pausing: **sleep**

usage: **sleep** seconds

You can cause the current process to pause for a specified number of seconds by issuing the **sleep** command. This is useful in shell scripts. For example, to execute a command every few seconds:

```
while true
do
    sleep 60
    command
done
```

The script running in the background ('&') executes the command every 60 seconds.

10.4.2.5 Waiting for Background Processes to Complete

usage: **wait**

At the completion of any child process, a signal is sent to the parent process. This can be tested with the **wait** command, which will resume processing at the completion of all background processes. If there are no child processes active at the time of **wait,** the shell immediately continues.

10.4.3 Interprocess Communication

Interprocess communication concerns the mechanism by which independent processes communicate with each other. Generalized communication techniques include the establishment of mailboxes and messages that can be sent, received, acknowledged, answered, etc. This usually involves the establishment of a list to contain the messages, called a *queue*, and operations that add, delete, and process messages in the queue. Several UNIX versions (e.g., System V) support general message handling at the system cell level.

The standard interprocess communication facility supported by all UNIX systems involves the concept of *pipes*, two-way channels set up by a parent process prior to spawning child processes with **fork.** This is illustrated in Figures 10.7a and 10.7b. The operation of **pipe** returns two file descriptors, one for reading and one for writing.

All children spawned by the process that creates the pipe will inherit the file descriptors and can therefore use the pipe for interprocess communication. The operation of the pipe involves the use of the I/O primitive operations **read, write,** and **close.** If a process writes to a pipe and the pipe is full, it waits. If a process attempts to read an empty pipe, again it waits. If a process reads a pipe that has been closed, it receives end of file. Thus, basic interprocess communication is implemented functionally as an extension of the file system.

parent:

```
pipe(filedescriptor);
pid = fork();
.
.
.
```

parent or child processes:

```
.
.
.
write(filedesc[0]);
.
.
.
read(filedesc[1]);
```

Figure 10.7a. Code Prototype for Pipe Processing

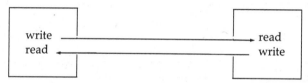

Figure 10.7b. Pipe Operation

10.4.4 Semaphores

We have already described the basic UNIX process synchronization technique that uses the **wait** system call to suspend the operation of a process until a child completes. This technique is rather primitive, since the process will resume when any child process completes, and special processing must be included to determine which process has completed. If the completed child process is not the one the parent is waiting for, it must wait again. Furthermore, there are synchronization situations that are not handled at all in earlier versions of UNIX. For example, shared access to a data structure was not supported at the system call level. Later versions of UNIX (e.g., System V) have remedied this problem by providing system call support for generalized synchronization primitives.

Semaphores are variables used to control access to shared resources and to implement other synchronization requirements. In its simplest implementation, a semaphore is a variable accessible by concurrent processes, which indicates the availability of a resource. For example, if the variable is 1 (non-zero), the resource is available; if it is 0, it is in use. Operations are provided to manipulate the semaphore variables, including allocation, initialization, and processing (testing and setting). Concurrent systems design requires the sophistication of semaphore operations, and if this is a requirement, you should check your system documentation for the availability of semaphore system calls and functions.

10.5 Interpreting Command Line Arguments

Another important programming activity concerns the interpretation of command line arguments. When a new process is initiated, two arguments passed to the main program are set for processing command line arguments:

1. *A Count of the Number of Arguments.* The count is always at least 1, since the first argument is always taken to be the name of the command. For example:

cmd1	count is 1
cmd2 arg1 arg2	count is 3

2. *A Pointer to an Array of Pointers to the Arguments.* This is illustrated in Figures 10.8a and 10.8b. The label program in Figure 10.1 reads in a file name and uses it to open the names and address file and create a label

Command Line:

```
cmd1 arg1 arg2:
```

main() header:

```
main(argc, argv)

    int argc;
    char *argv[]
```

Figure 10.8a. main Header

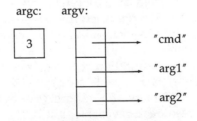

Figure 10.8b. main Arguments

qutput file. Line 34 in the main program checks for at least one file argument (**argc** must be greater than 1), then prints out the argument in line 39. Later statements use the argument for opening files.

This is the standard way in which all the commands and utilities handle command line arguments, and it should be used as a model for developing new commands or utilities.

10.6 Operating System Signals

In response to a variety of hardware and software activities in the system, the UNIX will generate one of fifteen basic signals. All versions expand on this primarily to take advantage of special software and hardware features, but all provide the basic signals listed in Table 10.7. Your program can respond to signals in one of three ways:

1. terminate
2. ignore
3. perform a defined function

You set up the response by issuing the system call **signal** indicating the signal and response. Figure 10.9 shows the C language statements. SIG__DFL and SIG__IGN are values defined in the include file, *signal.h,* which trap the signal, then either terminate the process or ignore the sig-

TABLE 10.7
UNIX Basic System Signals

SIGHUP	1	hangup
SIGINT	2	interrupt
SIGQUIT	3*	quit
SIGILL	4*	illegal instruction
SIGTRAP	5*	trace trap
SIGIOT	6*	IOT instruction
SIGEMT	7*	EMT instruction
SIGFPE	8*	floating point exception
SIGKILL	9	kill (cannot be caught or ignored)
SIGBUS	10*	bus error
SIGSEGV	11*	segmentation violation
SIGSYS	12*	bad argument to system call
SIGPIPE	13	write on a pipe with no one to read it
SIGALRM	14	alarm clock
SIGTERM	15	software termination signal

```
#include <signal.h>

int (*signal (sig, func))()
int sig;
int (*func)();
```

where:

sig has a value of 01-15

func has possible values:

```
SIG_DFL
SIG_IGN
function address
```

Figure 10.9 C Program Header for Trapping UNIX Signals

nal; **func** is the address of the function to perform when the signal is trapped.

In Table 10.7, signals with asterisks will create a core image dump upon process termination. The dump is placed in a file called **core** in the current directory. The debugging utility **adb** and its use in debugging programs and core image dumps was discussed in Chapter 9.

10.7 Further Exploration

This chapter has introduced some of the basic programming techniques you will need to begin designing systems on your UNIX system. For further references you should consult your system documentation, including the system call and subroutine sections and system file and administration sections. Try the following exercises:

1. Write a C program that prints out the message, "Hello *name*," where *name* is a parameter passed to your program.

2. Implement the name and address program.

3. Are interprocess message control subroutines part of your system? Design a C program that generates messages and another program to receive and print them.

4. Semaphores are very important systems programming–operating systems features. Design two processes that compete for the printer. Use a semaphore to represent the resource, and have each process loop repeatedly request the resource, print a message, then release the resource. Which process controls the resource most often? Do they alternate?

10.8 Manual References

close	close file system call
creat	create file system call
csh	C-shell command
exec	exec system call
fclose	close file library function
fopen	open file library function
fork	create process system call
fread	read file library function
fseek	seek library function
fwrite	write file library function
kill	kill process command and system call
lseek	seek system call
msgctl	message control system call
msgget	establish message queue system call
msgop	message operations system call
nice	set priority system call
open	open file system call
pipe	interprocess communication system
ps	process status command
read	read system call
semctl	semaphore control system call
semget	establish semaphore system call
semop	semaphore operations system call
sh	Bourne shell command
signal	trap signal system call
sleep	pause a few seconds
wait	wait for process completion
write	write file system call

PART III

Workstation Issues

The chapters in this part of the book address users at personal computer-based workstations. Issues relating to system administration and communications are discussed. A special section compares UNIX to MS-DOS.

11

System Administration

This chapter covers the basic functions you will have to perform as the system administrator of your personal workstation. Since many of the specific utilities and file names are dependent upon the version of UNIX you are using, we will try to give conceptual guidelines rather than step-by-step procedures, emphasizing the following functions:

Installation
Startup/Shutdown
User IDs and Passwords
Backup Procedures
File System Integrity
Special Files
Diskettes
Mountable File Systems
Daemons
cron, crontab

11.1 Initialization

This is the section you will turn to when you receive your PC-based UNIX system. Each PC-UNIX version has its own procedures and commands for installation, startup and shutdown. Unfortunately, we don't have the space to guide you through all the different systems; however, we can describe the overall process and guide you through your own system installation.

11.1.1 Installation

PC versions are usually distributed on diskettes, to be loaded onto a fixed or hard disk. There are four steps to installing a UNIX system:

1. *Boot the Installation Diskette.* This diskette contains a basic version of UNIX required to load the other diskettes to the fixed disk. It creates an empty file system, then loads all the UNIX software onto your system, usually using one of the UNIX dump/restore utilities. You use the same procedure you would use to boot other operating systems (e.g., CP/M, MS-DOS, etc.).

2. *Create the Fixed Disk File System.* Some systems will guide you through an automated installation procedure. By responding to questions about the size and structure of your file system, the hard disk will be set up and a basic UNIX system will be established.

The UNIX system can be divided into several subsystems, and depending on your needs, you load the appropriate software. For example, XENIX has the basic system (editors, basic commands, etc.), the program development system (C language, **lint, cb,** etc.), text development system (**nroff/ troff, eqn, tbl,** etc.), and the communications system (**uucp,** etc.).

3. *Copy the Installation Diskettes to Your System (Fixed Disk).* This creates a UNIX file system. This process uses UNIX utilities such as **tar** or **cpio** to load the diskettes distributed with your system onto the established file system. Depending on the version of UNIX you are installing and the parts of the system you are intending to load, this can vary from a few diskettes to 20 or 30.

The procedure for loading the files may vary. One type of load involves establishing the diskettes as mountable volumes. A more direct method uses the system dump/restore facilities, discussed in greater detail in Sections 11.3.1 and 11.3.2.

4. *Start the New System.* After creating the UNIX file system and loading the files distributed with the system, you start the system by going through the booting procedures outlined in your documentation.

11.1.2 Startup

UNIX can be started in three different operating modes.

1. The installation mode provides the utilities (system dependent) to create file systems and install UNIX and its subsets on your hardware.

2. The maintenance mode allows you to repair file systems and install utilities and devices. In this mode, the normal background processes that are usually started automatically are inhibited, and you are in an operating mode to perform different kinds of system maintenance without needing to be concerned about other concurrent activity. Furthermore, you are logged in as the superuser (see 11.1.4), which overrides UNIX security and protection modes and gives access to all the files and utilities in the system.

3. The normal mode brings up the production UNIX system and performs several functions:

(a) The UNIX boot program starts up the **init** process, the parent of all other processes.

(b) Then **init** executes the shell script call */etc/rc*. This script contains all the commands to be executed during system initialization. Eventually you may want to modify */etc/rc* to incorporate procedures specific to your installation, including the startup of those processes not associated with a terminal. These processes, called *daemons*, perform a variety of functions, including print spool management and scheduling of periodic jobs (see **cron** below). For now, display its contents to see some of the initialization activities.

(c) **init** starts up **getty** at each port which sets terminal characteristics and displays the system login message. **getty** will invoke the **login** process with the user name of whoever is logging into the system.

(d) The **login** processes the user ID and password information and establishes the session. Figure 11.1 shows the parent/child relationships of **init, getty, login,** and the user.

11.1.2.1 Setting Your Own Terminal Characteristics: stty

usage: **stty** [options] [stty-settings]

You may want to override the default terminal settings or tailor some of the keys to your own liking. This is done with the **stty** command. **stty** with no options lists some of the settings. The **-a** option lists them all.

Settings are placed on the command line separated by blanks. For some settings a minus sign in front of it turns it off. For example, **ignbrk** causes UNIX to ignore the break key on input; **-ignbrk** resets it.

Other settings take an argument. For example, to set the erase key you

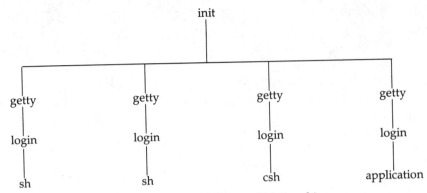

Figure 11.1. Initial Process Relationships

enter **stty erase** followed by the key you want to use to erase the last character of input. In this way you can take advantage of your terminal's special keyboard characteristics. The **stty** entry in the appendix lists common terminal settings.

11.1.3 *Shutdown*

When bringing down the system—you should carefully follow the procedures outlined in your system documentation. Errors at this point could permanently damage your file system and require extensive debugging and repair work.

In general, to shut down the system, all activity must cease. All users are logged off, and all daemons are terminated. Some systems will have a command to initiate the shutdown procedure.

From an operations point of view, the following steps should be taken, whether incorporated into an automated procedure or not:

1. Be sure all users are logged off (except the superuser).
3. Run any daily system maintenance procedures (backups, etc.).
3. Shutdown the system.

If your system doesn't provide automatic procedures, you can write shell scripts to perform the desired activities.

11.1.4 *Superuser*

A superuser is a user with access to the user ID ''root,'' which can override all file system protections. This means it has read/write access to all the files in the system and can run any program. Maintenance mode operation is within a superuser login. Additionally, when you log in, you can specify root as the user ID to get superuser privileges. When the root user logs in, a special prompt (#) reminds you that you are in the superuser mode.

A safer way to use superuser privileges is to enter the **su** command. You keep your current environment (HOME, PATH, current directory, etc.), but you can access any file. The **su** command will ask for the superuser ID password and, if correctly supplied, it will spawn a shell with a root prompt. To return to your own login ID, simply enter a *ctrl-D*.

11.2 User Administration

Even though your system may be for a single user more than likely you will be establishing several user IDs. If the system is multi-user, then different users can be on the system concurrently and the user base will be larger. Because UNIX is a multi-user operating system, you will have to establish and maintain the system by adding new users, deleting users, and changing user information. The following sections describe this process.

11.2.1 The User File System Hierarchy

Users are assigned login directories by the user-creation procedure described below. The placement of user directories in the UNIX file system hierarchy follows a loose standard, and while not enforced by the operating system, using the standard will make your system consistent with other UNIX systems.

User directories are placed subordinately to a directory in the root directory. On some systems they may be placed under */usr,* but on most modern large systems */usr* contains systemwide directories and another directory is used to hold the user directories (e.g., */usr1*). On a single-user or limited-user system, one level of user directories should be sufficient. In environments that may have users from different departments or groups, multilevel directories may be set up (see Figure 11.2).

11.2.2 /etc/passwd and Login

The system file containing information about individual users is called */etc/passwd.* There is a record for each user that contains seven fields separated by a colon, as shown in Figure 11.3.

The first two fields are used by the login program when you start a

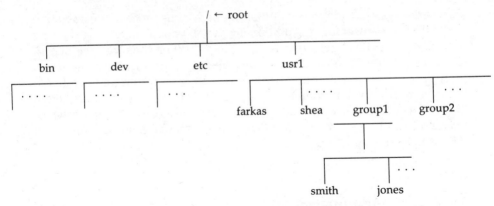

Figure 11.2. User Login Directory Hierarchy

UNIX terminal session. Both the login name and password are entered when you log in, but notice how your password is displayed. It is either in an encrypted format or, if you have no password, it is empty. There are no readable copies of your password on the system. The third and fourth fields, user and group IDs, are used by the file system to determine ownership and access rights. Associated with each file is ownership information, and as we have seen earlier, this can be tested against the group and user ID values to determine the different permission values of a file to a particular user. The fifth field, user name, contains your actual name, not the system or login name.

The sixth field is your login (home) directory. After logging in, the shell HOME variable is set to this value and it becomes the current directory. The seventh field is the program to run at login. In most cases this will be **sh** for the Bourne shell or **csh** for the Berkeley C-shell. Some versions may have their own shells and they or other applications can be substituted as well.

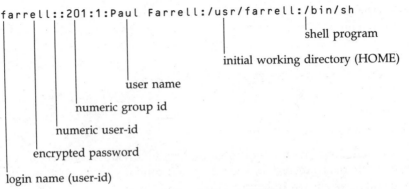

Figure 11.3. */etc/passwd* Entry

11.2.3 Adding, Deleting, and Modifying User Information

The simplest mechanism for adding new users involves editing the */etc/passwd* file, and adding, deleting, or modifying the individual lines representing users. Many systems have utility programs that will perform this action for you. For example, IBM's PC/IX **adduser** facility provides adding, deleting, changing, and listing functions. The command is also **adduser** in Berkeley UNIX, but **mkuser** in XENIX and **usermgmt** in AT&T System V.

11.2.4 Changing Passwords: **passwd**

usage: **passwd** [username]

Since the password is in an encrypted format you gain access to it through the **passwd** command line. Accessible by all users, **passwd** will ask you first for your old password. If correctly supplied you will be prompted for the new password. To be sure you haven't typed it incorrectly, **passwd** will ask for verification by prompting you for the new password again. If it matches, the new password will be stored in encrypted form in the */etc/passwd* file:

```
passwd
Enter Old Password:
Enter New Password:
Enter New Password:
Password Changed
```

The next time you log in, you will need to use the new password. If you are the superuser, you can change any password by giving the username on the **passwd** command.

It goes without saying, but we will say it anyway. If you are in a multiuser environment, it is a good idea to change your password often.

11.3 Backup Procedures

UNIX provides several techniques for copying all or part of your file system. Performing backups requires that you have some understanding of the different devices and how to access them, because the utilities will reference different backup media. Fortunately, since the commands used for file system backup can be tailored for default devices and file systems, your system may already be set up for taking backups with default command options.

11.3.1 *Backing Up by Name:* dump

usage: **dump -i** (filenames

The first type of backup is by name, in which you specify a list of files on standard input for copying. For example, you may want to copy an entire directory, or files in a collection of directories. The **-i** option of dump takes a list of filenames for backup. Used in conjunction with some of the other file utilities, different kinds of backups can be performed:

1. Backup of a directory:

```
ls | dump -i
```

2. Backup of a subtree of the file system:

```
find pathname -print | dump -i
```

In the first example, the filenames in the current working directory are piped into the **dump** command. In the second, the directories from the directory, *pathname* are recursively searched and the filenames are piped as standard input to the **dump** utility.

11.3.2 *Restoring a Dump:* restor, restore

usage: **restore** [options]   (e.g., PC/IX)

or

restor key [arguments]   (e.g., XENIX)

To restore the contents of a volume (e.g., diskette) created by the **dump** utility, you use the **restore** or **restor** command. This utility can be used to list the contents of **dump** volumes, restore by name, and restore an entire file system. Like **dump,** different systems have different formats for specifying the options, but the important key or option letters are the same. The **-t** option prints header or label information from the **dump** volume. In one format, **-T** also prints a table of contents.

To restore files, you use the **-x** (extract) option:

```
restore -x /dev/rfd0
```

In the above example, *rfd0* is the name of the special file (in the */dev* directory) of a floppy disk drive. Without any options, **restore** will extract the entire volume set from the default dump device. If there is more than one **restore** diskette, each one will be prompted until the entire set is restored.

11.3.3 Backup by Name: cpio

usage: **cpio** [options] [pattern]

cpio is a file archive utility that takes filenames from standard input and writes the files on standard output. The **-o** option takes filenames from standard input and places them on the archive file specified as standard output. In general, physical devices can be specified so as to create backups of the file system. For example, to backup the current directory, you use the **-o** option and specify:

```
ls | cpio -o >/dev/rfd0
```

Here *rfd0* is a special filename for a diskette drive. Device names are system specific and you will have to check your system documentation for the devices names you must use.

To recover files from a **cpio** archive, you use the **-i** option, which selects the filenames given in the form of a shell pattern for filename generation, and the **cpio** archive file or device as standard input.

```
cpio -i '*.c' < /dev/rfd0
```

In the above example, the C programs are restored from the diskette in the *rfd0* device. Other options of **cpio** will print a table of contents (**-t**), rename files (**-r**), modify access times, and efficiently block the archive.

11.3.4 Incremental Dumps: dump

usage: **dump** [options] [filesystem]

We have seen how to backup by name or by directory node. A second method backs up by dumping that part of the file system that has changed since the last dump. This is called an *incremental dump* and it saves only the part of the file system that has been modified recently.

The UNIX **dump** command has an option to select a dump number between 0 and 9, each value representing the next level in an incremental dump. Level 0 indicates a complete dump of the file system. Level 1 means dump all files that have been modified since the level 0 dump was taken. Level 2 dumps files modified after the level 1 dump, and so on. The **dump** command without any options except the level number will default to your running file system. If there is a maintenance mode in your UNIX system, you may be required to enter this mode to perform file backups on the main file system.

Depending on which UNIX you are running, there are two formats for specifying a dump. Fortunately, the formats are similar and their operation, options, and function are identical.

> **dump** [-u] [-level] [-v]   (e.g., PC/IX)
> **dump** [key arguments]   (e.g., XENIX)

The important keys or options are:

-u	record the date and level to **/etc/ddate**
-level	set current incremental level number
-f	set the target file or device
-v	verbose (descriptive)

We haven't indicated which file system to dump or where to dump it. Most systems have established the proper defaults for this. The hard disk filesystem is usually dumped to diskette or tape. Your system documentation of **dump** will describe exactly what the current defaults are, where they are located, and how to override or change them.

If we assume that the defaults have been set properly, the following commands illustrate a dump of your file system to the default media in the two different command formats:

dump -0   : dump entire file system (e.g., PC/IX)
or
dump 0   : dump entire file system (e.g., XENIX)

dump -u -1   : dump at level 1, storing date and level in a default file.
       (e.g., PC/IX)
or
dump 1u   : dump at level 1, storing date and level in a default file.
       (e.g., XENIX)

You can see that while the syntax of some of these commands varies in different systems, the command option letter is the same.

11.3.5 *Tape Archive:* **tar**

usage: **tar** [key] [files]

Tape archive is really a misnomer, since **tar** will operate on diskette as well as on tape or normal files. For workstation systems without tape backup, you may find that this is the backup/restore utility of choice, since it is used by the system during installation. The **tar** options are very similar to **ar** options (see Chapter 9). Furthermore, they are functionally similar to the options on the other backup utilities we have discussed.

The **tar** command reads a file, */etc/default/tar*, to determine the special file for the archive. By default, this may be one of your floppy disk drives. The options direct **tar's** action:

c	create a new archive
t	list the files on the archive (table of contents)
f*special*	override default device
x	extract files
v	verbose (descriptive)

11.4 *File System Integrity*

At a workstation, the file system may cause the most problems to the user of a UNIX system. As we have seen in Chapter 4, the UNIX file system is based on pointers and tables that are dynamically updated as the file system is modified. This can lead to inconsistencies in directories, file allocation, and free list allocation. Several utility programs are provided to check and repair file system consistency, based on an interaction with the system administrator. Some systems even have a file system debugging program, **fsdb,** which operates in a manner similar to **adb** to inspect and repair file systems.

11.4.1 *File Name Check:* **ncheck**

usage: **ncheck** [options]

ncheck searches through the file system generating a report of all the filenames associated with inodes. It uncovers allocated inodes with no directories pointing to them and directory entries pointing to unallocated inodes.

11.4.2 *Directory Check:* dcheck

usage: **dcheck** [options]

dcheck checks the consistency of link count field in the file inode by searching all the directories and ensuring that the number of directory entries for a specific file matches its link count.

11.4.3 *Free/Allocated Check:* icheck

usage: **icheck** [options]

icheck creates a bitmap of all allocated space and a bitmap of all free space, then checks for consistency (one is the complement of the other). Discrepancies are usually handled by recreating the free list.

11.4.4 *Clearing Inodes:* clri

usage: **clri** inode-number

clri clears an inode and returns it to the list of free inodes. The command is sometimes helpful in repairing a damaged file system.

TABLE 11.1
istat *Information Fields*

1. Device the file resides on
2. Inode number
3. File type
4. Protection modes
5. User and group names and ids
6. Link count
7. Size of the file
8. Dates of last update and access

11.4.5 istat

usage: **istat** filename or inode#

istat prints the formatted contents of an inode by specifying either an inode number or a filename. Table 11.1 lists the information provided by **istat,** and Figure 11.4 illustrates the output of **istat** on our telephone index. The **-i** option of **ls** prints filenames with their inode numbers.

11.4.6 File System Consistency Check: fsck

fsck incorporates **icheck** and **dcheck** checking, interactively suggests repairs, and checks for the inconsistencies listed in Table 11.2. A special root directory, *lost + found*, contains files found by **fsck** that have no directory references. The output of **fsck** with a bad free list is listed in Figure 11.5, which shows the different phases of a file system check.

fsck asks the user whether the free list should be salvaged and, after a yes response and fix operation, indicates that the system should be rebooted. The **sync** operation writes out the in-core version of the superblock, which has just been shown to be incorrect. Thus, no **sync** should be performed prior to rebooting.

11.4.7 File System Debugger: fsdb

usage: **fsdb** filesystem

fsdb allows the user to interactively inspect and modify a file system. Its operation is similar to **adb,** permitting the user to reference names, inode values, physical block numbers, etc. Like **adb,** fields can be set and listed in a variety of formats.

```
$istat telindex
Inode 1165 on device 0/0          File
Type 100000 file
Protection: rw-rw-rw-
Owner: 0(root)            Group: 1(staff)
Link count:    1          Length 217 bytes

Last Updated:    Fri Sep  7  19:50:42 1987
Last Modified:   Sun Aug 12  20:03:09 1987
Last Accessed:   Sun Sep 30  14:14:48 1987
```

Figure 11.4. Output of **istat**

TABLE 11.2
fsck *Consistency Checks*

1. Multiple pointers to the same block
2. Invalid pointers
3. Incorrect link counts
4. Incorrect inode format
5. Dangling Blocks (block not pointed to anywhere)
6. Dangling Directory References (point to unallocated inode)
7. Superblock checks
8. Free-block list checks

11.5 *Scheduling Periodic Activity:* **cron**

Daemons are active processes that are not associated with any terminal. These processes perform ongoing activities which manage and maintain the active UNIX system. We have already discussed the background print spooling process. In this section we describe the process of scheduling periodic activities. In general, daemons are started up when UNIX is initialized. The */etc/rc* initialization shell script contains the commands that start them.

cron is a process that periodically looks up a special table, *crontab,*

```
/dev/rhd0
File System: unlabeled fs

** Checking /dev/rhd0
** Phase 1 - Check Blocks and Sizes
** Phase 2 - Check Pathnames
** Phase 3 - Check Connectivity
** Phase 4 - Check Reference Counts
** Phase 5 - Check Free List
3 BLK(S) MISSING
BAD FREE LIST
SALVAGE? yes
** Phase 6 - Salvage Free List
1220 files 12502 blocks 481 free

***** MOUNTED FILE SYSTEM HAS BEEN MODIFIED - REBOOT (NO SYNC!) *****
```

Figure 11.5. Output of **fsck** with a Bad Free List

which contains entries describing the execution of regularly scheduled activities. Figure 11.6 illustrates the fields of a *crontab* entry. By adding entries to *crontab*, you can schedule a variety of activities to occur on a predetermined schedule.

The values of the first five fields can specify a single value, a list of values separated by commas, a range indicated with a dash, or all possible values indicated by an asterisk. In the example, the spelling dictionary is compressed at 2:45 AM every Sunday.

11.6 *I/O Devices and Special Files*

I/O devices are handled in a simple way by UNIX. Each available device is represented in the file system by a special file, and I/O activity is performed using file I/O operations on this special file. This unifying concept means that access to the devices is through the file I/O processing routines. For example, when redirecting I/O to a file, we usually specified files that were on disk (or diskette) and part of the UNIX file system:

```
$cat myfile > newfile
.
.
.
ctrl-D
$
```

We can access devices directly by referencing them symbolically through their special file names. For example, if the line printer special file is called

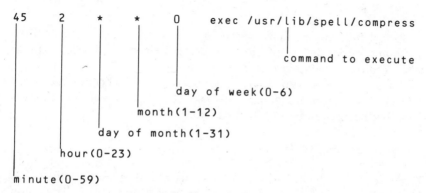

Figure 11.6. *crontab* Fields

lp and resides in the /*dev* directory, to list the file *myfile* directly on the printer you would enter:

```
$cat myfile >/dev/lp
```

Note that this bypasses the print spooling facility of your system, but it may be easier to use and it provides less system overhead. If you are the only user on the system, print spooling may not be necessary in all cases. To have the printer going while you are doing other work, simply indicate background processing by using the & notation:

```
$cat myfile >/dev/lp &
```

This representation of devices is quite general, and applies to all file operations that make sense (you can't use *lp* as standard input).

11.6.1 Adding New Devices: mknod

usage: **mknod** specialname [b] [c] major minor

When we say "adding new devices," we are talking about adding devices for which your UNIX system has supporting device drivers. Writing and installing new device drivers is beyond the scope of our discussion, and in most cases, the drivers accompanying your UNIX system will suffice. UNIX manuals have differing organizations, but one section will contain descriptions of the drivers in your system.

Associated with each driver are a major device number and a minor device number. The major device number identifies the device and entry point in the kernel for the device driver. The minor device number indicates either a specific device within the class of the major device number or device characteristics. The meaning of the minor device number will depend on the device.

Special files are symbolic names in the /**dev** directory which provide major and minor device information (device driver and device characteristics). Adding a new device on systems for which the driver is present and the hardware port is known involves using the **mknod** command to create a special file. For example, to create a special file for communications port 2 on the IBM PC under PC/IX, you enter:

```
$mknod /dev/ttynew c 5 17
```

This command will create the *ttynew* special file as a character I/O type file for the asynchronous adapter driver (major number, 5). The value 17 indicates that the second port is to be addressed with modem control enabled.

11.6.2 Formatting Diskettes: **format**

Many UNIX systems will have some mechanism for formatting diskettes. The simplest will be a **format** command that takes a device number as an argument and formats the diskette on the device:

```
$ format /dev/rfd0
```

Some versions provide a more general formatting utility that operates as an interactive subsystem, in which your responses determine the type and characteristics of the format.

11.6.3 Creating File Systems: **mkfs**

usage: **mkfs** device prototype

File systems, as defined in Chapter 4, consist of a superblock, inode list, data, and free areas. The **mkfs** command will create a file system on the specified device. (Our discussion will pertain to diskettes since, as a maintenance activity, you may want to create separate file systems on diskettes, then mount and dismount them.) The command assumes a properly formatted diskette. The first argument is the special file name of the diskette drive on which the diskette resides. The second argument, *prototype*, is a file which contains a description of the file system to be created. Prototype descriptions consist of tokens (strings separated by blanks or newlines), which describe the characteristics of the file system to be created. The first few tokens include:

boot program
size in blocks
number of inodes
root file description
$

For example:

```
/bin/unix
640 160
    .
    .
    .
$
```

The first three tokens are the boot program, size, and inode list size. Additional tokens would describe the root directory file. Since the characteristics of the prototype will vary from system to system, refer to your system documentation for a further description on the prototype. As in other UNIX utilities, sometimes there will be a prototype file already created which you may use as a model to create file systems.

11.6.4 *Accessing Alternate File Systems:* **mount, umount**

usage: **mount** specialfile directory

Once we have created a file system, we will want to access it as part of the current file system. This is accomplished with the **mount** command, which specifies the special file (device containing the diskette) and a directory name by which access to the file system is gained. For example, if a special file *rfd0* contains the new file system, we mount it by specifying:

```
mount /dev/rfd0 mydir
```

This creates an entry into the special table */etc/mnttab*, which contains a list of all mounted file systems; **mount** with no options lists the currently mounted volumes. Figure 11.7 illustrates the before and after **mount** file hierarchy. Prior to the mount, a directory listing of mydir yields an empty directory. After the mount, the root file system of the mounted volume is displayed as *mydir*.

The **umount** command (**unmount** on some systems) logically removes the named volume:

```
umount /dev/rfd0
```

You should be sure to unmount all volumes before physically removing them or shutting down the system.

11.7 *Automating System Administration*

In this chapter we have covered the types of activities which must be performed as system administrator. It is obvious that some of these tasks are important and require more than a beginner's understanding of UNIX. In order to make it easier for both new and experienced users, many vendors have incorporated administration procedures into subsystems. In fact, we have seen this in the **adduser** and **mkuser** utilities described above. As

Before **mount:**

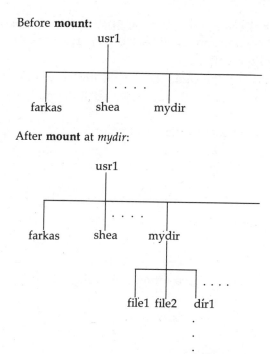

Figure 11.7. Effect of **mount** Command

another example, system accounting, which produces reports on system activity, may be a collection of shell scripts that collect information from system files and display it in an understandable format. AT&T System V has taken this even further by providing a menu-driven system, **sysadm,** for most of the system administration activities you will have to perform.

11.8 Further Exploration

This chapter covers some basic administration activities necessary to maintain your UNIX system. Because of the variety of versions, in many cases it is not possible to give exact procedures, but we have attempted to provide the necessary concepts to make your system documentation more readable. Try some of the following system administration functions:

1. Format a diskette (if your system supports diskettes).
2. Create a file system on the diskette.
3. Create a directory in your home directory and mount the new file system.

4. Backup a directory (one that will fit) onto the mounted volume. Note that this is another way to backup data from the main file system.

5. Unmount the volume.

6. Try backing up the same directory with **tar, dump,** and **cpio.**

7. Set up a new user with a different shell (if you have more than one shell available).

8. Which daemons are running in your system?

9. Use *crontab* to initiate a periodic activity (e.g., copy files from one directory to another as backup).

11.9 *Manual References*

acctcom	generate accounting reports
acct	turn on accounting processing
adduser	add new users
at	schedule future processes
ar	archive utility
clri	clear inode
cpio	copy standard input to output
cron	scheduling daemon
dcheck	directory check
dump	incremental dump utility
find	filename search and process
fsck	file system check utility
fsdb	file system debugger
icheck	inode check
init	UNIX initialization process
istat	display inode status
ncheck	generate names from inodes
passwd	set new password
restor	restore **dump** volumes
restore	restore **dump** volumes
shutdown	turn off a UNIX system
sync	write superblock to disk
tar	tape archive utility

12

UNIX Communications

UNIX contains a collection of comprehensive tools for intrasystem communication, intersystem communication with other UNIX systems, and facilities to communicate with other operating systems. The marketplace is rapidly augmenting UNIX communications capability by offering local area network support, a variety of operating system interfaces, and connections to existing communications architectures, such as IBM's SNA. In this chapter we look at some of the facilities and commands which are distributed with most UNIX systems.

Keep in mind that for these utilities to work, you must have appropriate hardware and UNIX device software support. Many systems provide support for common modems and communications devices, but you must check your system documentation to see what is required on your system. In this chapter we cover the communications features that are standard on most UNIX systems, including:

Electronic Mail
UNIX-to-UNIX Networking
Access to Remote Systems
UNIX-to-IBM Communications

12.1 Electronic Mail

Electronic mail is a systemwide facility for communicating with other users. It is used by some of the system programs to communicate the status of ongoing activities. It can also be used in a UNIX network to send and receive mail to and from other systems.

12.1.1 Mailboxes

All mail received is placed in a user mailbox (*/usr/mail* on System V and */usr/spool/mail* on Berkeley UNIX). The mailbox is accessed at several different times. When you log on, if the mailbox has been updated since the last login, you will be notified and a message will appear on your screen: ''You have mail.'' You may also check your mail by using the mail command and subcommands.

12.1.2 Sending Mail

The **mail** command sends messages to one or more users. It sends the standard input to the user login names on the command line. For example, to send mail to Smith and Jones, you enter:

```
$ mail smith jones
```

If you have a file to send, you then redirect the standard input:

```
$ mail smith jones < mailfile
```

Otherwise, **mail** will read standard input, a series of lines terminated by *ctrl-D:*

```
$ mail smith jones
Hi.
This note is to inform you
that I have resigned effective
today.
Bye.
ctrl-D
$
```

12.1.3 Reading and Processing Your Mail

The **mail** command has its own commands that read, store, forward, and respond to mail, and it has a set of subcommands to support functions that govern the way in which mail is handled. The **mail** subsystem is entered by typing in the **mail** command with no user names as arguments. If you have no mail, you will read "no mail." If there is mail in the mailbox, the **mail** subsystem will be entered and you will be given a ? prompt. A question mark entry at this point will list the available subcommands. The order in which messages are printed and the manner in which they are disposed of is governed by the options of subcommands specified when **mail** is entered. Table 12.1 lists the **mail** command line options. Table 12.2 lists **mail** subcommands.

12.1.3.1 Displaying Messages on the Screen.   Upon entering **mail** after the first message has been printed, you may continue to display messages either by hitting the carriage return or by typing in the **p** subcommand. The order of messages is determined by options to the **mail** command when it is initially entered. The default order is most recent first.

***12.1.3.2 Saving the Message:* s or w**

usage: **s**[myfile]

or

w[myfile]

Occasionally, you will want to save a message which has been sent to you, especially if it is a data file.

By default, the system will set up a file in your home directory called *mbox,* and messages are saved here. You may specify another filename for saved messages. The **w** command, which saves the message without the normal header (date, time, and sender), is a convenient way to save a file that has been sent by another user.

TABLE 12.1
mail *Command Line Options*

no option	display messages in last-in last-out order
−r	display messages in first-in first-out order
−p	prints the messages without entering the subsystem
−q	undeleted mail goes back into the mailbox

TABLE 12.2
mail *Subsystem Subcommands*

q	quit
x	exit without changing mail
p	print
s [*file*]	save (default *mbox*)
w [*file*]	save without header
–	print previous
d	delete
+	next (no delete)
m [*user*]	mail to user
! *cmd*	execute UNIX cmd

12.1.3.3 *Deleting the Message:* **d.** Usually, after reading messages, you will want to delete them. After the message has been displayed and the ? prompt has appeared, the **d** command will delete that message.

12.1.3.4 *Escape to the Shell:* **!**

usage: **!**UNIX command

In processing your messages, you may want to check something in your file system or perform another activity without leaving the **mail** subsystem. Similar to the way this was done by **ed,** you can execute any UNIX command by preceding it with an exclamation point. If you enter **!sh** you will invoke a new shell and you can enter any number if **Unix** commands until you exit with a *ctrl-D.*

12.1.3.5 *Forwarding Mail:* **m**

usage: **m** user ID list

You can reroute the current message by using the **m** subcommand with the user login name of the person or persons to which you are sending the message.

12.1.3.6 *Leaving the Mail Subsystem:* **q** or *crtl-D.* To quit mail, you simple enter end-of-file, *crtl-D* or the **q** subcommand.

12.1.4 *The Berkeley and AT&T System Mail Subsystems*

Berkeley, AT&T System V (**mailx**), XENIX, and other UNIX versions provide more comprehensive electronic mail facilities than we have just described. While providing the same subcommands described above, they also provide for:

Replying directly to mail.

Displaying a message summary.

Editing messages from within the mail subsystem.

Establishing a mail environment similar to the shell or **ex** environment.

Establishing distribution lists.

Establishing carbon copy lists.

Table 12.3 lists the expanded **mail** commands.

12.1.4.1 Replying to Messages. In addition to saving or deleting your mail, you can reply directly to the sender with the **R** command. This places you in the input mode, as if you had issued mail specifying the originating user. R (lower case) replies to all recipients as well as to the sender.

12.1.4.2 Message Summaries. The **top** command takes message numbers as arguments and may be used to summarize selected messages by displaying the first few lines.

top 1 2	summarizes messages 1 and 2
top $	summarizes the last message
top *	summarizes all messages

12.1.4.3 Editing Messages. For long messages, it may be desirable to use an editor rather than straight line-by-line data entry (you might make a

TABLE 12.3
Expanded **mail** *Commands and Their Abbreviations*

alias (a)	user alias list
cd (c)	change working directory
dp (d)	delete current message, print next
edit (e)	invoke editor
exit (x)	return to shell without updating *mbox*
file (fi)	displays the file being read; if *mbox* the owner
forward (f)	forwards the current message
headers (h)	lists message headers
list	lists **mail** subcommands
lpr (l)	sends messages to line printer
reply (r)	responds to messages
set (se)	displays and sets current **mail** options
shell (sh)	invokes a shell
top (t)	prints the top few lines of messages
unset (uns)	inverts the set for mail options
visual (v)	invokes **vi**
write (w)	saves the current message

typing error or want to change something). This is done by entering one of **mail**'s escape commands, which are indicated by a tilde (~) at the beginning of the line. To invoke one of the editors, you enter ~**e** (for **ed** or the default editor) or ~**v** (for **vi**). After editing the message, exiting from the editor leaves you *back in the message input mode* and you can continue entering the message. Table 12.4 summarizes the **mail** escape commands.

12.1.4.4 mail *Options*. Options to **mail** can be specified in a local file called *.mailrc*, which functions in a manner similar to the **ex/vi** or shell profiles. The options are either set and unset with the **set** and **unset** commands, or they are given string values. For example, to cause messages to print in chronological order, you would set **chron**. To be prompted for a subject during message preparation, you would set **asksubject**. String options may be used to describe the default editor or shell to invoke with the compose escape commands:

```
EDITOR /bin/ex
SHELL /bin/csh
```

The **mail** options are summarized in Tables 12.5a and 12.5b.

12.1.4.5 *Distribution Lists*. Distribution lists are set up by establishing aliases (in the C-shell manner) and including them in the *.mailrc* file. For example, to establish a distribution list for your friends, you might enter:

```
alias friends bill mary sue john
```

TABLE 12.4
mail *Escape Commands*

~?	displays escape commands
~.	EOF on new line
~!cmd	shell escape
~¦cmd	pipe to command
~_mail-command	escape to execute mail command
~:mail command	escape to execute mail command
~ alias	display aliases
~b name	adds name to blind carbon copy list
~c name	adds name to carbon copy list
~cc	same as ~c
~p	prints messages collected
~q	aborts message being sent
~Return name	adds name to return-receipt-to field
~s string	sets string as current subject
~t name	adds name to recipient list
~v	invokes **vi**
~w filename	saves message body in filename

TABLE 12.5a
Expanded mail *Options*

askcc	causes prompting for carbon copy recipients
asksubject	causes prompting for subject
autombox	defaults to saving messages in user mailbox
autoprint	causes delete command to delete the message and print it
chron	causes messages to be displayed in chronological order
dot	sets dot as EOF for message composition
execmail	sets sending of mail to background
ignore	sets ignore interrupt signals (@ displayed)
mchron	lists messages in received first order but display chronologically (when sent) order
metoo	include sender group expansions
nosave	aborted messages not appended to dead.letter
quiet	suppresses printing of mail version header
verify	verifies target mail recipients

TABLE 12.5b
mail *Options with String Values*

EDITOR pathname	sets the editor to use
SHELL pathname	sets the shell to use
VISUAL	sets the visual editor to use
escape	sets escape character if different from ~
page=n	lines/page when displaying text
record pathname	file to save outgoing mail
toplines n	sets number of lines to display with top

Assuming that the names are user names, entering mail with the username *friends* will send the message to all four users.

12.1.5 Electronic Conversations: write

The **write** facility initiates an on-line electronic conversation between users. You initiate your side of the conversation by issuing the **write** command with the ID of a user who is currently logged on. Once UNIX makes the connection, all subsequent lines entered at your terminal are displayed on the other user's terminal. The other user then responds with **write** and your user ID.

Once in the **write** mode, messages are interleaved, since lines are displayed as soon as they are written. It is a good idea to establish your own protocol or "handshaking" so that communication flows more consistently. This is similar to radio communications in which the operators use "over" to indicate the end of a message, and "over and out" when the conversation is to be concluded. For example, some users end all of their messages with a few asterisks. In this way, you know when the other party is finished, and you can begin. A typical dialogue is illustrated in Figure 12.1a. Rice enters **write,** which causes the initiation message to be displayed. Rice uses **o** on a line by itself as an abbreviation for "over," and **oo** for "over and out." When you wish to end the conversation, simply enter a *ctrl-D* which will display the EOF message and return you to the UNIX prompt.

12.1.6 *Sending Messages to All Users:* **wall**

The **wall** command operates like **write,** except that instead of targeting the message to an individual user, the message is sent to all users on the system. The message displayed identifies the sender and the text of his message, as shown in Figure 12.1b.

12.1.7 *Inhibiting Messages:* **mesg**

usage: **mesg** [y or n]

If you are in the middle of an activity and do not wish to be interrupted by system or user **write** messages, you may use the **mesg** command to disable them. The **mesg n** command prevents your terminal from receiving messages, while **mesg y** enables them. The default is to receive messages. If you try to initiate an electronic conversation with a terminal to which messages have been blocked, a message denying permission will be displayed.

```
$ write rice
Hello, BillieAnn, I just wanted to know if you
are interested in lunch
o
Message from rice tty0...
yes I am, how about 1:00
o
You're on. Bye for now
oo
ctrl-D
EOF
$
```

Figure 12.1a. Write Dialogue

Sent:

```
#wall
Please Log Off.
The system is coming down in 15 minutes.
ctrl-D
#
```

Displayed:

```
Broadcast from root tty0 ...

Please Log Off.
The system is coming down in 15 minutes.
```

Figure 12.1b. wall Operation

12.2 Remote Access to Other Systems

Your UNIX system has a number of facilities for connecting with remote systems such as Compuserv, the Source, Dow Jones, etc. Most UNIX systems have the **cu** command, used for dialing into other systems. IBM versions (PC/IX, AIX) use **connect,** which operates in a similar fashion. Both commands are used for remote login to UNIX or other computing systems.

12.2.1 Call UNIX: cu

usage: **cu** [options] telephone number

The **cu** command contacts a remote system by dialing the specified telephone number and setting transmission characteristics specified in the options. Once the connection is made, you can escape the transmission mode to perform a variety of activities by using the tilde (~) escape symbol. In this sense, **cu** operates as a subsystem of UNIX with its own set of subcommands. The options governing the transmission include:

    -s speed   set the transmission speed (110–9600)

    -a acu   specify automatic calling unit

Once the connection has been made you can interact with the remote system as a normal user or escape to the local environment and perform a variety of functions. The tilde (~) indicates local mode commands.

***12.2.1.1 File Transfer:* %take** *and* **%put.**   Files can be transmitted both to and from the remote system in a number of ways. The simplest technique is to use the **%take** and **%put** commands, which transfer files between your system and the remote one:

```
^%take remotefile [to localfile]

^%put localfile [to remotefile]
```

To use **%take** and **%put,** you must be communicating with another UNIX system and the terminal characteristics of both systems must have common attributes. If you are communicating with a non-UNIX system, it is still possible to transfer data, but you must use a variation of I/O redirection.

To send lines of data, you specify a file whose lines will be copied as if typed at the terminal. For example, on the remote system you might be in the editor's input mode. The following command would insert the local file into the remote one:

> ~ < localfile   takes the lines from the file specified
> as lines typed at the terminal.
>
> ~ >

A similar command is used at your end. By using I/O redirection, you indicate that the following lines are to be placed in the specified file:

```
~> localfile
  lines from the remote system
 ~ >
```

In this example, the opening command could also have been specified with an append notation, > >. In both cases, the operation is terminated with a greater than symbol (>).

```
      ~ >
```

12.2.1.2 *Local Execution of Commands.* There are several ways in which to execute UNIX commands during a remote terminal session. These may be summarized as follows:

> ~!   escape to a local shell
> ~!cmd   execute a single command on the local system
> ~$cmd   execute a single command on the local
>   system and send the output to the remote system

12.2.1.3 *Terminating a Connection.* After logging off the remote system, to terminate the physical connection, you enter either an end-of-file, *ctrl-D,* or the termination command, ~ .

12.2.2 *Connection to Remote Systems:* **connect**

usage: **connect** [options]

IBM UNIX systems (e.g., PC/IX, AIX) use **connect,** which performs the same functions as **cu.** To extract the communications parameters for the remote connection, **connect** uses a system file, *connect.con.* It first searches a local *bin* directory, *$HOME/bin,* for the symbolic connection name and, if not present, checks the *connect.con* file in a system-defined directory, */usr/ lib/INnet.* For example, to call an information service, Compuserv, there would be an entry in the *connect.con* file entitled ''compuserv.'' To initiate a connection, you would simply enter:

```
$ connect compuserve
```

The parameters of the transmission, speed, telephone number, etc., are established, and the connection is initiated. Similar to **cu,** once you have made a connection, you can escape to a local mode and execute a variety of commands. As soon as the connection is made, an escape sequence will be displayed. This is used to escape to a local mode. It is a good idea to write it down, since you will need to escape to the local mode to use local system UNIX commands, transfer files, and log off from the remote system. The default for most systems is three characters.

```
$ ctrl-Vu ctrl-M
LOCAL:
```

Once in the local mode, the LOCAL: prompt is displayed.

12.2.2.1 File Transfer. The **i** command writes the file specified to the remote system. It operates in the same manner as the redirected I/O in **cu.** To transfer the file, you set the remote system in the input mode (e.g., **ex,** **cat**), then escape to the local mode and transfer the file.

```
$cat > filename
$ctrl-Vu ctrl-M
LOCAL: ifilename
```

To download files from the remote system you would use the transcript command, **t.** This establishes a local file containing a transcript of the data passing through the connection. For example, to download a C program, *remote.c,* into the local system as *local.c:*

```
$ctrl-Vu ctrl M
LOCAL: tlocal.c
<CR>
$cat remote.c
$ctrl-Vu ctrl M
LOCAL: t-
```

In the example above, we first escape to local mode and open a transcript file called *local.c*. We then return to the remote session and display the file. The transcript is captured in *remote.c.*, and returning to local move **t-** closes the current transcription file. It could be reopened with **t+**, or a new file can be created with **t***filename*.

12.2.2.2 *Escape to the Local Shell.* When using **connect**, you first must escape to **connect**'s local mode by entering the break sequence (*ctrl-Vu ctrl-M*), then invoking the execute UNIX command (!), similar to **cu.**

```
$ctrl-Vu ctrl-M : remote system prompt ($)
LOCAL: !sh     : escape to SHELL
$  .           : enter local UNIX commands
    .
    .
LOCAL:<CR>     : return to remote mode
$
```

If you enter the **sh** command, you will escape to a local shell.

12.2.2.3 *Terminating the Connection.* To disconnect from the remote system after logging off, you must first enter the local mode, then use either the **quit** (q) or **disconnect** (d) command. This exits the **connect** subcommand mode as well:

```
$ctrl-Vu ctrl-M : escape to local mode
LOCAL:d         : enter disconnect
$
```

Since the effect of **d** or **q** is only to close the port, be sure to log off the remote system first.

12.3 UNIX-to-UNIX Network: *uucp*

uucp is the general name given to a collection of utilities for the creation and operation of a UNIX-to-UNIX network. The network involves systems connecting to other UNIX systems, either directly or indirectly, through other systems on the network. Connection to a network node may use any number of communications interconnection techniques, including dialup and direct cabling. Individual directories on remote systems are accessed by giving path names that include a system node path followed by a directory path name.

The syntax for accessing remote nodes is to follow a node name with an !, indicating that the name is part of a remote system reference. For example, a reference to a file, */usr/smith/file1*, on system *usys1* would be expressed as *usys1!/usr/smith/file1*. Keep in mind that some systems (C-shell) interpret the ! as a special character, and when used in a **uucp** file name, it must be quoted.

In a large network, it is not necessary for each system to be connected to every other one. When a request is received, **uucp** processing interprets the **uucp** system node path name, and if the request is not directed to it, it is passed on to the next node in the system. This assumes, of course, that the interpreting node is connected to the next appropriate node. Looking at Figure 12.2, to reach *usys3* from *usys1*, you give the intermediate node references, *usys2* and *usys3*:

```
usys2!usys3!/usr/smith/file1
```

In general, this mechanism works quite well. A typical example is a situation in which an organization has many machines. One system will be the interface to the outside world, say, on some public or private switching network. We will call it *usysout*. At each division there may be a system, *udiv1*, *udiv2*, etc., each of which are connected to usysout, and within each division, there may be several systems connected to their division systems.

Access to an individual directory in the organization from outside the organization is gained through the usysout and division systems. For example, the address of smith in division 2 is *usysout!udiv2!usys3!/usr/smith* (see Figure 12.3). Note that there may be multiple paths to a particular node. At each **uucp** site, there is a list of installations managed by **uucp,** to which a connection can be made. As requests are made, they are satisfied by calling or connecting to the appropriate system.

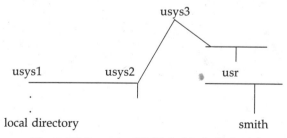

Figure 12.2. **uucp** Multiple Node Reference

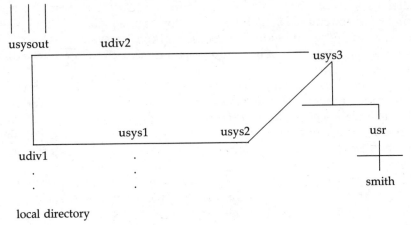

local directory

Figure 12.3. uucp Network

While it is beyond the scope of this book to describe how to set up **uucp** processing on your computer, it is important to understand how it operates from a functional point of view. If you have access to a system on a **uucp** network, you may actually be connected to thousands of users worldwide! Even if you are not a **uucp** site, you can use **connect** or **cu** from your system to connect with a system that has **uucp** installed.

In the next sections we look at the basic commands supported by **uucp.**

12.3.1 UNIX-to-UNIX Copy: **uucp**

usage: **uucp** [options] sourcefile ... destinationfile

uucp is a program that operates in a manner similar to **cp;** the difference is that **uucp** filenames may contain pathnames that include system names. The purpose of **uucp** is to collect the files from the systems specified in the *sourcefile* specifications and to copy them to the specified destination. Using our example in Figure 12.3, a user outside the network we have shown can copy files from his or her local system, as well as some of the shown systems, to the smith user:

```
$uucp file1 !sysout!div1!sys1!/usr/jones/jonesfile
sysout!div2!usys3/usr/smith
$
```

Using the mail facility **uucp** notifies the user that the **uucp** operation has been completed (**-m**), and also notifies the user in whose directory the copied files are placed (**-r***user*).

12.3.2 *UNIX-to-UNIX Command Execution:* **uux**

Another utility that uses the **uucp** subsystem and network is **uux,** which gathers source files from remote UNIX systems on the network and executes a command on a remote system. Standard output may be directed to a specified remote system on the network. For example, referring to Figure 12.3 again, if the user outside the systems shown wanted to use a specific print utility that was only available on system *usys3,* the following **uux** command would gather files from the local system, *f1* and *f2,* execute the command on the *usys3* system, and send standard output to the user's current directory. Optionally, a remote system could be specified for the redirected standard output:

```
uux !usysout!div2!/usr/smith/prutility f1 f2 >myfile
```

There are a number of other **uucp** commands and utilities that support the **uucp** environment. For example, to check the status of the **uucp** link, you use the **uustat** command. If you want to check the directly accessible **uucp** nodes, you list the known **uucp** system names with **uuname.**

12.4 *UNIX-to-Other-System Communications*

One of the major applications of your UNIX system may be as a front end, or workstation, to some type of mainframe computer. Many UNIX systems, especially those from manufacturers of mainframe equipment, will provide utilities for file transfer, interactive access, and remote job entry to mainframe hardware and operating systems. Most of these are not part of the UNIX system but are supplied by third-party vendors or the brand of hardware that the UNIX systems run on. We discuss some of these in Chapter 13.

One UNIX system connection we will discuss is UNIX-to-IBM, because several versions do contain IBM remote job entry (RJE) capability, and they provide the utilities to submit jobs and receive output from IBM mainframe hosts. The IBM system must include your UNIX system as an RJE station, and the RJE software must be in place on your system.

The command to submit a job to the IBM system, **send,** reads control statements and IBM Job Control Language (JCL) from standard input. You must have a valid job account number on the IBM system in order for your job to run. The **send** command processes arguments that determine the source of the input statements (e.g., a file, standard input, or the terminal), execute local UNIX commands, determine the host IBM system, and so forth. A status command, **rjestat,** will give you information about the availability of the rje link.

12.5 Further Exploration

As we have seen in this chapter, UNIX provides a broad set of utilities, systems, and tools for intra- and intersystem communications. Try out some of these features:

1. Which **mail** command is on your system? Send mail to another user.
2. Use **cu** or **connect** to dial out to another system. Try transferring files (download or upload).
3. Is **uucp** installed on your system? Which systems are you directly connected to (**uuname**). Send a message to someone on another system.
4. What other communications support is available? Is there a local area network? Are you connected to a non-UNIX host?

12.6 Command References

mail	electronic mail
mailx	electronic mail (AT&T System V)
mesg	enable/disable messages
rjestat	RJE status
send	submit RJE job stream
uucp	UNIX-to-UNIX copy
uupick	UNIX-to-UNIX copy
uustat	uucp status
uuto	UNIX-to-UNIX copy
uux	UNIX-to-UNIX execution
wall	send a message to all users
write	communicate with a single user

13

UNIX and Personal Computers

In this chapter we conclude our discussion of the UNIX operating system and address the trend in the computer industry, as well as the UNIX community, to put computing power at the user desktop. Several issues arise that are of interest to all users but specifically to users of workstations:

UNIX Workstations
UNIX Versions
Local Area Networks
Wide Area Networks
Connection to Non-UNIX Hosts
UNIX and MS-DOS

13.1 UNIX Workstations

By a workstation, we mean a UNIX system operated by a single user. This implies compact size as well as relatively low cost. They are machines that provide all the functions of UNIX at the desktop and that may be interfaced in some way to other workstations, UNIX systems, and non-UNIX systems, either in a network or to a host or file server. At the low end are personal computers and at the higher end are scientific workstations.

13.1.1 Personal Computer–Based Workstations

These systems provide the full function of a personal computer, having been designed primarily for that use. The portability of UNIX (that is, the ability to transfer it to different architectures) has allowed the system to be introduced on a variety of machines.

UNIX is available on these machines in one of two ways, either as a proprietary version of UNIX (licensed through AT&T directly or indirectly) or through a third-party UNIX vendor. A third approach, UNIX lookalikes, doesn't seem to have caught on. While there are too many UNIX PC-based workstations to discuss here, the next sections describe a few of the significant ones.

13.1.1.1 AT&T Personal Computer Workstations. AT&T offers UNIX on its entire commercial computer line and has two personal computer products. The AT&T 6300 Plus is an IBM PC compatible computer running UNIX on an additional board. The AT&T UNIX PC/7300 is a UNIX workstation with a fully-integrated graphics interface which provides a windowed menu-driven environment. Both systems run AT&T's System V, making it compatible with other systems in their computer line.

13.1.1.2 IBM PC/XT and IBM PC/AT. IBM's initial involvement with UNIX was on the IBM PC/XT with a version of UNIX from Interactive Systems Corporation called PC/IX. When the IBM PC/AT was introduced, PC/IX was upgraded to support the machine, and XENIX (see below) was introduced for the AT. Both systems are purchased through IBM and are currently System V compatible.

13.1.1.3 Tandy 3000. Tandy was one of the first personal computer manufacturers to introduce UNIX (as XENIX). Originally, these were proprietary. As of this writing, both Microsoft and the Santa Cruz Operation versions of XENIX run on the IBM PC/AT compatible TANDY 3000.

13.1.1.4 Hewlett-Packard Integral Personal Computer. The Integral PC is a single-user, multitasking MC68000-based system running HP's HP-UX. It includes a built in display, printer, and keyboard and weighs only 25 pounds.

13.1.2 Third-Party Vendor-Supplied UNIX

The second type of personal computer UNIX system comes from software publishers who develop, enhance, market, and distribute UNIX systems. While there are a number of these in the marketplace due to the popularity IBM personal computers and compatibles, IBM PC versions seem to dominate. There are two of interest.

13.1.2.1 XENIX.   One of the most popular UNIX systems is XENIX. Developed by Microsoft, XENIX runs on a variety of personal computers. XENIX is licensed either directly to the hardware manufacture (e.g., IBM PC/AT XENIX) or to value-adding software houses who then provide versions for different personal computer systems. One company, The Santa Cruz Operation (SCO), distributes its version of XENIX for IBM compatibles (PC/XT and PC/AT), Tandy Personal Computers, the AT&T 6300 Plus, among others.

Microsoft's next version of XENIX (by agreement with AT&T) will be System V Release 3.

13.1.2.2 VENIX.   VENIX, developed by VenturCom Inc., is a System V compatible version of UNIX that runs on IBM PC's and compatibles. A version of VENIX also has been developed for the Data General One laptop computer. Like XENIX, VENIX supports the C-shell and most of the Berkeley enhancements.

13.1.3 Scientific Workstations

When most people think of workstations, engineering or scientific workstations come to mind. In the past they have been midpriced mini-computers with high resolution graphics supporting applications that require a significant amount of computer power at the desktop (e.g., real-time graphics, cad/cam, scientific computation, engineering applications and scientific languages). UNIX became a popular operating system for these systems because it provided an existing standard development environment and because of its multiprogramming facilities.

In the past few years, the prices of engineering workstations have dropped to the point of competing with desktop personal computers in cost while continuing to provide the necessary performance. Most of the major computer manufacturers have products for the scientific workstation market, but two systems have gained significant attention.

The first, a recent entry into the workstation market, is the Berkeley 4.2-based Sun Microsystems workstation. One of the founders of Sun is Bill Joy, an original designer of Berkeley 4.2. The Sun Workstation is distinguished by high performance hardware supporting multiple users and high resolution real-time graphics.

The second is IBM's PC/RT. The RT incorporates a new type of processor design that reduces the size and complexity of the machine instruction set with the goal of improving performance. The concept is called Reduced Instruction Set Computer or RISC—hence PC/RT for RISC Technology. The PC/RT runs a System V compatible version of UNIX, AIX from Interactive Systems Corp.

13.2 INTEL 80386 Chip

As of this writing, the trade press is filled with articles about the next generation of microprocessors, which will bring high-speed computer performance to the desktop. It is anticipated that to support multiprogramming and multi-user environments, UNIX will emerge as the operating system of choice.

13.3 Connection to Non-UNIX Systems

The 1980s has seen an explosion in data and voice communication technology, and this has not been ignored by the UNIX community. In the last chapter we described the specifics of the communications tools available with UNIX. Here we describe some of the issues of concern when the communication is between UNIX and non-UNIX systems.

If UNIX is to be the operating system supporting nodes in both local area and wide area networks, it will be necessary to have software to communicate with the various types of common network protocols, including IBM's SNA and TCP/IP. Many vendors are offering interconnection hardware and software to provide these facilities.

Some vendors have homogeneous network systems to support the interconnection of UNIX machines, including AT&T's STARLAN local area network and Microsoft XENIX's MICNET for RS-232 connections of PC's. This is one area of significant change and you should be aware of your network needs before deciding on a basic UNIX workstation.

13.4 Developing Networked Applications

In a networked or distributed environment in which applications will access data that may be distributed in different parts of the network, strategies are necessary to incorporate distributed file processing into the UNIX file system. Three of these strategies are the TCP/IP based Network File System (NFS) from Sun Microsystems, the OSI based Remote File Sharing (RFS) in AT&T System V, and a distributed database management system, Prelude, which runs under VENIX, developed by VenturCom, Inc.

These software strategies make the accessing of distributed files transparent to the user by incorporating network file operations (e.g., read, write, etc.) into UNIX I/O system calls which integrate with the UNIX file and I/O systems (e.g., redirection of I/O, piping, etc.).

Users with distributed file processing requirements should explore these features in the systems they are using.

13.5 *UNIX and MS-DOS*

With the proliferation of IBM-PC compatible computers, and the MS-DOS operating system, the marketplace has indicated a need for some type of compatibility between UNIX and MS-DOS. That there should be a relationship between the two operating systems is not surprising, since both MS-DOS and XENIX have been written by Microsoft. In fact, from the user's point of view, the two systems have many similarities.

MS-DOS is the generic version of the operating system from Microsoft. PC-DOS is the IBM-PC version. Functionally the two are identical, so we will say DOS for MS-DOS or PC-DOS. DOS Version 2.0 and higher provide the support of hierarchical directories and many of the UNIX-like commands. Our discussion below concerns these DOS versions.

In the discussion of compatibility, we address two issues in the following sections:

1. A comparison of DOS and UNIX—their similarities and differences.
2. The hardware and software tools that have become available for the coexistence of UNIX and DOS on the same computer system.

13.5.1 *A Comparison of UNIX and DOS*

As indicated above, there are many similarities between the two systems. In fact, it is much easier for a DOS user to learn UNIX (and the other way around) than for users of other systems. Below we highlight the major areas of interest to the DOS user learning UNIX.

13.5.1.1 The File System. Both UNIX and MS-DOS have hierarchical file systems with a single root directory. The commands which manipulate the hierarchy operate in much the same fashion. Table 13.1 lists the file processing functions, UNIX commands, and associated MS-DOS commands. Notice how some of the command names are identical.

The major differences between DOS and UNIX are:

1. *Access.* DOS accesses multiple file systems on-line, rather than a single file system spanning multiple volumes.

In DOS, a file system (complete hierarchy) is limited to one fixed disk

TABLE 13.1
Comparison of UNIX and DOS Commands

Function	UNIX command	DOS Command
Directory contents	ls, l lc	dir
move files	mv	no move
copy files	cp	copy
rename files	mv	ren
delete files	rm	del, erase
display ascii file on terminal	cat,pr	type
print files	lpr, print	print
create a directory	mkdir	mkdir,md
delete a directory	rmdir	rmdir,rd
change directory	cd	chdir,cd
display current directory	pwd	cd no args

or diskette. It therefore can have several mounted, independent file systems at any one time. The drive designation changes the system from one file system to another, or it can be used to refer to files on drives other than the default drive. UNIX, on the other hand, has a single file system in which multiple volumes are mounted onto the single hierarchy. Furthermore, DOS has no user level file protection. This makes sense since it is presumably a single user system.

2. *File Naming Rules.* These are stricter in DOS. Unlike the filenames in UNIX, which can have up to 14 characters and contain any ASCII character, including upper and lower cases, DOS divides the name into two parts—1 to 8 alphanumeric characters followed by a period, then an optional extension of up to 3 characters:

    MYFILE.EXT

DOS filenames are all represented in upper case, and file specifications can be typed either in upper or lower case.

3. *File Specifications.* File specifications in DOS are similar to UNIX. The file hierarchy path is used to access files not found in the current working directory. The only difference is that DOS uses the backslash, \, as the name of the root directory and for specifying paths. UNIX uses the regular slash, /.

4. *File Names and Wildcard Characters.* DOS supports * and ? wildcard characters which function almost like their UNIX counterparts. The use of * in a file specification causes the rest of the filename to be ignored in the match with directory files. For example, a*b.x*y is equivalent to a*.b*. Thus, complex file specifications are not possible with DOS.

The ? matches a single character but will match trailing blanks. Thus,

???.∗ would match all files with 1, 2, or 3 characters before the period and any extension.

5. *File Manipulation Commands.* Like UNIX, DOS has basic file manipulation commands for copying, deleting, displaying, printing, and listing. The commands take file specifications of the type described above, so that all drives and paths are accessible from any directory. Table 13.1 lists the basic file manipulation commands.

13.5.1.2 The UNIX Shell and DOS COMMAND.COM. As described in previous chapters, the UNIX shell (**sh** and **csh**) is the user interface to the system, providing such features as I/O redirection, piping, and command interpretation. DOS utilizes many of the same concepts through its shell, called COMMAND.COM.

1. *Command Interpreter—COMMAND.COM.* The DOS commands are interpreted by COMMAND.COM, which provides an operating environment similar to the UNIX shell.

2. *The DOS Prompt.* The DOS prompt is by default the current drive designation (e.g., **C:>**). This may be changed to other values by setting the DOS environment variable, *PROMPT,* with the prompt command. Special arguments, key letters preceded by a **$,** are given special handling. For example, to set PROMPT to include the date and time:

```
C> prompt $d $t$g
```

The above sets the prompt to the date, time and greater-than sign:

```
Tue 12-05-1986 12:10:12.10>
```

More importantly, the prompt can be set to display the current directory:

```
C> prompt $p$g
C:\subdir>
```

When you change directories with the **cd** command, the prompt also changes, displaying the new directory. Setting the prompt is similar to setting the PS1 variable in the UNIX shell.

3. *PATH Environment Variable.* The DOS PATH variable establishes the directory search order for commands in the same way as in UNIX. The DOS PATH command sets the PATH:

```
C:\>path c:\;c:\dos;c:\bat
```

In the example above, the root (\), DOS (dos), and batch file (bat) directories are searched, in order, after a command is not found in the current directory. PATH without any arguments displays the current value of PATH.

4. *Redirection of Input and Output.* Redirection of I/O operates almost as it does in UNIX. The basic syntax is the same:

< file	use file for standard input
> file	use file for standard output
> > file	use file for appended standard output

For example, to sort the contents of filea and place the results in *fileb:*

```
C:\> sort < filea > fileb
```

5. *Pipes and Filters.* The concept of pipes and filters also is embodied in MS-DOS. Several UNIX-like filters are provided, and the | symbol is used to indicate a pipe. For example, to obtain a sorted directory listing:

```
C:\> dir | sort
```

The two other UNIX-like filters included with MS-DOS are **find,** which is used like **grep,** and **more,** which is similar to the UNIX **more** or **pg.**

The following expression prints a sorted DOS directory listing:

```
C:\> dir | find "DIR" | sort | print
```

6. *Multiple Shells.* DOS is not a multiprogrammed operating system, so it does not make sense to have truly concurrent processes. But it is possible to invoke a second shell which either replaces the existing process or stacks its environment for later restoration. From the DOS prompt, you can start a second shell by invoking COMMAND.COM. The **exit** command returns you to the original command processor environment.

COMMAND.COM can be invoked in three ways:

1. With no arguments, stacking the previous environment:

```
C:\> command
The IBM Personal Computer DOS
Version 3.10 (C) Copyright International Business Machines Corp
                                         1981, 1985
       (C) Microsoft Corp 1981, 1985
```

Then to leave the current COMMAND.COM:

```
C:\> exit
C:\>
```

2. A second way to invoke COMMAND.COM is with the **/P** option which makes the new version permanent. You can't restore the old environment.

3. The third way is to pass to the new command processor a command to execute:

```
C:/> command /C dir
```

Invoking multiple shells is embedded in some DOS packages allowing an 'escape' to DOS. This is similar to the way that UNIX escapes to the shell from **ex, vi, mail,** etc. After completing your DOS functions, you return to the place you left off by entering the **exit** command.

13.5.1.3 Batch Files. Just as the UNIX shell can be programmed by creating shell scripts, DOS can be programmed by creating scripts called *batch files*. Batch files in DOS are not as flexible as shell scripts, but they are nevertheless a powerful component of DOS.

Batch files have the extension **bat** and are invoked by giving their filenames only. There are 10 replaceable parameters, **%0–%9,** where **%0** is the name of the command and the rest are positional arguments on the command line. Note the similarity to UNIX shell command line parameters **$0–$9.**

The batch command language includes commands for argument processing (**SHIFT**), decision making (**IF, GOTO**), loops (**FOR**), and tailoring the interface (**REM, ECHO, CLS, PAUSE**).

13.5.1.4 Integration of I/O with the File System. In a manner much like the way UNIX gives names to devices in the */dev* directory, DOS also assigns names to devices that can be used in standard input/output operations. Table 13.2 lists the reserved names for DOS devices.

TABLE 13.2
Reserved Names for DOS Devices

CON	Console
AUX, COM1	Communications port
COM2	Communications port
LPT1, PRN	Parallel Printer
NUL	Null device

For example, to create a simple batch file at the terminal without using an editor:

```
C:\> copy con sortdir.bat
echo off
dir | sort
ctrl-Z
1 file copied
C:\>
```

In the example above, **echo off** turns off the echoing of commands, and the end-of-file indication ($\wedge$Z) is entered with the <F6> function key.

13.5.1.5 Program Development Tools. There are several DOS tools which are counterparts to UNIX program development tools. While they have different commands and operate differently, they perform the similar functions for DOS as their counterparts in UNIX.

1. **edlin** a line context editor similar to **ed**
2. **debug** an interactive debugger similar to **adb**
3. **link** the DOS linker similar to **ld**

13.5.2 UNIX and DOS Compatibility

The need for compatibility between the two systems leads to several approaches. In the first approach, data compatibility, we want to be able to create and access files on one system from the other. This usually involves having UNIX commands which perform the file and filesystem functions on a DOS hierarchy. Table 13.3 lists the commands for XENIX.

A second approach involves code compatibility, whereby applications written on one system can be run on the other system. Either they can run on both (true code compatibility) or the application has been cross-developed, that is, using one system for the development of an application

TABLE 13.3
XENIX Commands for DOS filesystem access

doscat	copy DOS files to standarrd output
doscp	copy files between DOS and XENIX
dosdir	display DOS directory in the DOS format
dosls	display DOS directory in the XENIX format
dosrm	delete DOS files
dosmkdir	create directory in the DOS file system
dosrmdir	remove directory in the DOS file system

on the other. In either event, if the application is written in the C language, there should be a high degree of compatibility at the source level. SCO XENIX System V, for example, provides the **cc** option **-dos** to generate DOS compatible modules.

13.5.3 UNIX and MS-DOS Coexistence

Coexistence of the two systems on the same hardware can take several forms. In the first and most common way, each operating system is resident on a portion of the fixed disk or disks. You run only one at a time, but, as indicated in the previous section, data can be transferred with special UNIX commands that manipulate the DOS file system. Partitioning fixed disks with the DOS FDISK command and its UNIX system counterpart will achieve this type of coexistence.

A second, more desirable approach is to be able to have the systems running concurrently. While the marketplace has yet to demonstrate a strong need for this, it is especially useful in UNIX environments using DOS personal computers as workstations. For example, the AT&T 6300 Plus provides hardware and software to support UNIX running as a full System V multiprogrammed system with a maximum of 1 login allocated to MS-DOS.

13.5.4 UNIX and MS-DOS Networks.

Another solution to providing UNIX and DOS within the same computing environment is to provide hardware and software connections for network support of the two operating systems. This option is especially attractive in environments with many IBM-PC compatible machines which need to communicate with each other and with UNIX (either on PC's or on larger systems).

Three products of interest in this environment provide communications solutions to UNIX vs MS-DOS problems. One company, Touchstone, has a product called *PCworks* which provides menu-driven interface for communication with other systems, UNIX in particular. UNIX operations, once connected, include electronic mail, file transfer, and remote login.

A second product, *WINPC*, from the Wollongong Group, is a TCP/IP compatible network interface also providing functions for electronic mail, file transfer, and remote login. The remote system, UNIX or any other, need only support TCP/IP.

A third product, *Synchrony*, from COSI, Inc., is a product that drives PC software from a UNIX host. This is ideal for applications which provide local application processing (at the PC), but periodically require centralized processing (at the host). *Synchrony* can be used to automate the DOS side (through batch files) by initiating program execution, as well as file transfer.

The three products mentioned here are examples of the increasing number of communications solutions to MS-DOS/UNIX compatibility at the time of this writing.

13.6 Conclusion

It is becoming apparent that UNIX will not replace the wide variety of systems in use today (although many would like to see that happen). With the introduction of faster and more powerful desktop workstations, however, the use of UNIX as the base machine in a larger heterogeneous environment seems likely. This author feels that there will be a surge in the use of UNIX precisely because of this movement.

New computers need operating systems, and UNIX provides the fastest and most comprehensive way to satisfy this requirement. As more and more programmers become familiar with this work environment, while we may not see the replacement of DEC VMS, IBM's CMS, MVS, etc., we will see more and more UNIX workstations used as the interface to these systems.

13.7 Further Exploration

This is not only the last section of this chapter, but it brings our discussion of UNIX to a close. As you must be aware by now, an introductory book on UNIX can only touch the surface of some of the more advanced topics. Depending on your requirements, you may want to explore advanced UNIX programming, **nroff/troff,** processing, or advanced usage of UNIX tools. I think you will find the process an adventure that is both productive and rewarding. Good Luck!

Command Reference

This chapter is a reference to most of the commands on your UNIX system. The organization is similar to your system documentation, except that it is abbreviated and intended for quick reference.

The format for an entry includes the command name, its generic usage, and important options, keys, or flags. Command entries are taken from the various UNIX versions discussed in the book (e.g., PC/IX, XENIX, AT&T System V, Berkeley 4.2) and so some commands and options may not be available on all systems. As of this writing, however, AT&T agreements with Microsoft and Sun Microsystems indicate that System V will move towards XENIX and Berkeley UNIX compatibility incorporating many of the unique features of both systems.

adb   interactive debugger

   usage: **adb** [options] [objectfile/coreimage]
   options:
   　　　　-w　　　　　create both object and core image files

adduser   create new user utility (PC/IX)

   usage: **adduser**

admin   create and administer SCCS files

usage: **admin** [options] [files]
options:

-n	Create a new SCCS file
-i[name]	Filename for new SCCS file
-rrel	First Delta Release Number
-t[name]	Filename for descriptive text

alias   set alias command string

usage: **alias** [name] [token list]

ar   file archive utility

usage: **ar** key [position] archivefile files
keys:

d	Delete files in the archive
r	Replace files in the archive
q	Append files to archive file
t	List contents of the archive file
p	Print the archive files
m	Reposition named files at end of archive file
x	Extract files from archive file
v	Give a verbose listing
c	Create a new archive file

as   target machine assembler

usage: **as** [options] sourcefiles
options: Options for the target machine assembler will be hardware dependent. Check your manual for options.

awk   pattern matching and file manipulation filter

usage: **awk** [program or **-f** programfile] file
options:

-f	awk program resides in a file

banner display string in large letters

   usage: **banner** string

bc interactive calculator

   usage: **bc** [options] [files]
   options:

-c	Compile only
-l	Specify math library

bdiff **diff** for big files

   usage: **bdiff** file1 file2 [n] [options]
   options:

n	Size of **bdiff** splits
-s	Suppress diagnostics

bfs big file read-only editor

   usage: **bfs** [-] file
   options:

                Suppress display of sizes

Note: Enters **ed**-like mode for read-only file scanning. See **ed**.

cal produce a monthly or yearly calendar

   usage: **cal** [month] year

calendar personal appointment calendar

   usage: **calendar** [-]
   options:

no option	Checks current directory for file, *calendar*
	Checks all login directories

cat concatenate files

usage: **cat** [options] files
options:
- **-u**   Inhibit output buffering
- **-s**   Ignore nonexistent files

cb ''C beautifier''; formats C programs

usage: **cb** [file]

cc invoke the C compiler

usage: **cc** [options] [object files] [C source files]
options:

-c	Suppress link edit, produce object file
-p	Create profile data in mon.out
-O	Optimize object code
-S	Create assembler output for each C program Saved in files with *.s* extension
-E	Run the preprocessor only
-P	Run the preprocessor, save the output in files with **.i** extension
-C	Leave comments after preprocessor
D*name*[= *def*]	Define name to preprocessor
-U*name*	Undefine name to preprocessor
-I*dir*	Set directories to search for #include files
-o*name*	Use this name instead of *a.out* as **ld** output
-l*name*	Define libraries for additional C and assembly language programs

cflow produce C language flow graph

usage: **cflow** [options] file
options:

-r	Reverse caller/called list
-ix	Include extern and static symbols
-i	include names beginning with '-'
-d*num*	Cut off depth at level *num*

chmod   set file access permissions

usage: **chmod** specification files
specification:
    ddd   octal digit mask for permissions

who op permission where:
  who: **u**   user
           g   group
           o   other
           a   all
  op: **+**   add permission
           —   deny permission
           =   assign permission
  permission:
        r   read
        w   write
        x   execute

chroot   change relative root designation

usage: **chroot** newroot command

clri   clear inode entry

usage: **clri** inode-value

cmp   byte-by-byte file comparison

usage: **cmp** [options] file1 file2
options:
    -l   Print byte number and differing bytes
    -s   No display for differing files, only return codes

col   filters reverse linefeeds

usage: **col** [options]
options:

-b	Output device does not process backspace
-f	Permits forward half linefeeds
-x	Inhibits white space to tab conversion
-p	Ignore unknown escape sequences

comm   compare sorted files

usage: **comm** [options] file1 file2
options:

-	Select file from standard input
-1	Suppress lines only in file 1
-2	Suppress lines common to both
-3	Suppress lines only in file 2

copy   copy files

usage: **copy** [options] source destination
options:

-a	Prompt before copying
-l	Use links when possible
-n	Destination must be new file
-o	Destination files set to source owner/group (default is to user invoking copy)
-m	Set modification/access time to source (default to time of copy)
-r	Perform copy on directories recursively
-ad	Prompt for directory processing (**-r**)
-v	Print messages during processing (verbose)
source	file, directory, special file
destination	file, directory (other than source)

cp   copy files

usage: **cp** file1 [file2...] target
note: Target may be a directory.

cpio   file archive utility

usage: **cpio** [options]
options:

-o	Copy out
-i	Copy in
-p	Copy out and in

note: **cpio** reads standard input and writes standard output.

cpp C language preprocessor

usage: **cpp** [options] [input file] [output file]
options:

-C	Strip C language comments
-Uname	Remove initial definition of *name*
-Dname	Define *name* to 1
-Dname = *def*	Define *name* to value
-Idir	Search for #include files enclosed in " " in directory *dir* after input-file directory

cref C or assembler cross-reference

usage: **cref** [options] files
options:

-a	Assembler format
-c	C format
-i	Specify *ignore* file
-l	List line number
-n	Omit context
-o	Specify *only* file
-s	List current symbol
-t	Specify temporary file
-u	Display only-once symbols
-x	Display only C external symbols
-1	Sort by symbol
-2	Sort by filename
-3	Sort by current symbol (or filename)

csh invoke C-shell

usage: **csh** [options] [arguments]
options:

-c *string*	Execute command from *string*
-s	Read commands from standard input

-i	Establish interactive shell
-e	Exit upon receipt of nonzero exit status
-f	Ignore *.cshrc* search and execution
-n	Read, but do not execute commands
-t	Read and execute a single line of input
-u	Treat unset variables as an error
-v	Print input lines as they are read with history substitution
-x	Set echo variable and print commands as executed
-V	Set verbose before *.cshrc* execution
-X	Set echo variable before *.cshrc* execution

csplit   split files by context

usage: **csplit** [options] file args
options:

-s	Suppress character counts
-k	In case of error, leave files already created
-f	Prefix set split files prefix

args: line selection criteria:

/RE/	current line to regular expression
%RE%	omit from current to RE
line no.	split to line number
{num}	follows the above as a repeat factor

cu   call a remote system

usage: **cu** [options] phone# or directory
options:

-s*speed*	Set baud rate
-l*line*	Select device
-h	Half duplex
-t	Dial auto-answer terminal
-d	Print diagnostics
-m	Select direct line with modem control
-e	Select even parity
-o	Select odd parity

cut   select fields of a file

usage: **cut** -c*list* [files] cut -f*list* [-d*char*] [-s] [files]
options:

-c	Character position selection
	list: pos1, pos2; pos1-pos2
-f	Field selection
	list: f1, f2; f1-f2
-d	Delimiter character
-s	Suppress lines with no delimiters

date   display and set time and date

usage: **date** [specification] [format]
options:

specification:	When present, sets time and date;
	format may vary by system: [mmddhhmm[yy]]
+format	When present, formats time/date
	display according to C language
	type format control

dc   arbitrary precision calculator

usage: **dc** [file]
note: **dc** is a UNIX subsystem with a complete set of interaction subcommands and facilities.

dd   file copy utility

usage: **dd** option = value
options:

if=*file*	Input *file* (standard defaults)
of=*file*	Output *file* (standard defaults)
isb=*n*	Input block size
obs=*n*	Output block size
bs=*n*	Input/output block size
cbs=*n*	Conversion buffer size
skip=*n*	Skip first *n* records
seek=*n*	Seek *n* records on output
count=*n*	Copy *n* records
conv=**ascii**	Convert EBCDIC to ASCII

conv = ebcdic	Convert ASCII to EBCDIC
conv = ibm	IBM map ASCII to EBCDIC
conv = lcase	Convert to lower case
conv = ucase	Convert to upper case
conv = swab	Swap bytes
conv–sync	Pad input to IBS
conv = "..,..,.."	Multiple conversions

delta   SCCS change control

usage: **delta** [options] SCCSfile
options:

-r*SID*	Specify *SID* release and version
-s	Suppress update messages
-g*list*	Specify delta *list* to ignore
-m[*mrlist*]	Specify modification request
-y[comment]	Comment the delta
-p	Print file differences

df   display free disk space

usage: **df** [options] [filesystem]
options:

-t	Display total allocated blocks
-l	Check free list
-f	Display free list only
-v	Display percentages
-i	Display inode percentages

diction   check language usage

usage: **diction** [options] files
options:

-ml	Skip lists
-f*patternfile*	User-supplied patterns
-n	Suppress default file

diff   compare file differences

usage: **diff** [options] file1 file2
options:

-b	Ignore trailing blanks
-h	Large file difference
-e	Produce editor output
-f	Produce editor output in reverse

dircmp compare directories

usage: **dircmp** [options] dir1 dir2
options:

-d	**diff** each paired file
-s	Report files same or different
-wn	Modify output line width to n (72 defaults)

diskcp copy floppy diskettes

usage: **diskcp** [options]
options:

-f	Format before copying
-d	Computer has dual floppy drives

DOS COMMANDS: PC/IX

dosdel DOS file deletion

usage: **dosdel** [options] DOSfile
options:

-m	Disk is a fixed disk
-v	Verbose
-Ddosdev	Named DOS drive

dosdir DOS file directory

usage: **dosdir** [options] [file]
options:

-a	Print information on all files
-d	Treat directory files as files

-e	Detailed listing (used with **-l** option)
-l	Long listing
-m	Treat named disk as fixed disk
-t	List directory tree from named file
-v	Verbose
-D*dosdev*	Named DOS device

dosread   read DOS file

usage: **dosread** [options] DOSfile [PC/IXfile]
options:

-a	Copy in ASCII mode
-m	Disk is a fixed disk
-v	Verbose
-D*dosdev*	Named DOS drive

doswrite   write DOS file

usage: **doswrite** [options] PC/IXfile DOSfile
options:

-a	Copy in ASCII mode
-m	Disk is a fixed disk
-v	Verbose
-D*dosdev*	Named DOS drive

DOS COMMANDS XENIX

doscat   DOS file concatenation utility

usage: **doscat** [option] files
option:
  -r   Copy without newline conversion

doscp   XENIX DOS file copy utility

usage: **doscp** [option] file1 file2
    doscp [option] files directory
option:
  -r   Copy without newline conversion

dosdir XENIX DOS directory listing (DOS format)

usage: **dosdir** directory

dosls XENIX DOS directory listing (UNIX format)

usage: **dosls** directory

dosmkdir XENIX DOS directory creation

usage: **dosmkdir** directory

dosrm XENIX DOS file delete

usage: **dosrm** file

dosrmdir XENIX DOS directory deletion

usage: **dosrmdir** directory

du display disk utilization

usage: **du** [options] [names]
options:

-s	Total for names only
-a	List each file
-r	Message for nonreadable entries

note: names are directories; if left out current is used

dump incremental backup utility

usage: dump [key [args] filesystem]
keys:

f	Use argument file instead of default
u	Date successful backup in */etc/date*
0–9	Backup level number

e invoke INed editor (PC/IX, AIX)

usage: **e** [filename [line [col [searchkey]]]]

echo echo arguments

   usage: **echo** [arg...]

ed UNIX line editor

   usage: **ed** [options] [file]
   option:
          -     Supress **r,w,e,q,** ! messages

env set environment for command execution

   usage: **env** [-] [name=value] [command args]
   where:

-	Ignore inherited environment
name	Environment variable
value	Value to be set
command	command to initiate
args	argument to command

eqn **nroff(neqn)/troff** equation preprocessor

   usage: **(n)eqn** [options] [files]
   options:

-d*cc*	Set eqn two-character delimiter
-p*n*	Set subscripts/superscripts to n points
-s*n*	Reduce subscripts/superscripts n points
-f*font*	Select *font*

ex invoke the **ex** line editor

   usage: **ex** [options] files
   options:

-	Suppress i/o error messages
-v	Enter **ex** visual mode (see **vi**)
-t tag	Enter **ex** positioned at *tag*
+*n*	Enter **ex** positioned at line number n

explain correct language usage

   usage: **explain**

expr   expression evaluation utility

usage: **expr** args
args: *expr1 op expr2*
where *op* is:

|	Returns *expr2* if it is null or 0, otherwise *expr1*
&	Returns *expr1* if neither null or 0, otherwise *expr2*
=, >, > =, <, < =, ! =	Returns result of integer or lexical comparison
+, -, *, /, %	Returns integer arithmetic result of operation
:	Match *expr1* with RE in *expr2*— return number of characters matched, otherwise *expr2*

factor   factor positive integer

usage: **factor** integer

false   return nonzero exit value

usage: **false**

fdisk   maintain fixed disk partition table (IBM PC based)

usage: **fdisk** [option]
option:
     -f*name*   Specify *device name*

file   return type of file

usage: **file** [options] files
option:
     -f   Use the argument as a file containing filenames

find   search directory hierarchy utility

usage: **find** directory [options]
options:

directory	Path to begin file search
-name *file*	Name of files to search for
-perm *value*	True if permissions match *value* in octal

-type *c*	True if type matches *c* (*b, c, d, p,* or *f*)
-links *n*	True if *n* links on file
-user *name*	True if file belongs to *user name*
-group *name*	True if file belongs to *group name*
-size *n*	True if file *n* blocks long
-atime *n*	True if file accessed in *n* days
-mtime *n*	True if file modified in *n* days
-ctime *n*	True if file changed in *n* days
-exec *command*	Execute *command* on selected files
-ok *command*	Execute *command* on selected files by response to prompt (y).
-print	Print pathname of current file
-newer *file*	True if current file newer than argument
(expression)	Use of *or* (**-o**), *and* (**-a**), and *not* (**!**) to create selection criteria expressions with above options.

format   format floppy diskette

usage: **format** [options] [device]
options:
      -f   Suppress confirmation prompt

fsck   file system check utility

usage: **fsck** [options] [filesystem]

options:

-y	Respond yes to all prompts
-n	Respond no to all prompts
-s*x:y*	Reconstruct new free list with
	x as blocks/cyl and *y* blocks interleave factor
-S*x:y*	Reconstruct free list if no discrepancies
-q	Suppress size check messages
-D	Directory check for bad blocks
-f	Fast check (Phases 1 and 5)
-rr	Recover root file system

get SCCS retrieve version

usage: **get** [options] file
options:

-r*SID*	Version to retrieve
-c*cutoff*	Do not include changes after
	cutoff: YY[MM[DD[HH[MM[SS]]]]]
-e	Retrieve for edit
-b	Create new branch delta
-i*list*	Forced delta list for **get**
-x*list*	Forced excluded delta list for **get**
-p	Write retrieved file to standard ouput
-s	Suppress standard output
-m	Display delta information line by line
-t	Access most recent release delta

getty set terminal characteristics

usage: **getty** [options] line [speed [type] [linedisc]]
options:

-h	Suppress forced hangum
-t *n*	Set timeout time to *n* seconds
line	tty special name
speed	Baud rate
type	Terminal type
linedisc	Line discipline

grep pattern matching utility

usage: **grep** [options] pattern files
options:

-v	Select lines that don't match
-x	Select exact line matches only
-c	Display count of matched lines
-l	Display filenames with matching lines
-n	Display relative line number of matched lines
-f *file*	Take patterns from *file*

haltsys bring down the system, halt CPU

usage: **haltsys**

hd hex display

usage: **hd** [options] files
options:

-a	Address format
-c	Character format
-b	Byte format
-w	Word format
-l	Long format
-A	ASCII format
-x	hex base
-d	Decimal base
-o	Octal base
-t	Text format
-s *n*	Begin at *n* byte offset
-n *n*	Process *n* bytes

head print first few lines of file

usage: **head** [options] file
option:

-n	number of lines to print from beginning

help command and error message reference

usage: **help** [args]
args:
  help reference strings:
  message numbers
  command names

history display previous commands list

  usage: **history**

hyphen display hyphenated words

  usage: **hyphen** file

init create process for enabled terminals

  usage: **init**

install install packages and commands (PC/IX)

  usage: **install** [options] file dirlist
  options:

-c *dir*	Install command in *dir*
-f *dir*	Override command in *dir*
-i	Ignore default directory list
-n *dir*	Place file in *dir* if not found in search list
-s	Suppress messages other than errors

join join on relations in two files

  usage: **join** [options] file1 file2
  options:

-a*n*	Display lines for unpairable lines in file *n* (1 or 2)
-e *s*	Replace empty output fields by string *s*
-j*n m*	Join on the *m*th field of file *n* (1 or 2)
-o*list*	List display output with fields in list (*m.n*): the *m*th field in the *n*th file
-t*c*	Use *c* as a delimiter

kill terminate a process

  usage: **kill** [-signal] pid

options:

    -signal   Termination *signal* set to process

l list a file, screen by screen (PC/IX)

usage: l [options] files

options:

-n	Line numbering
-f*n*	Start at line *n* (default 1)
-p*n*	Page size (default 23)
l*n*	Same as **-p**
-q	Suppress 'waiting' message
-c	Suppress clearing screen between pages

l identical to "**ls -l**" (XENIX)

usage: l [options] [files]

lc list directory in multiple columns. (XENIX)

usage: **lc** [options] files

options:

-1	One entry per line
-A	Display files beginning with . except (. and ..)
-C	Force display in columns
-F	Trail directory names with /, trail executable files with *
-R	Recursively display subdirectories
-a	List all entries
-b	Print nongraphics in octal (*ddd*) format
-c	Sort by file creation date
-d	For directories list only the name
-f	Force interpretation as a directory
-g	Long format without owner
-i	Prints inode
-l	Long format (mode, links, owner, group size, time of last modification
-o	Long format without group
-m	Stream output
-n	Long format with user ID instead of owner name

-q	Print nongraphics as ?
-r	Reverse sort order
-s	Give size in blocks
-t	Sort by time modified
-u	Sort by last access
-x	Sort columns across page rather than down

ld   invoke linkage editor

usage: **ld** [options] files

options:

-i	Create separate instruction and data spaces
-l *x*	Select system library */lib/libx.a*
-m *name*	Create link map in file *name*
-n *n*	Truncate symbols to length, *n*
-o *name*	Set executable output to name, *name*
-s	Strip the symbol table
-u *symbol*	Name designate *symbol* as undefined

notes: **ld** is a highly machine- and version-dependent program development utility. For a complete command summary, see your system documentation.

lex   generate C language lexical analysis program

usage: **lex** [options] files
options:

-c	C options
-t	Create lex.yy.c
-v	Display 1 line summary of statistics generated
-n	Inhibit summary

li list directory in multiple columns (PC/IX)

note: See description of **lc**

line   read a line from the terminal; write to standard output

usage: **line**

lint   C-program checker

usage: **lint** [options] files
options:

-a	Suppress long value assignment messages
-b	Suppress unreachable break messages
-c	Suppress questionable portability messages
-h	Suppress heuristic tests
-u	Suppress used/defined messages on functions and external variables
-v	Suppress unused arguments messages
-x	Suppress nonreferenced external declarations
-n	Suppress compatibility checks against standard and lint libraries
-p	Check portability to C dialects

ln   link files

usage: **ln** file1 [files] target

login   sign onto system

usage: **login**

logname   display login name

usage: **logname**

logout   sign-off system C-shell

usage: **logout**

look   find lines in a sorted file

usage: **look** [options] string [file]
options:

-d	Use dictionary order
-f	Fold cases

lorder   find ordering relation of an object library

usage: **lorder** library

lpr   line print spooling program

usage: **lpr** [options] [files]
options:

-c	Copy file to be sent
-r	Remove file after sending
-m	Report completion by mail
-n	Suppress completion messages by mail

ls   list directory contents

usage: **ls** [options] files
options:

-l	Long format list
-o	Long format, suppress group
-g	Long format, suppress owner
-t	Sort by last modification date first
-a	List silent entries
-s	Give size in blocks
-d	For directories display name only
-r	Reverse order of sort
-u	Sort by last access date first
-c	Sort modification date of inode first
-i	Print inode number
-f	Treat arguments as directories
-p	Put a / after directory names

m4   invoke macro processor

usage: **m4** [options] [files]
options:

-e	Interactive mode
-s	Enable line sync output for C preprocessor
-D*name*[= *val*]	Define *name* (default to null)
-U*name*	Undefine *name*

mail   electronic mail (BASIC)

usage: **mail** [options][-f file] [users]

options:

no option	Persons sent mail from standard input
-e	Suppress printing of mail
-p	Print mail with prompting for disposition
-q	Terminate mail, rather than current message on interrupt
-r	Print mail first-in first-out order
-f *file*	Use *file* as mailbox for default disposition

mail   electronic mail (Berkeley)

usage: **mail** [options] [users]
options:

no option	Persons sent mail from standard input
-u *user*	Read *user* system mailbox
-f *file*	Read *file* as user mailbox
-e	Permits escapes from compose when input comes from file
-R	Session set to read only
-i	Ignore terminal interrupts
-s*subject*	Set *subject* field for messages

mailx   AT&T System V expanded electronic mail

usage: **mailx** [options] [users]

make   program management utility

usage: **make** [options] files
options:

-makefile	Name of **make** description file
-p	Print macro definitions
-i	Ignore command errors
-k	Respond to errors by continuing on unaffected dependency branches
-s	Suppress printing of commands as executed
-r	Do not use built-in rules
-n	Print command, but do not execute
-e	Environment variables override makefile assignments
-t	Touch target files
-d	Print detailed information

-q	Return success (zero) or failure (nonzero) status if file up-to-date
-b	Compatibility mode for old makefiles

man   online manual reference

usage: **man** [options] [section] title
options:

-t	Typset using **troff**
-n	Print using **nroff**

mesg   turn on/off terminal messages

usage: **mesg** [n] [y]

mkdir   create a directory

usage: **mkdir** directory

mkfs   build a file system

usage: **mkfs** [options] blocks [:inodes] [gap blocks]
      mkfs [options] special proto [gap blocks]
options:

-y	Prompt for confirmation if file system exists
-n	Terminate if file system exists
special	Special file to create fs blocks, file size in blocks
: inodes	Number of files in file system
proto	File containing file system description
gap/blocks	Interleave factor

mknod   create special file

usage: **mknod** name type
type:

c	Character-oriented device
b	Block-oriented device
p	Named pipe
s	Semaphore
m	Shared memory

mkuser   create new user utility (XENIX)

usage: **mkuser**

mm   mm macro document processor

usage: **mm** [options] [files]
options:

-c	Invoke **col**
-e	Invoke **neqn**
-t	Invoke **tbl**
-E	Invoke **-e** option of **nroff**
-y	Use noncompacted version of **mm**

mmt   typeset documents with **troff**

usage: **mmt** [options] files
options:

-e	invoke **eqn**
-t	invoke **tbl**
-a	invoke **-a** option of **troff**
-y	use noncompacted version of **mmt**

more   list a file, screen by screen

usage: **more** [options] file
options:

-n	Window size in lines
-c	List from top
-d	Prompt for next screen
-f	Count logical rather than screen lines
-l	Ignore *ctrl-L* (form feed)
-s	Squeeze multiple blanks
-u	Suppress underline processing
-r	Suppress printing of noninterpreted control characters
-w	Wait at EOF before exiting
+*n*	Start at line number *n*
+/*pattern*	Start two lines before *pattern*

mount   mount a file system

usage: **mount** [special-device directory [option]]
option:

      -r   mount as read only

mv   move files

usage: **mv** file1 [files] target

ncheck   display filenames from inode numbers

usage: **ncheck** [options] [filesystem]
options:

    -i*numbers*   Inode number list
    -a   Include . and .. names
    -s   Include special and set ID files only

news   print news

usage: **news** [options] [items]
options:

    -a   Print all items
    -n   Report item names without contents
    -s   Report number of current items
    items   Selected news items

nice   set process priority

usage: **nice** [-increment] command [arguments]

nl   line number a file

usage: **nl** [options] file
options:

    -b*type*   number logical page body
    -h*type*   number logical page header
    -f*type*   number logical page footer
                where *type* is
                   a–number all lines
                   t–number printable lines only
                   n–suppress line numbering

-p		suppress renumbering at page delimiters
-vn		start number at n
-in		increment line number by n
-sc		separate text and number with c (default is tab)
-wn		use n as width of line number (default is 6)
-ln		n blank lines counted as 1
-nformat		format line numbers with format:
		ln–left justified
		rn–right justified
		rz–right justified (with zeros)

nm   print name list (symbol table) of argument list

usage: **nm** [options] [+ offset] [files]
options:

-a	Print absolute symbols
-c	Print C program symbols
-g	Print global (external symbols)
-n	Sort numerically
-o	Display file name to each line
-O	Print symbol values in octal
-p	Print in symbol-table order
-r	Reverse sort order
-s	Sort by size of symbol (display size)
-u	Print undefined symbols
-v	Display object file/symbol table format

nohup   run command with hangups/quits ignored

usage: **nohup** command [arguments]

nroff   invoke line printer text formatter

usage: **nroff** [options] [files]
options:

-olist	Print page numbers in list
-nk	Set first page number to k
-sk	Stop every k pages
-mname	Use macro file /usr/lib/tmac/tmac.name

od   octal dump

usage: **od** [options] file
options:

-b	interpret bytes in octal
-c	interpret bytes in ASCII
-d	interpret words in decimal
-o	interpret words in octal
-x	interpret words in hex

pack   compress files

usage: **pack** [-] file
options:

- prints statistics

passwd   change user password

usage: **passwd** newpasswd

paste   merge lines of several files

usage: **paste** [options] file file ...
options:

-d*list*	*list* is the replacement to the tab character used to concatenate lines
-s	Merge lines rather than concatenate
-	When used instead of a filename, reads a line from standard input

pr   formatted print

usage: **pr** [options] [files]
options:

+*n*	Begin printing with page *n*
-*n*	Print with *n* columns
-a	Print multicolumn output
-m	Merge and print files
-d	Doublespace
-e*ck*	Expand input tabs to multiple of $k+1$ position using *c* as the input tab; if

omitted, default tabs at 8 characters, tab as tab character.

-icn	Replace output white space with tab characters (c) every n + 1th position.
-ncn	Provide n digit line numbering following each number by a tab (c).
-wn	Set line width to n characters
-on	Offset each line by n characters
-ln	Set page length to n lines
-h arg	Set header to arg
-p	Pause at each page break
-f	Use form-feed character for each page
-r	Inhibit diagnostic messages
-t	Inhibit standard header/trailer
-sc	Separate columns by tab (c)

prep   tokenize a file into words

usage: **prep** [options] files
options:

-d	Display word number
-ifile	Ignore words in file
-ofile	Select-only words in file
-p	Include punctuation

print   line printer utility

usage: **print** [queue] [options] [files]
queue: symbolic designation for system print queues
options:

-ap=n	Set priority to n (existing print files)
-bp=n	Set interfile separator pages where: n=0 no headers/trailers n=1 headers before each file n=2 headers/trailers printed
-bp	Headers/trailers printed
-ca	Cancel printing
-cp	Copy file
-fi	Use print as a filter
-nb	No headers/trailers

-no	Notify user after print
-pr=*n*	Set priority to *n* (new print files)
-rm	Delete file after printing
-q	Display queue and print status
-ti=*title*	Title a specific print request
-to=*name*	Label output for delivery

printenv   print environment variable contents

usage: **printenv**

prof   profile a program's execution

usage: **prof** [options] file
options:

-a	Report all symbols
-l	Order listing by symbol

prs   print SCCS file

usage: **prs** [options] files
options:

-d*spec*	Specify SCCS data *spec*
-r*SID*	Specify *SCCS IDentification*
-e	Display information earlier and including **-r** option (SID)
-l	Display information later and including **-r** option (SID)
-a	Display removed and existing delta information

ps   process status

usage: **ps** [options]
options:

-e	Print information about all processes
-d	All except process group leaders
-a	All except process group leaders and processes not associated with a terminal
-f	Full listing
-l	Long listing

-t *list*   Restrict to processes associated with terminals in *list*
-p *list*   restrict to processes with PID in *list*
-u *list*   Restrict to processes with user ID or login names in *list*
-g *list*   Restrict to processes with group in *list*

pstat   report system status

usage: **pstat** [options]
options:

-a	Display all process slots
-i	Display the inode table
-x	Display the text table
-p	Display active entries in the process table
-t	Display terminal table
-u	Display information about a user process
-f	Display the open file table

ptx   permuted index

usage: **ptx** [options] inputfile outputfile
options:

-f	Fold upper and lower case
-t	Prepare for phototypesetter
-w *n*	Set line width to *n*
-g *n*	Define index gap length
-o *file*	Use keywords from *file*
-i *file*	Ignore keywords from *file*
-b *char*	Use *char* as a word separator
-r	Use leading word as an identifier

pwd   print working directory

usage: **pwd**

restore,restor   incremental restore utility

usage: **restore** key [args]
key:

f	Use first arg as backup device
r,R	Load archive onto file system (**R** for multivolume sets)

    x   Extract by name (arguments)

    t   Display date archive written and date file system backed up

rm   delete files

    usage: **rm** [options] files

    options:

                -f   Overrides prompt for no-write files

                -r   Recursively searches directories

                -i   Interactively verifies deletions

rmdir   delete directory

    usage: **rmdir** directories

rmuser   remove user utility (XENIX)

    usage: **rmuser**

rsh   restricted shell

    note: Limits placed on commands; directory access set by system administrator. See **sh** for full capabilities.

sddate   display/set backup (dump) dates

    usage: **sddate** [name level date]

    arguments:

                name   Device name

                level   Level number (0–9)

                date   In- **date** command format

sed   stream editor

    usage: **sed** [options] files

    options:

                -n   Suppress default output

                -e *string*   Use *string* as sed command string

                -f *file*   Use *file* for sed commands

settime   set access/modification time

usage: **settime** mmddhhmm[yy] [option] files
option:
                    -f*name*   Get setting from file *name*

setkey   set function keys (IBM-PC)

usage: **setkey** key string

sh   Bourne shell

usage: **sh** [options] [arguments]
options:
  -c *string* Execute command from *string*
    -s   read commands from standard input
    -i   Establish interactive shell
    -e   Exit upon receipt of nonzero exit status
    -k   Place keyword arguments in the command environment
    -n   Read, but do not execute commands
    -r   Restricted shell
    -t   Exit after executing one command
    -u   Treat unset variables as an error
    -v   Print input lines as they are read
    -x   Print commands as executed

shutdown   terminate all processing

usage: **shutdown**

size   display program size

usage: **size** [options] file
options:
                    -o Print sizes in octal
                    -x Print sizes in hex

sleep   suspend execution

usage: **sleep** seconds

sort   sort/merge utility

usage: **sort** [options] [+pos] [-pos] [-o file] files
options:

-b	Ignore leading blanks
-d	Use only letters, digits and blanks
-f	Fold upper case onto lower case
-i	Ignore unprintable characters
-n	Initial numeric strings treated arithmetically
-r	Reverse order of sort
-t*c*	Use *c* as the tab character
-c	Check already sorted
-m	Merge sorted input files
-u	Discard duplicate lines
-o	Use next argument as output file name
+*m.n*	Use field beginning at field *m*, character *n*
-*m.n*	Terminate field beginning before field *m*, character *n*

spell   spelling check

usage: **spell** [options] [files]
options:

-v	All words in the file, but not in the spelling list, are printed
-b	Check British spelling
-x	Display possible stems

split   split a file

usage: **split** [options] file name
options:

-*n*	Split file into *n* pieces
name	Use *name* suffix to new piece names

strings   find ASCII strings in object file

usage: **strings** [options] files

options:

-	Check initialized data space
-o	Display offset of strings
-n	Minimum string length (4 defaults)

stty   set terminal characteristics

usage: **stty** [options] [settings]

options:

-a	Display all settings
-g	Report settings for input to stty

settings: Setting preceded by a dash (-) turns the setting off.

note: Different versions may define additional **stty** settings. Below are common user-oriented terminal option settings. Check your system reference.

input:

inlcr	map NL to CR
igncr	ignore CR
icrnl	map CR to NL
ixon	enable start/stop (*ctrl-Q/ctrl-S*)
ixany	enable any character to restart output

output:

opost	postprocess output
olcuc	map lower case to upper case
onlcr	map NL to CR-NL
ocrnl	map CR to NL
onocr	do not output CR at column 0
onlret	have NL perform CR function at terminal
ofdel	file characters are DEL (-ofdel:NUL)
icanon	enable KILL/ERASE
xcase	enable processed upper/lower case
echo	echo back typed characters
echoe	echo ERASE character as backspace-space-backspace string
echok	echo NL after KILL

miscellaneous:

tabs	preserve tabs on when printing
ek	set ERASE and KILL to # and @
sane	establish reasonable values

style   analyze document characteristics

usage: **style** [options] files
options:

-mm	Use **mm** macro package overriding **ms** default
-ml	Cause **deroff** to skip lists
-a	Print sentences with length and readability index
-e	Print sentences beginning with an expletive
-p	Print sentences containing a passive verb
-l_num_	Print sentences longer than _num_
-r_num_	Print sentences with readability index > _num_
-P	Print parts of speech of words in the document

su   change to another user (default is superuser: root)

usage: **su** [-] [user-name] [command]
arguments:

-	Invokes new shell with login environment
user-name	Login user (root is default)
command	Command with arguments

sync   update superblock

usage: **sync**

sysadm   AT&T System V. Administration system

usage: **sysadm**

tail   display last lines of a file

usage: **tail** [options] [file]
options:

+**n**[lbc]	Number of lines (_l_), blocks (_b_), or characters (_c_) from beginning (_l_ defaults).
-**n**[lbc]	Number of lines, blocks, or characters from beginning.

tar   archive utility

usage: **tar** [key] [files]

key:

r	Append named files to archive
x	Extract named files
t	List files in the archive
u	Add new files to archive
c	Create new archive
0, ..., 7	Select archive drive
v	Display files as processed (verbose)
w	Prompt for confirmation
f *arg*	Use *arg* as archive name (for - use standard output)
b *n*	Set blocking factor to *n* (1 defaults)
F *arg*	Use *arg* as file for next arguments
l	Display error messages for link resolution
m	Set modification time to extraction time
k *n*	Set size (in bytes) of archive
e	Inhibit splitting files across volumes
n	Indicate not mag tape
p	Extract with original permissions
A	Suppress absolute filenames

tbl   invoke **nroff/troff** table preprocessor

usage: **tbl** [options] [files]
option:

-TX	use full vertical line motions

tee   capture a copy of standard input

usage: **tee** [options] file
options:

-i	ignore interrupts
-a	append output to file

test   test conditions

usage: **test** expr [expr]
expr: true if:

-r *file*	*File* readable
-w *file*	*File* writable

-x *file*	*File* executable
-f *file*	*File* regular
-d *file*	*File* is directory
-c *file*	*File* character special
-b *file*	*File* block special
-u *file*	Set-user-ID bit set
-g *file*	Set-group-ID bit set
-k *file*	Sticky bit set
-s *file*	Size greater than zero
-t *filedesc*	Open file associated with terminal
-z	String string length zero
-n	String string length nonzero
s1 = s2	Strings equal
s1 != s2	String nonequal
s1	String not null
n1 *-op* n2	Comparison true where *op* is: eq, ne, gt, lt, le, ge
!	not
-a	and
-o	or
(expr)	parenthesis grouping

time   time a command

   usage: **time** command

touch   update modification and access time of a file

   usage: **touch** [options] [mmddhhmm[yy]] file
   options:

-a	Update only access time
-m	Update only modification time
-c	Inhibit creating a file

tr   translate characters

   usage: **tr** [options] [string1 [string2]]
   options:

-c	Complement *string1* character set
-d	Delete characters in *string1*

-s   Squeeze string1 repetitions into
a single character on output

troff   typeset documents

usage: **troff** [options] files
options:

-o*list*	Print page numbers in *list*
-n*k*	Set first page number to *k*
-s*k*	Stop every *k* pages
-m*name*	Use macro file */usr/lib/tmac/tmac.name*

true   return zero exit value

usage: **true**

tset   set terminal modes

usage: **tset** [options] type
options:

-e*c*	Set erase character to *c*
-E*c*	Same as **e** for terminals that can backspace
-k*c*	Set kill character to *c*
-	Display terminal type
-s	Display 'setenv' commands for **csh**, 'export' commands for **sh**
-S	Display environment variable strings
-r	Display terminal type on diagnostic output

note: See documentation for additional options

tsort   topological sort

usage: **tsort** [file]

tty   return terminal name

usage: **tty** [options]
options:

no option	Display path name of **tty**
-s	Test exit code: 0 - if standard input is a terminal 1 - otherwise

umask set default protection modes

usage: **umask** [octal string]
argument:
   no argument   display current default mode
   octal string   set mode to complement of 3-digit octal string

umount unmount special file

usage: **umount** special-file

uniq test of repeated lines in a sorted file[

usage: **uniq** [options] [+n] [-n] [infile [outfile]]
options:
-u	Nonrepeated lines selected
-d	Select one copy of repeated lines
-c	Output contains a line count of the occurrence of repeated lines
-n	Ignores the first *n* fields in comparing lines
+n	Ignores the first *n* characters after the first *n* fields (if any)

units units conversion utility

usage: **units**

unpack expand packed files

usage: **unpack** files

uucp UNIX-to-UNIX copy

usage: **uucp** [options] sourcefiles destinationfile
options:
-d	Create necessary destination directories (default)
-f	Do not create intermediate directories
-c	Use the source file directly rather than copying to a spool file (default)
-C	Copy source to spool directory
-r	Inhibit start of spooling program
-g*x*	Prioritize spool files with alphabetical value *x*
-m	Send mail to requestor upon completion of copy

-nuser	Notify remote user that file was sent
-esys	Execute **uucp** on system sys

uustat uucp status and control

usage: **uustat** [options]
options:

-mmachine	Display status of machine
-mall	Display status of all known machines
-kn	Display status of job number n
-cn	Remove status entries older than n hours
-uuser	Display status of user's requests
-ssys	Display status of requests to system sys
-on	Display status of entries older than n hours
-yn	Display status of entries younger than n hours
-jall	Display status of all requests
-v	Verbose display

uux UNIX-to-UNIX execution

usage: **uux** [options] command
options:

-p	Standard input for the command
-c	Use the source file directly rather than copying to a spool file (default)
-l	Link rather than copy files to spool
-z	Inhibit mail for successful completion
-n	Inhibit mail
-r	Inhibit start of spooling program
-gx	Prioritize spool files with alphabetical value x

vi invoke the screen editor, **vi**

usage: **vi** [options] [file]
options:

-t tag	Positions editor at tag in file
-r file	Recovers after a crash
-l	Sets LISP options
-wn	Sets window size to n
-x	Prompts for encryption key
-R	Set read-only option

view   invoke **vi** editor in read-only mode

   usage: **view** files

vsh   invoke the visual shell (XENIX)

   usage: **vsh**

wait   wait for the completion of background processes (&)

   usage: **wait**

wall   broadcast messages to all users

   usage: **wall**

wc   character, word, line count

   usage: **wc** [options] file
   options:

-l	Gives the line count
-w	Gives the word count
-c	Gives the character count

what   identifies files

   usage: **what** files

who   display logged in users

   usage: **who** [file] [am I]
   arguments:

file	checks alternate system file for logins
am I	prints who you are logged in as

whodo   determine who is doing what

   usage: **whodo**

write   converse with another user

   usage: **write** user [tty]

xref   cross-reference

usage: **xref** [files]

yacc   yet another compiler-compiler

usage: **yacc** [options] file
options:

-v	Produces grammar description file *y.output*
-d	Produce #define file *y.tab.h*
file	Context free grammar

yes   repeat a string indefinitely

usage: **yes** [string]

Index